More praise for R. D. Lawrence's
In Praise of Wolves

"His charmingly written book will make any animal-lover long to know more—if not yet all—about wolves."

—*The Atlantic Monthly*

"Lawrence is unique because he has spent a lifetime doing both field and captive wolf studies, and his book reflects the depth of his passion."

—*Natural History*

"The book's power derives from the author's rendering of moments of mental union between wolf and man.... Readers will almost certainly experience something of the mystical communion with wolves that the author celebrates."

—*San Francisco Examiner*

IN PRAISE OF WOLVES

R.D. Lawrence

BALLANTINE BOOKS • NEW YORK

http://www.randomhouse.com

Library of Congress Catalog Card Number: 97-93182

ISBN: 0-345-41802-6

This edition published by arrangement with Henry Holt and Company

Manufactured in the United States of America

First Ballantine Books Mass Market Edition: December 1988
First Ballantine Books Trade Edition: May 1997

10 9 8 7 6 5 4 3 2 1

This book is dedicated to the memory of Douglas H. Pimlott, Ph.D., a biologist with whom I had the honor to work for a short time and a man whose commitment to his science, and especially to the study of wolves, won the admiration and respect of all those who knew him or who were exposed to his writings. Douglas Pimlott spent many years observing wolves in the field, a period during which he acquired a deep respect for the species. But, more than that, Doug became a champion of wolves; he wanted to see them protected and he wanted to ensure that future generations would have the opportunity to hear the wolf sing in the wilds of North America. The conclusion of an article that he wrote for the Winter 1971 issue of *Science Affairs* speaks of his hopes and issues a challenge to his readers which I now take up on his behalf by including it with this, my tribute to him:

"I have high hopes for the future of wolves in North America. Many men will cease to think of them as vermin and see them as they are—one of the most interesting and intelligent animals that have ever lived on our globe. Do you dare to become involved in such a noble cause?"

ACKNOWLEDGMENTS

A lot of people have helped me in many ways during the years that I have devoted to the study of the wolves and the environment of North America. To all I am grateful, but I regret that space precludes my naming every one of them. Some, however, *must* be named, for their cooperation, interest, and encouragement have greatly contributed to the writing of this book.

My thanks go to: Ed Addison, a biologist with the Ontario Ministry of Natural Resources; Sylvia and Ed Altman, Seattle, Washington, friends and fellow conservationists who keep me informed; Clement W. Alspach, Columbus, Ohio, who fights hard on behalf of animals and the environment; Robert A. Jantzen, Director, U.S. Fish and Wildlife Service, Washington, D.C., who welcomed me to his headquarters and gave my various inquiries his blessings; Steve Kuntz of Wolf Haven, Tenino, Washington, who gives sanctuary to wolves that have run afoul of humans; Janet Lidle, Clifton Heights, Pennsylvania, publisher of *WOLF!* newsletter; Roxanne Mas-Proux, of the Canadian Wildlife Service, Ottawa, who has been a great help in many matters; Ken Robertson, Ministry of Natural Resources, Toronto, an old friend and colleague who has assisted me during many years; Sharon Sauvee, Haliburton, Ontario, for typing so industriously and cheerfully; Bertrand Tetreault, Director General, Canadian Wildlife Service, Ottawa, whose assistance has been invaluable; Larry Vanlieshout of Haliburton, Ontario, who "loaned" his computer for the typing of this manuscript; Wayne Wood, Haliburton, purveyor of wolf meat! To all of these, I am deeply grateful.

I would also like to compliment Robert E. Hess, Acting Coordinator of the Endangered Species Program, and Edward J. Mikula, Chief of the Wildlife Division, Michigan Department of Natural Resources, for the encouragement they have given me during my study of Jim Wuepper's wolves.

Finally, although they are mentioned in this narrative, I must offer a special "thank you" to Dr. Allyn Roberts of Madison, Wisconsin; Dr. Danny B. Pence, Texas Tech University, Lubbock, Texas; Michael Collins, Gooderham, Ontario; Murray Palmer, Douro, Ontario; Dr. Rolf Peterson, Michigan Technological University, Houghton, Michigan; Dr. Laurie M. Brown, DVM, Haliburton, Ontario.

ONE

The leader of the wolf pack is a big, creamy-fawn animal whose kin still hunt the tundra of Canada's Northwest Territories. His name is Shawano. He was six years old when I sought to win his trust during an afternoon in early April of 1983 in Michigan's Upper Peninsula while Lake Superior winds blew chill through the forested land.

I was crouching, one knee resting in the snow, speaking softly to the five wolves; my words inconsequential, my tone neutral and intended to offer reassurance. Deliberately, I kept my gaze away from Shawano, knowing that direct visual contact with wild animals during the early stages of acquaintance is most often looked upon as a threat or a challenge, and that if I was to win this wolf's trust I could only do so with patience, allowing him to seek eye-to-eye unity of his own volition and in his own time.

As he continued to make his slow approach I waited, realizing that he was angling toward my back, but that he was doing so without sinister intent, his direction of travel dictated by the fact that wolves are supremely cautious animals who rarely use a frontal approach when they are investigating anything unusual within their territory. Had Shawano been motivated by aggression, he would have signaled his intentions by the way he carried himself: his hackles would have been raised, his gait stiff-legged, his tail held high; a deep, rumbling growl would have further emphasized his belligerence. As it was, he moved fluidly, if at a measured pace; his tail was held low, at the almost fully relaxed angle, and he was neither growling nor erecting his mane. Seeking to declare my own neutrality, I ignored the pack leader, pretending instead to be interested in the doings of one of the other wolves, who was standing about fifteen paces away, partly concealed by the trees and watching the action, his eyes alternately swiveling from me to Shawano with nearly metronomic timing. Perhaps a minute went by in this fashion. Then, by peripheral sight, I noted that Shawano had come to within three feet of my right shoulder, there to pause with raised head.

It was clear that he was now seeking eye contact. I began to turn my head slowly toward him, observing wolf etiquette by smiling openmouthed to reveal my teeth; as I was doing so, the big wolf closed the distance between us to about two feet. Our eyes met. He too was smiling, mouth agape and showing his own great fangs, to which small fragments of raw chicken still adhered, remnants of a recent meal and rather stark reminders that I was in close proximity to a powerful carnivore. But the interest and twinkling humor that I saw in the wolf's almond-shaped, yellow-amber eyes belied any threat that might have been inherent in the ivory teeth and in the bloody shreds of meat decorating them.

As we studied each other, I became aware that although he was prepared to be friendly, he was also still subjecting me to intense scrutiny. And as always happens when I look deeply into the eyes of a wolf, I found myself drawn into another realm, an altogether different plane of mystical dimension far removed from the material norms that today mold the affairs of mankind. Hypnotically impelling, Shawano's glowing eyes probed into my being, reading me, looking for weakness, for fear, for aggression—above all, for honesty.

2

No one can deceive the eyes of a wolf. They always know. They can strip away the shams of civilization. I knew that only if Shawano was satisfied by what he saw in me would he allow future encounters to develop into friendship; if it were otherwise, he would wheel away swiftly and lead his pack into the privacy of the trees.

The wolf's next move signaled that he was willing to trust me. Continuing to hold my gaze, he slid his front legs forward and downward, as if he were bowing; then, with that graceful swiftness so typical of his kind, he leaped at me, trying to steal the woolen cap that I was wearing. Knowing wolves, I had been expecting some sort of mischievous prank and had been watching him as keenly as he had been studying me. His body gave no clue to his intent, but his eyes did, even to the point of telegraphing the target that had been selected. With bare millimeters to spare, his teeth clicked emptily as I moved my head out of reach, chuckling while doing so and pretending to scold him in a quiet voice.

Half-sitting and still as a statue, his head tilted to one side, Shawano found my eyes again, telling me without words that I had been tested and that if he had managed to secure my cap, he would have taken it away, perhaps to chew it to pieces or, more likely, to bury it within the shelter of the trees and bushes. A moment later he rose to all fours, made a half-turn, wagged his tail, and moved on. But after seven paces he stopped to inspect me again, his eyes still reflecting that gleam of puckish humor which is so characteristic of wolves, who love to tease and do so frequently.

Following my close encounter with their Alpha male, the other four wolves that made up the pack at that time turned their attention away from Shawano and transferred it to me, openly curious, as all wolves are, but cautious, not yet willing to trust the strange human who had arrived so unexpectedly. I, in turn, took the opportunity to make special note of each of them.

To my right, some twenty-five paces away, was Denali, Shawano's black mate and the Alpha female of the pack. Statuesque and in her prime, her muzzle salted on both sides by pure white hairs, Denali stared at me almost arrogantly, her entire being proclaiming her high rank.

Near her, but a respectful distance away, stood Thor, a two-year-old of brindled coat, the Beta, or second-ranking male. Almost as large as Shawano, Thor seemed an intense wolf who took life seriously and who one day might well challenge his leader's authority. Toivo, the third male of the pack, stood the farthest away, a yearling who had earlier caused my wife, Sharon, to exclaim: "Look at him! He's *so* scruffy. And *funny*! I bet he's a Dennis the Menace kind of wolf." Looking at him now, I had to agree with my wife's assessment; he clearly gave the impression that even if he were to be carefully groomed by brush and human hand, he would instantly revert to full scruffiness. He wasn't dirty, nor was his fur matted, but every guard hair along his mane stood up, each aiming in a different direction, and the rest of his coat, although in good condition, gave the impression that it had been obtained two sizes too large from some not-so-stylish thrift store. Toivo, I decided, was a natural comic, and like all good clowns, he had an intriguing personality, an air of charming insouciance that invited further acquaintance.

The fifth member of the pack was another black female. Her name was Brigit; she was six years old and had been relegated to the lowest position of all. Brigit, I had been told, was having a hard time, but before I could do more than notice that she was standing well away from her companions, Shawano took his eyes off me and began to lope toward the trees, only to be immediately converged upon by Thor, Denali, and Toivo. They mobbed him, each smiling as though to applaud his short but daring exchange with the human intruder. Shawano, standing erect and curtly as a monarch, accepted the homage of his subjects, allowing his muzzle to be nibbled but advertising his status by holding his tail high, his head up, his ears erect, his mouth partly open. His lips were wrinkled by a benevolent grin. This in contrast to the other wolves, who were careful to keep their tails low and who flattened their ears and whined as they sought their leaders's approval and reassurance. The exchange was typical of wolves everywhere, an interaction often mistaken by human observers for a manifestation of dictatorial tyranny on one side and fawning subjuga-

4

tion on the other. What soon followed would have served to confirm that impression, for Shawano suddenly stopped grinning and peeled back his lips in a seemingly ferocious snarl as he concentrated his attention on Toivo, who, in his enthusiasm, had become overly bold, allowing his tail to rise as he pressed too tightly against his leader.

Shawano's snarl turned into a rumbling growl. He sidestepped with his back legs, raised his shoulders so as to tower over Toivo, and then leaned on his subordinate. The young wolf, realizing his trespass, immediately dropped to the ground, there to lie with his tail pressed tightly against his groin and his uppermost back leg raised to expose the stomach and inguinal region. At the same time, he arched his neck, offering his throat. As this was going on, Denali and Thor imitated their leader and began snarling at Toivo, whose previous overconfident smile had turned into a mild grin of submission.

It would have been easy to conclude that a really savage contest was taking place and that blood was about to flow. Thirty years earlier I might well have drawn such an inference, but by now I knew that I was watching a frequently repeated and most important interaction, one genetically designed to preserve peace and good order in the pack. During this sort of exchange, a dominant wolf displays ritualistic aggression and a subordinate animal willingly exhibits fully submissive behavior, deliberately exposing its most vulnerable parts: the groin, the stomach, and the throat. Simultaneously, other members of the pack will rally to their Alpha's side and copy his behavior, in this way reinforcing his leadership during a mild altercation that usually lasts only a few seconds and ends, as it did that afternoon, when the dominant wolf fastens his fangs on the subordinate's muzzle, a hold during which the pressure is just sufficient to dimple the skin.

The mobbing of the leader by his subordinates, on the other hand, which is a frequent, daily occurrence, fulfills a pack's need for physical contact, strengthens the bonds between individuals and reinforces their leader's self-confidence. Far from being a display of tyranny and sub-

jection, such behavior represents an outpouring of affection that maintains social unity.

When Shawano released his hold on Toivo's nose, the four wolves separated, remaining near each other but momentarily busying themselves to work off the excitement generated by the mob display and by the ritualistic confrontation. Now there was much sniffing, yawning, urination, and body-shaking to resettle displaced hair; and there were many comings and goings as individuals sniffed at each other's wet deposits and somehow managed to produce a little more of their own fluids to add to the total. Presently, after scratching vigorously with his back paws, Shawano walked away, heading west. The other three wolves followed him and moments later they all disappeared within the trees.

Still kneeling, I returned to watching Brigit, who had elected to remain in my vicinity. It was obvious that she was seeking my attention, but it was also clear that she was afraid to come near me. Studying her, I noted that her coat was in poor condition and that she was thin, but it wasn't until she turned her back on me to go and sniff at the place where Shawano had disciplined Toivo that I noticed the open sore at the base of her tail, an area almost three inches in diameter that was devoid of hair and blood-red in color. Knowing that the other wolves had begun to harass Brigit in late January, at the start of the breeding period, I surmised that her injury had been inflicted by her companions, who were in the habit of nipping at the same place from time to time, keeping the sore open and enlarging it.

Based on the information that I had been given, I calculated that the black bitch had now been subjected to constant punishment for almost six weeks, even to the point where she was frequently denied access to food, so I was not surprised by her poor condition, nor by the appearance of general malaise that she exhibited. Neither did I find it remarkable that Brigit should now be behaving in a contradictory way, at one moment anxious to attract my attention, at the next seeking to avoid it. Having been denied the companionship of her pack, she was eager to socialize with *something*, even a human. Yet the deeply rooted inhibitions imposed by wolf hierarchy were

6

forcing her to remain in exile, even in the absence of the other wolves; she wanted to come to me, but she dared not.

That Brigit had been subjected to harassment at the onset of the breeding season was not abnormal, for only rarely will a second female in a pack be allowed to mate. To prevent such a union, the Alpha male and the Alpha female keep a close watch on their companions and are quick to subdue any other female that appears to be seeking the interest of a subordinate male. The vigilance of the Alphas is especially acute during the height of the estrus or female reproductive cycle, a time during which they will be quick to punish subordinate bitches for even the most minor transgression. In this, Alphas are often helped by the other males, who, despite any latent breeding desires that they might themselves have, are so committed to pack discipline that they subjugate their urges and follow the examples set by the Alphas. This is one of the inherent ways in which wolves control their populations and thus keep their numbers in balance with their food resources.

What was unusual in Brigit's case, however, was the intensity of her persecution and the length of its duration. Hitherto, during extensive studies of wild wolves as well as of four other captive packs, I had noted that although the estrus could last more than a month in the absence of pregnancy, the mere presence of an undisputed Alpha female considerably shortened the cycle of a subordinate, sometimes even appearing to inhibit it altogether. In the former case, lower-ranking females were harassed only during their curtailed sexually active time; in the latter situation, I had noted that in the absence of estral hormones subordinate bitches were not regarded as breeding competitors and were therefore left in peace. Why, then, was Brigit still being harassed? To try to find an answer to this question, I reviewed first the characteristics of the pack's home range, which earlier that afternoon I had toured with Jim Wuepper, the young man who keeps the wolves.

The enclosure consists of a two-acre quadrangle located just outside the town of Ishpeming, a community of some eight thousand people that lies 177 miles west of Sault Ste. Marie, Michigan. The land occupied by Shawano and his companions is part of a ten-acre lot bought by Jim and his wife, Kaye, for the express purpose of keeping wolves. The Wueppers and their seven-year-old son, Jason, share the property with the pack, for their pleasant bungalow home is located less than fifty yards from the eastern perimeter of the sanctuary. Here, too, lives Chico, a large, shaggy dog of mixed breed who watches the approaches to the house from the vantage of his own kennel near the entrance driveway and who is quick to advertise, with deep barks, the arrival of strangers.

During our inspection of the enclosure, while Jim was telling me how he and Kaye had come to settle on the outskirts of Ishpeming, I carefully examined the pack's habitat and noted that it contained all those features that wolves require for their well-being and contentment. In fact, it was the best of its kind that I had seen to date. The dominant trees were conifers, but there was a scattering of birches and other deciduous species as well as shrubs and bushes. The land sloped and rose haphazardly, containing hillocks and isolated rock outcrops of respectable proportions that offered sentinel heights much prized by wolves. Deadfall trees and branches were not constantly removed from the enclosure and these obstacles provided variation and challenge for animals that delight in romping and climbing when they are not engaged in more serious affairs. Last, but of vital significance, I had seen that the terrain offered areas of clay-sand soil ideal for the digging of dens. So, all in all, this habitat was a miniature representation of typical wolf range that would not in itself be expected to cause serious behavioral modifications during the breeding period, a time when even the best regulated wild packs undergo considerable stress.

After this brief review, aware that a reassessment of the enclosure could not yield the answer I was seeking, I began marshaling my knowledge of wild packs in general, of these captive wolves in particular, and of the people who are so committed to them. And as is my habit when seeking to understand any of the numerous conundrums that nature tosses my way at regular intervals, I

8

started at the beginning, recalling the first of those events that were to combine to bring me to the U.P., as this part of Michigan is most often called.

During an evening in December 1979, not long before Christmas, the telephone rang as Sharon and I were still sitting at the dinner table discussing our plans for the forthcoming holidays. Upon answering the ring, I was greeted by a man who identified himself as George Wilson and who in the same breath informed me that he was calling from "Marquette, Michigan, the Queen City of the U.P.," a statement that ended with a dry chuckle. Rather inanely, because I didn't quite know what else to reply, I said, "Oh? How interesting . . ." But before I had time to collect myself and phrase a more suitable comment, George plunged into the reason for his call.

"Well . . . *here!* Let's get down to it . . . I'm halfway through your book *The North Runner*. My brother Bill gave it to me today; he said, 'Here, you've got to read this man.' Well, anyway, I'm reading it. I'm halfway through it. You know, I used to keep wolves and I'm still involved with the pooches. I'm a filmmaker . . ."

I get many letters and more than a few telephone calls from people who have read my books and are kind enough to want to let me know that they found some interest in my work. But this was the first time that a total stranger had called intent on dragooning me into the service of his own special conservation project. Despite the stubborn streak that develops in me when I feel I am being pushed in a direction I have not personally selected, I found myself interested in George and in agreement with his views. I even shared his goal, which was to present the wolf to the general public in a realistic, sympathetic way, avoiding show-business exaggerations and steering clear of the rigidly dogmatic approach taken by most biologists.

I explained to George nevertheless that I was too busy just then to consider new work, although I might manage to do so at some later date. Undaunted, George continued to talk about wolves at some length and by the time our conversation ended, I had promised to visit him in Marquette after he returned from London, where, at the

9

invitation of the British Broadcasting Corporation, he was going to attend an international symposium of wildlife filmmakers.

Christmas had faded into the New Year and winter had turned into early spring before I heard again from George Wilson, this time by mail, a little note written, as he himself said, "in intellectual shorthand." He was back, I read; there followed a few succinct lines describing his welcome in London by the BBC and by a number of people whose names meant nothing to me. But included with the note was a veritable mass of other material, some of it referring to George's experiences with his own wolf pack and some dealing with the making of wildlife films. Buried amid this material was a postscript that said: "When you come, telephone me. We'll meet you in the Soo [Sault Ste. Marie]. Wolves mated. Small pooches expected May."

As matters turned out, I was too busy to go to Michigan in 1980, but George continued to send his succinct memos, to which I replied. And we telephoned each other from time to time, trading wolf information while discussing the animals in a general way. Thus began a long-distance relationship that gradually developed into friendship, even though we were not to meet in person until more than three years after our first telephone conversation.

In December of 1982, again shortly before Christmas, George called to chat. As usual we discussed wolves, but on this occasion my friend referred to a particular captive pack with whom it appeared that he had developed a close rapport, although because of his penchant for switching from topic to topic without preamble, I was unable to determine where in Michigan the wolves were located, or who really owned them, believing initially that they were under his care. By then I knew George well and had realized that the only way to bring him back to a topic was to ask for specific information and to interrupt firmly whenever he wandered off the subject, a habit due, I believe, to his keen brain, which always seems to be working overtime. In due course, I learned for the first time about Shawano and his companions and about Jim Wuepper. I found myself growing extremely interested in the

10

wolves and in those people who were so obviously committed to them.

As he had done at the end of all telephone conversations, George again urged me to visit him in Marquette. As usual, I was too busy and I again refused so that we concluded our talk by exchanging season's greetings. Afterward, however, I found that I could not stop thinking about George and the wolves. On the third day after our conversation, I felt compelled to go to Michigan to meet this energetic champion of wolves and to spend a little time with the Ishpeming pack. I was also curious about Jim Wuepper and especially about his reasons for keeping wolves. There and then I telephoned George and gave him the news. He seemed delighted. Then he immediately began to plan the book about wolves that he expected me to write after our visit! Apart from flitting blissfully from subject to subject during general conversations, George appears to have trained his mind to reject the word *no*. He simply ignores refusal and continues talking and planning as enthusiastically as ever. I was therefore not surprised that he took no notice of me when I tried to tell him that I was far too busy to consider another book at that time. In the end, not wishing to increase the earnings of the telephone company's shareholders, I let the matter drop, naively believing that I could deal with it on arrival in Marquette.

Having decided to go to Michigan, I went to my desk calendar to pick suitable dates for the journey. I was aghast by what I had taken on for 1983! I had to put the finishing touches to a book; I had to write an article on winter camping for a Toronto magazine; Sharon and I were due to go to Massachusetts in early March to do shark research; on our way back from the coast, we had committed ourselves to call on an elderly lady who has been operating a sanctuary for beavers in upper New York State for more than fifty years; in early May, I was due in Washington, D.C., to meet with officials of the U.S. Fish and Wildlife Service to begin research for another book; then my publisher had arranged for me to go on a seven-day, cross-Canada tour to promote my latest published work. And there was more! I had three books to structure and outline; a neglected correspondence file that

11

bulged with letters from readers; a second book was to be published in June and I was to go on another promotion tour. What should I do? My first move was to consult Sharon. My wife has an incisive way of dealing with problems, and although she scolds me occasionally for taking on more work than can properly be managed, she is good at peering into dark tunnels and seeing the distant daylight. Listening quietly until I had finished explaining my predicament, she asked if I couldn't postpone the trip to Michigan until autumn.

I told her that I felt impelled to go in the spring. I had been putting off this journey for three years. I felt I couldn't put it off much longer.

"Well, we're due back from Massachusetts and New York on March 25. Why don't we spend two days at home—you'll *have* to rest for a bit—then leave on the twenty-eighth, it's a Monday. We can spend a night in Sault Ste. Marie and drive the rest of the way on the morning of the twenty-ninth. But I don't think we can stay longer than a week," was Sharon's verdict.

When we eventually arrived in Marquette in accordance with Sharon's timing, I still did not have the heart to tell our friend that this was to be a brief, one-time visit and that, on no account, as we both had firmly repeated to each other, would I allow myself to become involved with writing about wolves that lived almost five hundred miles from our home.

George, who seems to know everybody everywhere, had booked us in to the Tiroler Hoff Motel, located just outside Marquette on the Carp River Hills, a charming establishment with a grand view of Lake Superior (icebound at that time). The proprietors gave us a truly royal welcome. Here, later that afternoon, we at last met George Wilson; over six feet tall, if somewhat stooped, of Aztecan features and serene presence, he arrived bearing gifts: a flowering plant for Sharon and a bottle of Courvoisier cognac for me—he had read in one of my books that I enjoy a tot of this elixir on special occasions. Sharon instantly hugged him; I shook his hand; our long-distance friendship blossomed wonderfully. George is a very special man. His warm personality, his lively sense of humor, and his effervescent enthusiasm for the cause

12

of wolf conservation touched us both deeply. Beyond these things, if it had not been for his stubborn refusal to take "no" for an answer, this book would never have been written!

No real naturalist assumes that he knows all about any mammal species. If he ever reaches that point, he is promptly disillusioned by acquaintance with an individual that behaves as no others of his kind have acted before. . . .
                                        —Victor H. Cahalane,
                                        Mammals of North America

TWO

On the afternoon during which Sharon and I were introduced to Shawano and his pack, we arrived with Buck LeVasseur, producer-cameraman for WLUC-TV in Marquette, a man greatly interested in wildlife and conservation. He wanted to film our meeting with the wolves. With this in mind, Buck came equipped with a video camera and a large tripod and began setting up just outside the enclosure as we approached the fence. The wolves became nervous, retreating into the trees.

Standing silently between Sharon and Jim Wuepper, I readily identified Shawano as the leader by his behavior and by the way that he carried himself. His movements were assured; his general demeanor broadcasted confidence tempered by caution and proclaimed that he would study the new developments in his territory before deciding his next moves. In like manner, I was soon able to determine the social standings of the other members of the pack. Although it is normal for such sensitive and intelligent animals to be reserved in the presence of strangers, Shawano's subordinates were displaying a greater degree of apprehension than I might have expected. Hard upon this observation it struck me that the manner of our arrival must have inhibited the wolves. This caused me some annoyance; I should have anticipated the effects of our visit at a time when the pack was still gripped by the excitement and tensions of the breeding season.

Instead of coming quietly, preferably in Jim's car, the sound of which was familiar to the wolves, we had driven into the yard in three separate vehicles. The clatter of the combined engines announced our approach even before we had turned into the Wuepper property. Then, instead of going into Jim's house, there to wait until the wolves had been given time to adjust to our noisy invasion of their domain, we had immediately approached the enclosure. Chico's noisy barks also heralded our arrival, the dog having become equally excited. No wonder the pack reacted as it did! Tame wolves will readily accept most strangers if these are properly introduced by the humans in whom they have reposed their trust, but these animals were only semisocialized toward people and more inclined to react like their wild kin, as George Wilson had told me long before our arrival in Michigan. I had stupidly allowed myself to be carried away by my eagerness to see the pack. That after thirty years of experience with wolves I should have been guilty of such a gross error of judgment was humiliating. Of more concern, however, was the very real possibility that my blunder would cause Shawano to distrust Sharon and me now and in the future, in which case our journey would be wasted, for wolves literally follow their leader. In such an event, I would be denied the opportunity to study the pack's behavior and compare it with that of wild wolves, which was another reason why we had journeyed to the Upper Peninsula. Fortunately, Shawano was good enough to forgive my trespass once he had the opportunity of "reading" me.

Jim brought my self-recrimination to an end by opening the box of raw chicken he'd brought, taking out a piece, and holding it aloft. Shawano and his family observed keenly, and soon afterward the leader trotted forward, followed more cautiously by the others. While the

15

Alpha was still some fifteen paces from the nine-foot-high fence, Jim threw the first piece of meat. It sailed high over the wire and Shawano went into swift action.

Running toward us, the big wolf leaped, stretching his lean body to the fullest, his muscles and sinews bunching fluidly and becoming visible even through the dense coat of creamy-fawn hair. Up and up he went, his great jaws gaping, his amber eyes fixed on the descending target. It was like watching a slow-motion movie, although in reality the entire action did not last more than a few seconds; but the picture of that lithe wolf leaping so wonderfully for the food is still as vivid today as it was at the time. And I can still hear the great *thunk* of his jaws closing on the prize while it was still a foot or so higher than the fence!

Shawano landed facing us, but turned about quickly. It was then that I noticed Thor, who had moved from a position beside a spruce and was at that moment rushing toward his leader. Now, I was sure, a fight would take place, for no Alpha wolf that I had ever observed would have permitted a subordinate to approach at such a moment. Shawano ran toward Thor without emitting the usual growls of warning, a silence I interpreted as a sure sign that he was going to attack immediately. Then, to my utter astonishment, when the distance between the two wolves had closed to about ten feet, Shawano literally *threw* the chicken at the Beta male, whose jaws opened and closed on the offering as noisily as the Alpha's had done moments earlier. "This," I thought, "is highly unusual!"

Jim, seemingly quite unconcerned by the extraordinary behavior, reached into the box, took out another piece of chicken, and heaved it over the fence. Again, Shawano rushed forward, leaped as mightily and gracefully as before, snapped up the food, and turned. This time his mate, Denali, ran toward him. Again at about a ten-foot distance, he threw the chicken at her. She fielded it as easily as Thor had done and retreated into the trees to eat in concealment. Jim threw a third piece of chicken; Shawano repeated his moves, on this occasion throwing the meat into the jaws of Toivo, who had also anticipated the gift and was running to get it. Only then did Shawano take the fourth piece of chicken and keep it for himself, trotting away to join the other three wolves. Brigit was left to get her own food, which Jim threw to her. For some minutes after this, the only sounds to be heard were the champing of fangs in meat and the cracking of bones.

We all stood silently for some minutes. I don't know what the others were thinking, but I was busy reenacting Shawano's expert throws, lupine field passes that were made with force and bull's-eye accuracy, the movements of which I had entirely missed during the first throw, but which I carefully noted during the next two. The wolf had run with his head held high and his shoulders erect, the food clamped firmly in his mouth. When he judged the distance to be right, he suddenly snapped his head and chest forward, at the same time opening his jaws. Evidently he sighted down his nose, for when this was pointing directly at the approaching target wolf, he released the chicken, an example of perfect coordination that produced extreme accuracy.

In the wild, the male and female Alphas usually eat first, followed by the other pack members in descending social status, although the entire family will often congregate around a carcass after the leaders have at least partially satisfied their hunger. Usually, if a subordinate approaches a higher-ranking wolf too closely, the latter will snarl, a deep and rumbling sound that normally causes an underling to retreat; if it does not, the dominant animal will likely snap at the interloper, sometimes fastening its jaws on the latter's muzzle, a bloodless bite that almost always suffices to intimidate a lower-ranking animal. These generalizations notwithstanding, it should be noted that social interactions within each pack, or family, though they conform to certain basic and inherent characteristics, vary considerably in all behavioral aspects, just as they do among human families, no two of which conduct their affairs in exactly the same ways.

It is safe to say that the parent wolves, the two Alphas, most often eat first, but it would be presumptuous to state that they always do; and those observers who dare to ascribe to all wolf packs those traits witnessed only in some groups will surely come to regret their brashness if they continue to study wolves.

17

Be that as it may, those dominant wolves that insist on taking first place at the dinner table do so not out of selfishness, but rather because they are the guardians of the pack and must remain strong for the good of all. And I have often noted that Alpha males that jealously guard their right to eat first are also the first to face a threat, or even the suspicion of one. Similarly, such dominant wolves are often the first to initiate an attack on large, potentially dangerous animals. Then, too, Alpha wolves will conscientiously bring back food to their nursing mates during the denning time, either carrying pieces of meat in their mouths or regurgitating the food, feeding in this manner the nursing mother and the pups, if these have begun to eat meat. This sharing of food is not unique to the Alphas, however, for all wolves, no matter what their status may be, engage in it with more or less frequency, even after the pups have grown to hunting size and are no longer in need of individual attention. I have also observed one adult wolf regurgitating for another on being solicited, usually in summer. A pack may split up, foraging over a particular area, each animal hunting for itself. Luck or experience may favor some of the wolves, who become replete; others may eat only enough to still their hunger pangs for a time. It is not uncommon, then, for one adult to feed another on demand. Nevertheless, I had not until that day witnessed a lead wolf actually feeding each of his subordinates in turn before he had satisfied his own hunger. But when I remarked about this to Jim, he seemed surprised that I should even mention the matter.

"Yes, he does it all the time when strangers come to visit," was his reply.

It became clear to me that Shawano, with the unfailing intelligence and sensitivity of his kind, had long ago realized that although he was not personally intimidated by newcomers, his pack members were; so for their sake, if strangers were around when food was being distributed, he deliberately faced visitors on his own, feeding the pack members in turn so that they could eat unmolested. By the time we arrived in Michigan, all the wolves had become accustomed to their leader's routine, knowing

18

that as they rushed toward him one at a time, he would feed them.

Between autumn and spring, Jim's wolves feed largely on the meat of deer and other animals that are killed on U.P. highways, but from late spring and through summer, when road-kills become scarce because animals remain within the shelter of the forests, the wolves are given meat purchased at a local supermarket, mainly chicken parts and raw liver. The pack is fed near the fence, usually by Jim but sometimes by George Wilson or Scott Stewart, another wolf enthusiast who has developed a close relationship with Shawano and his companions. (To those dog and cat owners who are careful to avoid feeding chicken bones to their pets because splinters may pierce the animals' intestines, let me say that this would be a rare accident for a wolf. Unlike their domestic counterparts, these wild dogs crunch up such small, hollow bones and, additionally, appear to have a superb digestive system capable of voiding even the many strange objects pups tend to swallow, including quite large stones, rolled-up pieces of birch bark, and chunks of wood chewed off dead branches.)

On the occasion of our first visit with them, after Shawano and his three companions finished eating, they moved away from the fence area and disappeared into the forested part of their enclosure, leaving Brigit alone. The low-ranking bitch, having finished her own meal, began to solicit my attention. Undecided about whether to come to be petted or to run away, she seemed nonetheless to find some solace or reassurance in my presence, so I remained near the fence, watching her and occasionally speaking softly to her, observing her behavior while at the same time thinking about this pack in particular and wolves in general.

Meditating in this way, I thought that those of us who have knowledge of the wolf and have deep empathy with the species discover to our frequent amazement, and despite our knowledge, that this much-maligned animal possesses the best of human attributes but few, if any, of our weaknesses. Furthermore, judging by those few people who still live in small, closely knit tribal units, it seems to me likely that wolf hierarchy is not much different from that by which early hominids probably governed themselves, when related individuals lived and worked together under strong male *and* female leadership and cooperated conscientiously to ensure the family's survival.

Long before my introduction to the Ishpeming wolves, I had concluded that the wolf reached his evolutionary plateau by the simple expedient of always exercising his full potential. That is to say, his mind, his spirit, and his body have become blended into a single natural and highly efficient instrument that functions in harmony with the environment. No matter what his hierarchical standing, a wild wolf is always in command of himself and is aware of his strengths and his limitations. These things allow the wolf to conform to the disciplines of the pack while at the same time preserving his individuality and his self-respect. Unlike contemporary humans, who consider that to be of low rank is debasing, the wolf readily accepts his social position, whatever this may be, because he is inherently aware that the success of his species is based upon full intragroup cooperation. This means that an individual wolf must be subservient to the pack and that the pack cannot function effectively without those rules that cause its members to work to their full potential.

Occasionally, however, a wolf seems to require solitude. It will then leave the pack, most often wandering off somewhere nearby and lying down alone, there to doze or merely to watch the forest. Sometimes such a wolf may go off to explore farther afield, usually following known trails as he gradually increases the distance between himself and his companions. During such solo journeys, he will often pause to hunt, stalking, killing, and eating small animals, but unable alone to pull down the large prey found within his territory.

During the summer of 1971, in the mountains of British Columbia, near the source of the Nass River, I watched one such temporary loner leave the pack and make his way along the valley floor. He followed an ancient, well-defined trail that led northwest to thread a twisting course between the Skeena and Cassiar Mountains, a pathway used by animals and man and known

20

topographically as the Old Telegraph Trail, which in that area follows the course of a waterway named Muckaboo Creek. I had been in contact with the pack for almost a month and had been accepted by the wolves, although now that they had taken that year's litter of five pups to a summer rendezvous, the Alphas occasionally came near my place of vantage and howl-barked at me—a not uncommon display that wolves resort to when humans intrude, the main intent of which, I believe, is to cause the interlopers to go away. Nevertheless, if an observer has been circumspect in his or her behavior and has been accepted as harmless by a pack, the rather intimidating outcries of the two leaders will usually cease after fifteen or twenty minutes, when the wolves will return to their family.

The evening before, the pack, which consisted of nine animals, had made a kill and had returned bulging with food about 8:00 P.M. The five pups and their babysitter, a small female wolf whom I thought of as an aunt, had alerted me to the return of the pack by howling noisily, the voices of the young high and often yappy, their sitter's deep and long-drawn. Seconds after this outbreak, the returning pack howled in response, a chorus of throaty songs that continued intermittently until the male and female leaders came into view, followed closely by the other wolves. I had no means of knowing what kind of animal the pack had killed, but guessed that it had probably been a moose, judging by the pack's bulging stomachs.

As the pack entered the boundary of the rendezvous, a sparsely treed area of relatively flat land located along the flanks of a five-thousand-foot-high mountain, the pups and their guardian converged upon them, each soliciting food, the "aunt" whining and nibbling at the muzzle of the Beta male, and the pups mobbing their father and mother. Within seconds, dark red meat was being regurgitated. The stay-at-homes were soon as bulgy as the hunters.

My very spartan little camp was located farther up the mountain in direct line of sight, about five hundred yards from the rendezvous, but more like one thousand yards up the gradient. From here, with field glasses, I had an

21

excellent view of the rendezvous and of the wolves and could by then recognize each member of the pack and know its hierarchical standing.

The loner was a young animal, probably a two-year-old, a male of low rank, but not in the least inhibited by his social standing. He was active, playful, and at times downright cheeky, whereupon the big male leader, a dark gray animal with a pepper-and-salt head, would pin the unmannerly wolf to the ground, grasping his muzzle, a task at which he was often joined by the lead female and the Beta male. None of these reprimands had much effect on the young male, however. He was never bitten hard, and although he whined and showed submission while being roughed up, he always sprang to his feet immediately after the ordeal was over and galloped away, sometimes rushing about at full speed, on other occasions picking up a piece of gnawed bone or a chewed stick and soliciting play from one of his companions.

The day before he left on his personal walkabout, I had noticed that he spent a considerable time lying quietly in the shade of some bushes, snoozing quite a lot, yawning widely, and, between naps, staring fixedly downward, toward Muckaboo Creek. In the afternoon, when the pack gathered amid great excitement, then set off on their hunt, the loner followed, as intent on the business at hand as were his companions. But early next morning, as the sun was blooding the eastern peaks, I saw him rise from his bed, stretch and yawn mightily, then, without a glance at any of the other wolves, begin to trot downward. I watched him until he disappeared from view around Muckaboo Rapids, thinking that he would probably return by evening. An hour later, the pack left as well, but in a different direction, this time the aunt going with the group and the mother staying with the pups. Four hours after departure, the main body of wolves returned. They had gone back to the kill and were as replete as they had been yesterday. Again they fed the stay-at-homes. But the loner was not with the pack.

On the evening of the fourth day following his departure, the loner announced his return by howling, a cry evidently emitted while he was several miles away and received faintly by my ears. Indeed, had the pack not become electrified by the call, I would have disregarded the distant howls, believing them to be uttered by a wolf from another group. But even before the first notes alerted my hearing, the wolves I was observing reacted, obviously having been able to detect the very beginning of the call. Chorusing, the thirteen wolves exhibited a high degree of arousal. The Alphas came together, the female holding her head close to her mate's, her muzzle more horizontal than his, which was upraised. Her mouth was open wide; her call was high. The male's mouth was tunneled, only about half-open, his voice deeper and modulated by the enclosing lips. The combined voices from the rendezvous made it impossible for me to hear the loner's call, but then, almost in unison, the pack stopped howling. Now there was much coming and going, some soft growling as one or another wolf mouthed a companion. The pups rushed around, two of them chasing each other, a third, the biggest and a male, trying to catch his own tail while the remaining two ganged up on the aunt and play-bit at her neck. She endured the mauling with the kind of typical forbearance that adults always display toward the young.

I had started my stopwatch as soon as the wolves replied to the loner. By its timing, the missing pack member howled again four minutes and eleven seconds later. This time, although some of the wolves yelped excitedly, particularly the pups, the Alpha was the only one to reply. But he didn't howl. Instead, he gave what I call a howl-bark, a sound that begins with a deep, throaty *ooooh* note, turns into a high-pitched half-growl-half-bark, and ends in a mournful, long-drawn howl. Again there was silence and, as before, great excitement gripped the pack. Two minutes later, the male and female leaders trotted to the northwestern side of the rendezvous and stood waiting, stiff-legged and tails erect.

The loner now appeared. He stopped on seeing the leaders; then, tail down, ears flattened against his head, and back arched, he moved forward, his mouth gaping in a wide smile, his head bobbing up and down and moving from side to side alternately, a sort of exaggerated bowing movement. The two Alphas went to meet their subordinate and began growling, not the full-throated,

23

deep growl sparked by aggression, but a more ritualized vocalization quite different from the sound that I have come to term "the real thing." The loner and his leader met, whereupon the newcomer immediately flopped on his side and was set upon by the Alphas. They muzzle-bit him, growling in that controlled way, while he whined, licked at them, and, right leg lifted high, wetted himself. For about a minute he was mildly roughed up by the Alphas, who were now ringed by the rest of the pack, until the male leader pounced upon his underling. This signaled a general mobbing of the returnee, a free-for-all accompanied by much growling and yapping in which even the pups joined. After some moments the loner regained his feet and began to run round and around the open area, pursued by several of his companions. The two leaders, however, went off on their own, followed by the pups. The father, mother, and young stopped. The adults lay down side by side and the pups began romping with each other. The loner continued to run and leap as he led the chase. But this was clearly a game now. Each wolf ran with sheer abandon, mouth open, tongue lolling out, the white teeth showing in that age-old lupine smile. Then, one by one, the chasers got tired and went off to lie down. In the end, the loner, now fully welcomed into the pack again, flopped on his side near two of the pups, who immediately began to play with him, climbing on his back, biting at his tail, and generally having a joyous time.

Before that day in British Columbia, I had seen other examples of a wolf's need for solitude and had noted, on those occasions when I had been able to observe the return, that the packs involved always acted in pretty much the same way as the group I observed in the Nass Valley. Such behavior suggests to me that the family is glad to welcome back the wanderer, but I get the feeling that a mild reprimand is also intended.

Thinking about these things while I was watching Brigit, I remembered that I had seen two examples of females being temporarily chased away from their packs during the breeding season, the first in 1968 and the second in 1969. Although each female belonged to a different pack, both instances had occurred in Ontario, on land

24

I had bought in 1963. These seventy-five acres of forested domain backed onto government wilderness in which wolves, coyotes, foxes, moose, deer, and other animals made their homes.

In August of the year I bought the land, I completed construction of a one-room cabin. There my late wife, Joan, and I spent as much time as possible. One Friday afternoon in mid-November, after I had hauled in five hundred pounds of coal for our stove, leaving it outside the cabin, Joan and I went shopping at a local store four miles away. The weather was already cold, some twenty degrees below the freezing point;* a light fall of snow covered the landscape.

When we returned, we discovered that a pack of wolves had inspected our building, tracking all around it; they had urinated copiously on the coal sacks. Interested but not greatly surprised—we had heard this particular pack howling on a number of occasions—I put the coal away in a shed and we had our supper. Before bedtime it began to snow again, a sleety white driven by a westerly wind. In the morning it was still snowing, a fine, blowy, niveous curtain that swirled through the forest and formed patterns against the western sides of the tree trunks. I went outside. As I stood within the trees, I heard the high-pitched barking of wolves coming from the northeast, the calls being fairly constant and seeming to be issuing from one location, suggesting that the pack was more or less stationary. Knowing the country well by now, I felt sure that the wolves were on the ice of one of our largest beaver ponds, located three-quarters of a mile away. Without bothering to have breakfast, I took my camera and set out for the pond, guided by the continuing barks. The excited sounds puzzled me, for they suggested that the pack was worked up over some particular thing that it had found in the area of the pond. The closer I got to the area, the louder and more agitated were the barks. Soon I could see the screen of trees that surrounded the frozen water, and I began taking advantage of whatever cover I could find. Minutes later, I had squeezed myself within the low branches of a large bal-

*All temperatures throughout are Fahrenheit.

25

sam tree, concealed from the wolves but commanding a good view.

Although visibility wasn't great, I had no difficulty seeing the eight gray-fawn wolves that were dashing about over the ice, at times bunching up, on other occasions spreading out over an area of some four hundred square feet. The wolves were playing! Using the field glasses to confirm my first impression, I was immediately able to determine that a definite game was in progress. Seven of the wolves were chasing a large individual, clearly the pack leader, each trying to make body contact with him. The Alpha was dashing about wildly, at one moment running at full speed, at another coming to an abrupt, sliding stop that swiveled his hindquarters, much as an automobile skids around when braked abruptly on a slippery surface. The result of this maneuver was that the big wolf turned about, sliding sideways. This caused the pursuers to run right past him, all of them sliding also as they tried to stop in order to turn and continue the chase. Recovering his balance, the leader would then charge into the rearmost of his pursuers, hitting it with his chest and sending it rolling over and over, skidding helplessly on the snowy ice. When this happened, the seven chasers would bark shrilly, including the one that had been bowled over, as though registering their pleasure and amusement. Then the whole show began over again.

The wolves were about 150 yards from where I was crouching, but although I had brought a telephoto lens for the camera, poor light and the snowy curtain precluded photographs. In any event, I was much too engrossed with the spectacle to run the risk of alerting the wolves by moving or making even the faintest sound, knowing that such things would cause the pack to disappear into the forest.

I watched those wolves for seventeen minutes. They ran, skidded, rolled, and leaped over the ice in complete abandon, remaining in more or less the same part of the pond and behaving, it seemed to me, like children newly let out for recess. Quite suddenly, the leader halted in his tracks and stared directly at my place of concealment. I may have made some slight sound, or he may have scented me, or, more likely, his finely tuned senses registered my alien presence because of certain influences that my own dull faculties could not detect. In any event, after staring fixedly for a few seconds, an interval during which the other wolves became statue-still and also stared at my hiding place, the big wolf turned fluidly and led the pack across the ice and into the forest.

Soon afterward, I became aware that the wolves were regular visitors who seemed to find something of special interest in and around our cabin. Apart from the many tracks left in the snow, they always urinated on our walls and front step; if I left something outside, such as an axe, it would be singled out for the same treatment. In effect, the wolves had turned our rustic dwelling into a giant scent station. This told us that the pack considered the land we had bought, including the location of the cabin, as part of their personal territory.

When the wolves began visiting at night while we were in residence, I began buying food for them: stewing beef, bones and fat, commercial dog food; we also saved all our table-meat scraps. By now I had christened the leader Lobo, for no particular reason other than that the word is Spanish for "wolf," and so I thought of the pack and wrote about it in my notes as the Lobo Pack.

I always placed the food offerings on a bare rock that was about twenty-five yards from the east window of the cabin and in direct line of sight, for I was hoping to get a glimpse of our visitors. At first, however, they came only at night, the disappearance of the food and the big tracks left in the snow telling their own stories. Then, early one morning toward the end of winter, Lobo appeared on his own. The sun was not yet tipping the trees, although the eastern sky was flushed with its nearness. I had gotten up about fifteen minutes earlier, stoked the fire, and put the coffee water on the stove. Waiting for the kettle to boil, I walked to the east window to look outside, using field glasses to search the area around the food cache. It had snowed the previous day; there were no fresh tracks to be seen. The meat and bones were still there, except for a few scraps that the gray jays were even then filching from the pile. One of these charming and companionable northern birds had just landed on the ground and was hopping toward the frozen meat when it

27

suddenly flapped up, settling itself high in the branches of a white pine and scanning the forest. Moments later I caught a glimpse of gray fur, then another. Lobo had come. He now stood peering at the cabin, most of his body concealed behind the trunk of a large poplar. I remained stock-still, my heart thumping with the thrill of the moment. Then Lobo stepped away from the tree and trotted to the food. After one more look in my direction (I suspected he knew I was there, but of course I have no proof of this), the wolf began to feed, at first standing astraddle, the frozen pile between his front feet. He was using his lower incisors to scrape pieces off the mass, but presently he lay down, occasionally digging at the hard meat with one front foot and in this way dislodging chunks that he chewed up. Ten minutes later Lobo had ingested all the meat and had left, carrying in his mouth a large beef knucklebone.

Our acquaintance with Lobo and his pack ripened eventually into a sort of mutual trust, for, following that first daylight appearance of the big wolf, he came quite regularly to take the food we put out. But when visiting during the day, he always arrived alone, although whether he shared his meal with the pack, or more probably with the Alpha female, I do not know. Today, however, having seen Shawano feed his pack, I suspect that Lobo did share with at least his mate.

Between 1963 and the spring of 1967, we saw Lobo and his companions on many occasions. Because I regularly traveled the wilderness, I sighted the wolves more often than Joan did, and as time went by, I was followed by the pack quite frequently. Lobo often showed himself at such times, and on occasion I also caught a glimpse of one or two of the other wolves. Then, in October of 1965, after an entire day in the wilderness, I had camped in the open, bedded on a mattress of evergreen boughs and sleeping fully dressed inside a down bag, a small tarpaulin spread over me as a cover to keep out moisture.

I was awakened at dawn the next morning by a sound that I at first thought was made by falling rain, but when I raised my head from its concealment within the sleeping bag, it was to see Lobo in the act of lowering one of his back legs after he had urinated on the foot of my bed!

My immediate impulse was to yell at him, for I do not like being piddled on by anything! But I controlled the urge, completely fascinated by Lobo's behavior. Had I raised my head quickly, I might well have startled the wolf and caused him to run; as it was, I looked up slowly, still half-bemused by sleep. Lobo now gazed directly into my eyes from a distance of about six feet. Then he backed away slightly, scratched vigorously at the ground, and turned around. At this point I noticed that six members of his pack were clustered among the trees about fifteen feet away, every wolf watching the action with thoughtful gaze.

Lobo next trotted toward his pack, reached the group, turned, and gave me one more glance. The wolves then disappeared, silent as drifting feathers.

In the spring of 1967 we bought an additional 350-acre farm eight miles north of our seventy-five acres. By early summer we were living there full time. We thought that we would only see the Lobo Pack on those rather rare occasions when we visited our woodland cabin. But Lobo found us.

I spent most of July and part of August exploring our own wilderness and some of the many thousands of acres of government forest that lay at our back door and stretched to the north and east of our new location. During the course of these explorations I found many wolf tracks and droppings; on three occasions I discovered the remains of old hunts, but I did not see a single wolf. Then, in the autumn, as Joan and I were strolling through our large stand of sugar maples, we heard some faint sounds at our back. On turning, we spotted Lobo, who was standing beside an exceptionally large maple. As we looked at him, he backed away, concealing most of himself behind the big trunk, but keeping his head out, giving us that intense wolf stare. Moments later he trotted away.

We started putting food out once more, this time just on the edge of the maple woods, at a place we could watch from our kitchen window and about two hundred yards from our house. Again the Lobo Pack came routinely, but at irregular intervals. By this time, however, the adults of the pack had been reduced, consisting now of the leader and his mate, a rather small, light-colored wolf, as well as one adult male and a dark gray female who had always been of low rank. Trapping, I knew, had reduced the adults. But five young wolves, born that spring, almost made up the losses.

When we took up full-time residence at the farm, we bought a malamute pup, Tundra. By autumn he was six months old and as large as the young wolves in Lobo's group. The pack now showed considerable interest in the dog's tracks and urine deposits, invariably covering these with their own. Tundra always accompanied me in my wilderness wanderings, a guide whose keen nose and ears frequently led me to make discoveries I would have missed had he not tugged me off my own course in order to investigate sight or sound. In this way, during the breeding season of 1968, Tundra dragged me to a height of land, a large upthrust of Cambrian granite on which grew only a cover of blueberry bushes and a few tenacious pine trees. One of these was a giant, a squat tree of massive girth that grew on a sharp drop-off overlooking an expanse of meadow, which many years earlier had been a large beaver pond but was now abandoned by its builders and covered in rushes, stunted willows, and alders. From this vantage I was able to see Lobo's pack trotting northward in single file; but there were only three adult wolves. The low-ranking female was missing. The pack was about five hundred yards away, aiming for a second granite rise almost opposite the one on which Tundra and I stood. Watching through the field glasses, I noticed that Lobo and his mate often looked behind them, but although I scanned their backtrail with the glasses, I could not see anything out of the ordinary.

As the pack began to climb the rock rise, however, Lobo stopped, turned around, and began running downslope, followed by his mate and the rest of the pack. It was then that I saw the gray bitch. She had just entered the beaver meadow and was walking slowly toward the pack, her entire being showing total submission. Her tail was tucked between her legs, her spine arched, her ears held flat against her head, and her mouth open in a submissive grin. I turned the glasses on Lobo. His hackles were up, his ears erect. His mate copied his actions.

30

When the wolves reached the gray bitch, Lobo and his Alpha ganged up on her, ignoring her submission as they knocked her down. I couldn't see clearly, but it became obvious they were biting her. Tundra, whose ears were so very much better than mine, could obviously hear the growling that was beyond my senses. He howl-barked. This caused Lobo and his pack to turn away from the bitch and to streak for the shelter of the forest. The unfortunate female, meanwhile, got up swiftly and disappeared in the same direction from which she had emerged.

From tracks and occasional sightings of the Lobo Pack as well as of the ostracized female, I learned that she remained in exile until after the birth of that year's cubs, a time during which she often followed the pack at a respectful distance and even managed to eat leftovers from some of the kills after Lobo and his group had departed from the sites of the remains.

At first, I felt sure that the gray female had been forced right out of the pack, but in June when I found the place where the weaned cubs had been relocated (there were only two pups in the litter that year, both males), I discovered that the gray wolf had again become an active member of the pack and was, in fact, babysitting the cubs when I found their rendezvous.

While Lobo's pack ranged the wilderness that lay to the west of the central portion of my farm, a second, smaller pack occupied a territory to the east, its western boundary overlapping the Lobo Pack's eastern limits. Later I was to theorize that this East Pack, as I named it, was related to the Lobo Pack, for on three separate occasions I was fortunate enough to witness meetings between the two groups, all of which, although beginning with raised hackles and aggressive body postures displayed by the two leaders, ended with tail-wagging and a general intermingling. Some of the younger members even played together.

The following February, I discovered that one of the three females belonging to the East Pack was also chased away during the breeding period, this information again being determined by tracking and some sightings. But I did not manage to locate the rendezvous of this group, so I was unable to determine whether the ousted female had, as in the previous case, acted as a cub-sitter. Nevertheless, in July of 1969, I saw the entire East Pack traveling along a granite ridge within some seventy-five yards of where I was sitting. Aided by the field glasses, I saw that the outcast bitch had been readmitted to the group.

My studies of these two wolf packs ended soon after this sighting, for Joan had died in June of that year and I was unable to continue living at the farm, which I sold in 1970.

Now, kneeling in the snows of Michigan's Upper Peninsula and watching Brigit, I realized that the harassment to which she was being subjected by Shawano and Denali was the result of the wolf's strong and inherent need to keep its numbers balanced with the food supply, a natural form of birth control inherently exercised by the species, which, in the wild, prevents overpopulation and continues to assert itself even in captivity. This characteristic of wolves has been known for some time, but more recently scientists have begun to argue about the mechanisms that combine to inhibit breeding by subordinate females. Later I will examine this important part of the biology of wolves in detail. Here I will note only that Brigit's *continued* harassment—long after the estrus period—occurred because she had no option but to remain with the pack; she could not leave for a time and return after the pups were born, when she almost certainly would have been made welcome in a wild state. As it was, I learned later from Jim Wuepper that Brigit's persecution ended when the pups were born, and after these had been weaned, she appointed herself their guardian, a task at which she excelled and which was approved of by Shawano and Denali.

Having reached these conclusions, I began to take careful note of the way in which Brigit was carrying herself, reading what George Wilson would have called her "body English" and which I have long thought of as body language.

Brigit moved in a semicrouched position; her head and neck were carried low and her back legs were slightly bent, a posture that caused her spine to arch. Her tail

32

was tucked between her thighs, almost pressing against the stomach, her ears were flattened backward, and her lips were parted in a solicitous grin. She studiously avoided eye contact and she whined constantly, but softly.

In human terms Brigit would have appeared pathetic, but within the strictures of wolf hierarchy, her behavior advertised her total submission. Such voluntary and sustained subservience should have been sufficient to defuse the aggressive behavior of the Alphas, but for the fact that her continued presence within the pack contradicted the messages that her posture and manner were telegraphing. For these reasons, Shawano and Denali continued to punish her.

I seek acquaintance with Nature—to know her moods and manners. Primitive nature is the most interesting to me. . . .
—Henry David Thoreau, *The Journal*

THREE

Jim Wuepper's fascination with wolves and the wilderness began while he was still in high school in Lower Michigan, when he became influenced by the writings of James Oliver Curwood. Four years later, when he was twenty-one and working as a photographer in Marquette, he happened to print some negatives for George Wilson; but it wasn't until the pictures were finished and examined under the light that he realized they were portraits of wolves.

His reaction was immediate. Stimulated by the photos, Jim went to meet George, whose apartment is full of wolf photos, lupine souvenirs, and filmstrips, an organized clutter further accentuated by cinematographic equipment and by stacks of cans containing processed wolf footage, some fifty thousand feet of it!

In the photographic studio that Jim now owns and operates in Negaunee, a town some twelve miles west of Marquette, I interviewed him. George Wilson was there taping our conversation.

Describing his first impressions of the Wilson apartment, Jim looked at our mutual friend, aimed a thumb in his direction, and said, "You know what it's like in George's pad . . . wherever you look, you see wolves, or stuff dealing with them, and those labels pasted on his cupboard from outfits like Disney Studios, the BBC in England, and all that . . . I left in awe!"

Some months later, Jim went to Shawano, Wisconsin, to visit Larry and Joan Gehr, a couple who at that time kept some eighteen wolves.

"It was just unbelievable! I can still remember driving up to this guy's house and seeing better than a dozen wolves trotting around this enclosure. Light gray, *beautiful* creatures. It was April, and there was no snow on the ground; a great spring afternoon. And those wolves just looked *gorgeous*! It was at that point that I *knew* I was going to do something like that.

"While I was down there, I learned that they had two litters of pups, so I asked Larry if it would be possible to buy two of them. He said, 'There's no way that I would sell them! I'd sooner put them under first.' He said that there was some man in Texas who wanted to buy two of them as well, but Larry's concern was that he had to be sure that whoever got any of his wolves would know about these animals and would be able to do a good job raising them. He wouldn't even *consider* selling them to some knucklehead like me because he didn't think that I would be able to do a good job with them."

Although he was disappointed at not being able to obtain two wolf pups, Jim's enthusiasm was always rekindled whenever he remembered the Gehr pack. Eventually, obsessed by the thought of working with wolves, he realized he needed to learn a great deal more about the animals. He bought books dealing with the species and began to study them intently. He also went to see George Wilson on a number of occasions, listening with eager attention to the older man's stories about wolves and about the pack that George had kept in St. Louis, Missouri.

Eventually, feeling that he had tapped all possible sources of wolf information, Jim decided to act. First he got in touch with the Michigan Department of Natural Resources, to inquire about getting a permit to keep

35

wolves in the state. The reply was disappointing. It said, in part: "The importation of wolves into Michigan, though an infrequent act, causes anxiety for the neighbors of the permittees, makes trouble for the local police agency, and causes poor public relations for the Department [of Natural Resources]. . . . Possession permits to keep wolves as 'pets' will not be issued." Import permits could be issued, however, to educational and research institutions. Would it be possible, Jim wondered, to secure the interest of scientists at Northern Michigan University?

With this in mind, he worked out a proposal in which he offered to provide the land, erect a safe and suitable fence around it, and feed and care for the animals at his own expense if the university was interested in conducting a long-range study of captive wolves. He and Scott then presented this proposal to the university's department of psychology, where it received favorable interest. In due course, the plan was tentatively approved by the university, the Michigan Department of Natural Resources, and the U.S. Fish and Wildlife Service in Washington. But in anticipation, before all the paperwork was completed and the permits issued, Jim bought ten acres of well-forested land near the village of Ishpeming. There he started building a home for himself, his wife, Kaye, and their infant son, Jason. But while he was doing this, he kept on thinking about the wolf enclosure, drawing diagrams on paper and walking the area to determine where he would put in fenceposts, counting the number that would be needed.

Eventually, the university submitted to the local state authorities its completed proposal for "a study of captive wolf *(Canis lupus)* behavior." This was forwarded to headquarters of the Department of Natural Resources in Lansing, Michigan, where it was approved, although the permit from the state, and a second permit that had to be issued by the federal government to comply with the requirements of the Endangered Species Act of the United States, would not actually be granted until some months later. Nevertheless, Jim decided to get ready to receive the wolves, and early in 1977 he built the two-acre enclosure that is now home to the pack.

36

It was a big day in Jim's life when the two softly furred, wobbly puppies came into his care. One was a male, the other a female. At first, because they had not yet been weaned, the pups were kept in the house, for they had to be fed by bottle every four hours, a task that kept Jim and Kaye busy and was to continue to be a part of their routines for several weeks to come. But by the time the two were forty-two days old, the pups no longer needed milk and were then capable of eating meat, a task that they performed with eagerness, efficiency, and gusto. Now they were put into the enclosure and Jim decided to name them.

The male was called Shawano in memory of the place where Jim had seen his first wolves; the female he named Brigit because he had recently been impressed by French actress Brigitte Bardot's fight to save the seals that were annually being slaughtered on the ice off Canada's East Coast.

The pups were from different litters. Shawano had been sired by a wolf from Canada's Arctic. His mother was an eastern timber wolf, but the pup, born that year on April 19, was destined to favor his father in size and coloring. He grew up to weigh somewhat in excess of one hundred pounds and to sport a honey-blond coat. Brigit's parents were both eastern wolves, but she was born black and destined to remain so, a gorgeous animal with a white star on her chest and a frosting of white around her muzzle. Born April 8, Brigit was eleven days older than her future mate.

The gestation period of wolves is about sixty-three days (as it is with domestic dogs), but pups may be born two or three days before or after that time, depending upon the physiological constitution and health of the mother. The availability of prey animals and their kind and size exert considerable influence upon pregnant wolves, especially during the early development of the embryos. As might be expected, miscarriages may take place in times of famine, and accidental injuries can kill embryos within the womb—even relatively minor mishaps such as a fall against a downed tree trunk. In such cases, the mother, as well as the embryos, may die.

Wolves are sexually active only once a year. Most

commonly, mating takes place during late February or early March, but the height of the breeding season is likely to vary in accordance with the latitude of the pack's territory. Wolves in the extreme north will probably mate in early April, but those in the south may breed in early January; temperature and the amount of daylight appear to have some influence on the onset of estrus as well as upon the sexual readiness of the males, which, though they may show great interest in the hormonal scents of a female in estrus, will not engage in the business of mating until their own urges are aroused. (In contrast, domestic dog females come into estrus twice a year, while males are sexually motivated at all times.) The birth of the cubs, therefore, can take place between the first week of March and the first week of June, with a mid-time of late April to early May occurring in the region roughly contained between 45 and 55 degrees north latitude.

Newly born wolf puppies look more like tiny bears than like members of the dog family. They are blind, their hearing is poor, their ears are flattened forward, and their noses are squashed, as though someone had pressed them down with a forceful thumb. The legs are short and underdeveloped and the beautiful, plumelike tail sported by the adult bears no resemblance to the short, skinny appendage of the wolfling. These babies come into the world wearing dark brown or slate-blue coats of fine, woolly hair, except for those of their kind that are black, the coats in such cases being of a glossy sable shade. Jim, of course, did not get to see Shawano and Brigit immediately after birth, but from his studies he knew what they must have looked like as they emerged into the world: wriggly, mewling little bundles that weighed about one pound, each of which was to experience immediately the pleasantly warm stimulation of their mother's tongue and then, perhaps abruptly, the small, sharp pain that stabbed them briefly when the maternal incisor teeth nipped through the umbilical cord to liberate the newborns from their embryonic ties, although it is not unusual for the cord to break on its own.

By the time Shawano and Brigit were settled in the Wuepper household, their eyes had already opened, an important event in the life of every wolf pup, and one

38

that appears to be as fraught with anxiety as it is full of wonder. Before that magic moment, the little wolves are only vaguely aware of their surroundings, but keenly cognizant of the caressing tongue of their mother, the warmth of her body, and the solace of her rich milk. But when their birth-blue eyes are first liberated from the embrace of their lids, and even though little light reaches the den chamber, the experience of first sight is intimidating, puzzling, and exciting.

How well I remember sitting up all night with my wolf Wa* after I noticed that one of his lids had become slitted, suggesting that the pup would soon be opening both eyes. Hour by hour I watched the slow process until, at last, the little animal's eyes were uncurtained and he raised a wobbly head to stare myopically at his surroundings.

Wolf puppies open their eyes between nine and twelve days after birth, the variance accounted for by individual rates of development. More precise timing, therefore, cannot be determined, and it is not even possible to estimate average timing for this process because only a relatively few wild young have been monitored from the moment of birth to the moment of sight. Nevertheless, from observations made by George Wilson, Jim, myself, and other investigators, it seems reasonable to assume that the majority of wolf cubs are gifted with vision when they are eleven days old, although they are extremely nearsighted and will remain so for several weeks. Even then, their perceptive abilities are not fully developed; the cubs will not attain real visual efficiency until they are about four months old, at which point the color of their eyes has changed from blue to amber.

The quality of sight, which the vast majority of people can only measure through personal experience, is a subject that is too loosely dealt with by many of those who study animals and subsequently write about their findings, perhaps because such observations measure acuteness of vision from the standpoint of their own perspectives.

As a rule, human beings see that which they *want* to

*R.D. Lawrence, *Secret Go the Wolves* (New York: Holt, Rinehart and Winston, 1980).

look at, such perceptions being consciously noted. But for the most part, humans do not use their eyes as do wolves and other wild animals, who *must* look at everything in their world and take conscious note of it, no matter how small or insignificant an object may be. People don't need to be so constantly alert. Compared with other mammals, we live in relatively unchanging environments in which such things as our safety, our home, our food supply, and our mode of travel are usually assured. We do not constantly scan our territory for signs of enemies or for the presence of food; and more often than not, we can usually avoid latent dangers because of the very order of our society. When we walk, most us do so on clear, level surfaces; when hungry, we can eat practically at will; we rest and spend much of our leisure time in comfortable and secure "dens." Because of these things, most humans do not make proper use of their visual capabilities.

During the last fifteen years I have been trying to exploit the full potential of my own eyes and for this reason I have been making careful field observations of animals, and especially of wolves, as well as researching the physiology and function of vertebrate vision. My findings are by no means complete, but I have attained a much better understanding of the capabilities *and* limitations of sight, particularly of those receptors that are hidden behind each eye lens. I have come to realize that this subject has been greatly neglected by those who study the behavior of animals (and of humans, for that matter!) and because of this failure, a very important part of the biology of wolves has gone unrecorded. As a result, I feel that a brief explanation of the internal workings of the eyes of wolves, and a comparison with those of our own species, may fill an important behavioral gap.

The interior of a vertebrate's eye is lined by a light-sensitive, layered membrane—the retina—in the rearmost, central portion of which is located the site of clearest vision. In humans, primates, diurnal birds, and lizards, this spot is furnished with a small pit known as the *fovea*. The eyes of most other vertebrates, including wolves, lack such depressions; nevertheless, the same rearmost area of each retina, called the *macula* in such animals, is also the center of best visual definition. Eyes furnished with concave retinal foveas are capable of seeing distant objects in greater detail than eyes that lack the depression. The reasons for this difference are explained by the science of optics, and need not be examined here. Suffice it to say that because their eyes lack foveal pits, wolves are relatively nearsighted. They can see details clearly up to a distance of about seventy-five feet; beyond that limit, objects probably become blurred. This means that wolves cannot identify by sight faraway, *unmoving* objects, although the acuteness of their hearing and scent more than compensates for the visual lack. Movement is another matter. Because the outer perimeters of the retinas of all vertebrates are exceptionally sensitive to movement as well as to dim light, wolves are quick to notice any kind of activity occurring in their neighborhood, even at long distance in areas of open landscape. Such peripheral vision allows wolves and all other wild mammals constantly to monitor the *moment-to-moment* events taking place in their environment.

Frontal sight, on the other hand, serves to alert the animals to the presence of trail obstructions, permits them to recognize each other's features, and guides their actions while hunting, especially during the actual attack. Frontal sight is also used in conjunction with peripheral vision when distant events are being observed. In this context it is important to note that all wolves can immediately recognize previously encountered shapes and movements; they are well able to remember the differences that exist between, say, a moose and a deer by the general shape of each animal and by the distinctive ways in which they walk and run and feed. Indeed, I know from personal experience that wolves are acutely sensitive to the *rhythms* of movement, and are able to recognize each other, or a human with whom they relate, by the appearance of an individual's motion as well as by the sounds made during locomotion. Time and again I have deliberately altered my shape, height, and walk and have in every case created confusion in the minds of my lupine friends. Although they have been able to scent me, and to recognize my scent, the changes in stance, rhythm, and height have always caused them to back away

41

cautiously until the distance between us has closed enough for them to read my features clearly. Beyond serving to demonstrate that wolves are, indeed, frontally shortsighted, this also shows that they employ all their senses in equal measure at every opportunity. That is to say, no wolf is ever satisfied about any unknown influence encountered in its range until *all* of the messages received by its eyes, by its ears, and by its nose have been properly coordinated in its brain. But there is one aspect of the vision of wolves and that of most other mammals that for me remains open to question: color perception.

Although it has been clearly established that humans, primates, monkeys, birds, and a few other species can definitely see colors, the scientific literature states unequivocally that all other animals are unable to perceive the hues of the rainbow. According to this thesis, wolves and most other mammals are held to be color-blind, which suggests that they see all things in shades of white, black, and gray. I cannot accept this belief. Many experiments have shown that most mammals do not perceive color *in the same way that it is seen by human eyes*, but I am nevertheless convinced that wolves can detect color in ways that have not yet been identified.

I have noticed on a number of occasions that wolves become interested in those colors that have red as a base when these are perceived in good light. The truth is that we just do not know what a wolf (or any other animal) sees when it looks at a green tree, a setting sun, or a lady, like my wife, Sharon, wearing a violet or mauve coat—colors that she favors and that often captured the interest of Shawano and the other wolves. Matta and Wa, the two wolves that I raised in the 1960s, also showed considerable interest in red tones and, to a lesser extent, in shades of blue. Some humans are said to be color-blind because they may see red as green and blue as some other color. Of course they are not color-blind. They merely see color in another way. Is the world of the wolf and his companion animals made up solely of grays and blacks and whites? I do not think so; but until more and better research is done in this field, the question cannot be answered with assurance.

When it comes to hearing, wolf observers are on firmer ground. As adults, these animals have acute auricular perception and can detect sounds that are much too faint for human ears, even in the total absence of wind. But, as pups, their hearing is poor until about the third week of life, when it begins to improve rapidly. It has been said that wolf pups are actually deaf at birth—I myself have said so, at the time placing too much faith in the available literature—but evidence I have gathered through the years appears to deny this claim, and more recently, Jim Wuepper and Scott Stewart, who have both crawled into wolf dens within hours of the birth of pups, discovered that the wolflings were able to hear, and discern as alien, the noises made by the intruders as they scuffed their way through the tunnel that led to the nesting chamber.

In the matter of sound, I think it likely that wolves can also *feel* the vibrations of movement. On three occasions, while wolf-watching in mountain country in the Yukon Territory and in British Columbia, I saw packs that were running along lowland areas suddenly change direction and head for prey that appeared to me, watching from a height, too far away for the animals to hear or scent. On two of these occasions the prey animals were moose and, on the third, caribou.

Although they cannot see and do not hear too well, newborn wolflings have an excellent sense of smell and this, very soon after they have been licked clean by their mother, guides them unerringly to the milk supply, although during this first, purposeful journey, they are also drawn toward the mother's body heat.

As Jim was to learn from Shawano and Brigit, baby wolves begin to develop their teeth by about the third week after birth, when the needle-sharp tips start to poke through the gums. From then on, the teeth grow rapidly and about one week later they are quite capable of injuring human fingers, although this is not because the pups intend to bite the hand that feeds them, but simply because the canines, curved and very sharp, can cut almost as well as a surgical scalpel.

By their fourth week of development, the pups become very active. They love to play, staging mock combats

43

between themselves that are accompanied by much youthful growling and controlled biting. When one pup is bitten too hard during these rough-and-tumble games, it whines, whereupon the aggressor usually lets go immediately, undoubtedly knowing that if it does not, a real fight may develop and, in any case, when its own turn comes to feel pain and it cries its own anguish, its sibling may not let go, either. At this stage, too, the puppies are intensely curious and determined to explore their den and its environs, a task that is undertaken with great interest but tempered by infinite caution. If a sight or sound is perceived suddenly, a pup will back away immediately, torn between avid curiosity and an inherent sense of apprehension. Curiosity usually wins out, but it may take a pup considerable time before it actually reaches the object of its interest. In the interval, it moves forward a step or two, backs away, moves forward again, stops, stares, sniffs, and listens. In this way, step by step it approaches, gaining confidence with each advance until it finally reaches its objective, which, if chewable, is immediately grasped and bitten, a procedure that appears to give much pleasure and causes the discharge of copious amounts of saliva, and one that clearly relieves some of the discomfort caused by the budding teeth. At about this time, sibling rivalry, present from birth and manifested by competition for the hind teats (which produce the most milk), begins to intensify as the pups test one another, each seeking to dominate its siblings. Gradually, after many mock fights during which two or more antagonists roll about, using the weight of their bodies to pin down an opponent and their teeth to secure a whine-producing hold, the "pecking order" begins to emerge and what can be termed an "Alpha pup" emerges and is followed in descending order of dominance by its litter mates. Nevertheless, all pups in the pack are themselves subservient to all the adult wolves and will remain so for at least two years, in some cases for their entire lifetimes.

Shawano and Brigit, inasmuch as they were the only pups in Jim's mini-pack, were to settle their status relatively quickly, with Shawano, by virtue of his larger size and more determined character, emerging the clear win-

44

ner. In such a situation, however, when one wolf is male and the other female, both become Alphas even though one of them is slightly more Alpha than the other. It is not unusual for a female wolf to dominate a male, or even for a female to emerge as pack leader, despite the fact that males are usually about 20 percent larger than females. Size is important, of course, but so are determination, intelligence, and aggressiveness.

In any event, by the time Shawano and Brigit were five weeks old, the male pup had emerged as the leader and it was he who claimed the first and choicest bits of meat, although Brigit tried at such times to take his food away by artifice, creeping up to Shawano, pretending to be intimidated by his growls, then lying down near him and slowly inching her way closer and closer to the target. Using such tactics, she managed to sneak the meat away from her mate-to-be quite regularly, often playing with it but not eating it. Eventually Shawano recovered his lost prize, somewhat the worse for wear, and consumed it. But it was not long thereafter that both pups began to eat meat daily; and they started to wean themselves, a process that in a wild state is initiated by the mother when the pups are about thirty-five days old and is usually completed when they are about fifty days old.

Wolf cubs grow rapidly. At one month, they will weigh between five and six pounds and will measure some seventeen inches in length from the root of the tail to the end of the nose, the tail itself measuring about five inches. At ten weeks, a cub will probably weigh between thirty and thirty-five pounds, and at twenty weeks it will have grown to about half the size of the adults and will probably weigh about fifty-five pounds, such rapid development being necessary to prepare the young wolves for the rigorous life of the northern predator, for those pups that survive (and many do not live beyond the third or fourth week after birth) must be ready by August to accompany the hunting pack, learning from the adults as they go and, by late autumn, being expected to become effective members of the pack during hunting forays.

Shawano and Brigit, however, although they developed as rapidly as their wild kin, did not go hunting, their food needs being provided by Jim on a regular basis. By September 1978, the two had become pair-bonded, viewing Jim and Kaye and Scott Stewart as their pack, but yet behaving toward one another like an adult, mated pair, except that they were not yet quite ready for sexual relations.

By mid-February of 1979, however, when they were twenty-two months old, their behavior was such that Jim believed they were going to mate, a rare event between subordinate animals in an established pack led by two Alphas, but quite usual when a pair of young wolves come together to form their own group.

Jim, eager to film every aspect of wolf courtship and mating, set up a scaffold outside of the enclosure. From there, he hoped to record the action, but, although he spent many lone and cold vigils, movie camera ready, the wolves did not intensify their relationship, and believing that he had misread their intentions, Jim put away his equipment, convinced there would be no pups born in his enclosure that year.

In early March of that same year, Shawano became interested in a raven that flew down and landed on one of the enclosure's fenceposts. Jim happened to be watching from outside the wire and he noted that bird and wolf stared at one another for some moments. Then Shawano heard something in another direction and, distracted, turned to look. Immediately upon the wolf's eyes leaving the raven, the large black bird flew down and actually landed on Shawano's back, causing the almost fully grown, future leader of the pack to jump as though he had received an electric shock. The raven merely touched down on the wolf's back and immediately afterward flew up again, but the experience quite unnerved Shawano, who had yet to realize that these big, tough northern birds have enjoyed a special relationship with wolves since time immemorial.

By the end of the first winter of their lives, however, Shawano and Brigit learned to ignore the ravens on those occasions when they were feeding on road-killed deer, or whenever Jim would toss chicken parts into the enclosure, the young wolves knowing by now that if one or the other of them charged at a raven that was intent on

46

stealing some of its food, other birds would swoop down and take the unguarded meat. At the same time, the wolves and the scavenging birds also developed that special communion which is common to the two disparate species, in due course even howling whenever the ravens called. But that was later, after Shawano and Brigit had become adults.

By mid-March of that year, since Jim had not seen any actual mating behavior between the young wolves, he assumed that Brigit was not pregnant, but in early April he noticed that she had become rather thick in the waist and stomach. Two weeks later he discovered that the wolves had dug a den, and almost simultaneously he saw that Brigit's mammae were swollen, indicating that she was already producing milk. Had the pair mated after all? His question was answered on May 4, when Brigit gave birth to two black female puppies. All the humans involved with the Ishpeming wolves were astonished. Shawano and Brigit were delighted.

Whereas before the birth of her pups Brigit had displayed very submissive behavior toward Shawano and the humans in her life, motherhood appeared to make her confident and even assertive. She made it clear to all concerned, including her mate, that the business of giving birth was entirely her own show. So was the responsibility of caring for the two tiny puppies, upon which she lavished attention. Jim and Scott Stewart did manage to crawl into the den to have a look at the newborns, an action that their mother tolerated with thinly veiled hostility. But the father was not allowed to enter the nesting chamber until the wolflings were some two weeks old and already starting to move about within the darkened den.

When Jim first saw the two little wolves in full daylight, he immediately realized that one of them was bigger than the other, showed more confidence, and had already acquired dominance over her sibling. At this time, Jim also named the two. The big one he called Denali, which was the name given by the Indians of Alaska to Mount McKinley: it means "the great one." The smaller cub he christened Siskiwit, a name given to three locations found on Isle Royale, the big island in Lake Superior that lies 48 miles northwest of Michigan's Upper Peninsula.

47

Ceded by the British to the Americans in 1783, it was declared a national park in 1940, and has since figured prominently in the study of wolves and moose.

As matters turned out, Denali was aptly named. She did, indeed, become "the great one." Growing rapidly, maintaining her dominance over her exceptionally submissive sister, Denali showed from a very early age that she had that special something which, in time, produces a leader.

Discussing the newborns with psychologists from the university made it clear that no attempt should be made to socialize the two pups, the upbringing of which was left entirely to Brigit and Shawano. Perhaps because he felt the responsibilities of fatherhood, or because he was overprotective of his offspring, Shawano at this time took to nipping the bottoms of psychology students who approached the den too closely, sneakily delivered reprimands that could not possibly be mistaken for real attacks (which would have inflicted serious injuries). Nevertheless, the nips were more than sufficient to discourage the researchers, who thereafter took care to stay a respectful distance from the den, or from the pups when these played outside, a state of affairs acceptable to Shawano, who thereafter tolerated the scientific voyeurs.

Wolves will nip each other in reprimand, or affectionately; in either case, the bite, delivered by the incisors, causes them no damage and, because of the dense fur and thick hide, elicits little if any pain. But, as Sharon and I can testify from personal experience, when a wolf nips a human during an excess of affectionate zeal, such love-bites can sometimes bring uncontrolled tears to the eyes and they will surely produce purple welts by the next day. Neither of us have been nipped in reprimand, but I am sure that there is little difference between a pinch of love and one of admonition. Nevertheless, I do not propose to prove my point through personal research . . .

As Denali and Siskiwit grew, Brigit was a typical wolf mother. Although she pampered them a lot, she also took care to emphasize her dominant status over them, even though by this time she had again reverted to her former submissive behavior when dealing with Shawano and humans.

48

Nevertheless, Brigit, an intelligent wolf not averse to scheming, often got what she wanted from Shawano, as she had as a puppy, by employing calculated deviousness. Nothing illustrates this better than her behavior during the winter of 1979, when Jim Wuepper threw a deer head to Shawano. Brigit salivated, but did not dare try to take it from her mate by direct means. Instead, she trotted over a small hill, behind which Denali and Siskiwit were resting, and brought the yearlings back with her, standing by while the gangly young wolves dashed up to their tolerant father, who allowed them to take the deer head away from him, a liberty that did not even elicit a mild growl. Brigit must have quite clearly known beforehand that this would be the outcome of her scheme; no sooner had the yearlings dragged the head out of sight of Shawano than their mother took it away from them and kept it for herself!

As the 1980 breeding season approached, Jim noticed that Brigit seemed extremely concerned about maintaining her Alpha status. Up to this time she had been a devoted mother, but now she began to harass her yearling daughters on an almost constant basis, demonstrating by her behavior that she saw Denali and Siskiwit as rivals, but particularly picking on Denali, who was by now a large wolf of imposing appearance and assured mannerisms. Shawano at first ignored the noisy goings-on, but later he occasionally joined Brigit in her attacks, almost as though seeking to reassure her about her status by approving her harassment of her daughters. By the end of February, however, and presumably because Brigit was no longer in estrus, life among the Ishpeming wolves had returned to its usual tenor. But Brigit did not conceive in 1980, although she and Shawano had mated. No satisfactory explanation for this failure has been found. It is possible that the she-wolf's great preoccupation with status raised the level of Brigit's stress to such a degree that it prevented ovulation. That is only a guess, but it is backed by medical and biological evidence, which shows that high levels of stress can prevent conception in human females and in other mammals (just as it can cause males to become impotent).

During the year that followed Brigit's failure to produce young, the pack continued to strengthen its ties under the leadership of the two Alphas, its day-to-day affairs monitored by psychology students as well as by Jim and Scott. But although the wolves were studied on a regular basis, observations were made from a reasonable distance, to allow the animals to behave in natural ways. Unlike many present-day studies, where the wolves are anesthetized (usually by being darted) in order to monitor vital functions, to measure endocrine levels, or to examine the animals physically, the pack was not experimentally abused. The wolves were, of course, photographed by still and movie cameras, but picture-taking did not distress them—Shawano and Brigit had been photographed since they were puppies and so did not take alarm when the equipment was displayed, and since their parents showed no concern, Denali and Siskiwit did not react either.

Nevertheless, because they had not been socialized toward people, the two young wolves exhibited all the inherent cautions common to the species when strangers approached the enclosure. Jim and Scott, because they worked with the wolves practically every day, could approach the sisters closely, but neither Denali nor Siskiwit would allow herself to be handled. Nor did Jim and Scott try to do so in any event, for this would have been contrary to the intent of the study.

In late January 1981, the restlessness that develops in all wolves two to three weeks prior to the breeding season began to show up in the pack. It later became evident that all three females were in estrus. Now Denali began harassing Siskiwit, who, submissive as she was, offered no resistance to her formidable sister. Soon afterward, during an occasion when Denali was again attacking Siskiwit, Brigit, exerting her Alpha status, interfered, trying to intimidate Denali by defending the smaller female. At this, Denali turned on her mother, hackles raised, teeth bared, and deep threat-growls issuing from her throat. There followed a skirmish that was soon to end in Brigit's defeat. From that moment on, Denali became the Alpha female of the pack, her mother accepting a very subservient role.

When Shawano also became sexually ready, he unhesitatingly mated with Denali and, indeed, combined with his daughter to harass his onetime mate. The two dominant wolves now made it a practice to chase Brigit whenever they saw her, meanwhile almost totally ignoring Siskiwit, whose extremely submissive nature evidently ruled her out as a breeding competitor. Then, in late February, Denali and Shawano chased Brigit into her old den and kept her there for three days, ostracizing her completely and preventing her from feeding.

On the third day, as Brigit, driven by hunger, was trying to emerge, Jim, who had brought food for the pack, witnessed the way in which the two Alphas were treating the now submissive wolf. He became angry with Shawano and Denali, entered the enclosure, and literally charged at the two wolves, who, looking upon him as a sort of super-Alpha, ran away. At this, Brigit shot out of the den, her hackles up, growling. She charged with Jim and tackled Denali, who dropped to the ground submissively. The alliance between dominant human male and submissive female wolf had turned the tables. This kind of interaction is common in wild packs, except, of course, that no human is involved. But if a dominant wolf takes the part of a subordinate animal against those that are harassing it, the low-ranking wolf joins with its high-status rescuer and, quite literally, "gets its own back." Of course, in the absence of the dominant animal, the low-ranking wolf continues to be put down by its higher-ranking companions whenever it forgets itself and commits a trespass—which was what happened in Brigit's situation.

Jim later regretted his anger-generated interference, realizing that his behavior had been motivated by human emotions rather than by objective, scientific reasoning. Nevertheless, his actions unwittingly produced very positive experimental evidence. At that time, Shawano must have weighed between ninety and ninety-five pounds and Denali probably about eighty pounds, both of them immensely strong, fully dominant wolves that singly or together could easily have killed Jim had they decided to meet his charge. That they did not do so speaks volumes for the rigid disciplines imposed by the hierarchical laws that have been regulating wolf societies probably since

51

before the advent of man. Furthermore, the unplanned "experiment" also showed that under the proper conditions, wolves can readily imprint on humans and look upon them as bona fide members of the pack, even to the point of accepting one or more individuals as ultra-dominant superiors. Let it not be supposed, however, that I am advocating that persons who have dealings with wolves should engage in similar behavior! Jim's actions were spontaneous and, as he himself realized afterward, rather foolhardy; the results were positive from an investigative standpoint. But whenever humans have close contact with wild animals, no matter how tame and people-oriented these may be, it must always be borne in mind that every one of them is an individual in its own right. Whatever one of a kind may do, it does not necessarily mean that all members of the same species will also do it.

In contrast to Jim's experience, my wolf, Wa, decided to challenge my status just as Denali challenged her mother's. He was ten months old at the time and he and his sister, Matta, had been allowed into the house when they scratched at the door for admission. We were just finishing supper, the main course of which that evening included T-bone steaks. After the wolves entered, accompanied by our malamute dog, Tundra, who was treated by the yearlings as a Beta male, Wa came to my place at the table, sniffed, and decided to help himself to the steak bone that was on my otherwise empty plate. This was a liberty that an Alpha would not tolerate, so I reacted by aiming a light slap at his muzzle with an open hand, a perhaps too-mild reprimand. Before my fingers made contact with his nose, he growled deeply and fastened his jaws on my right forearm, a crushing bite that produced a deep puncture, the scar of which I still carry. There was only one course open to me. I had to defeat the wolf in his own way. For perhaps ninety seconds we rolled about on the floor, until I was able to scissor my legs around Wa's waist while securing a stranglehold around his neck. Finding himself unable to move, and becoming short of breath, the wolf capitulated, whining his submission. I let him go immediately and he went to lie down in a corner. Matta and Tundra, meanwhile, had been very interested spectators, and my wife a very frightened witness. Now, although bleeding and feeling quite apprehensive, I knew that I had to reinforce my Alpha status, so I went to Wa, leaned over him, growled as I showed my teeth, and pushed his head against the floor, securing a hold on the scruff of his neck. He reacted by raising a back leg, tucking his tail against his belly, and wetting himself; then he whined. I released him immediately and patted his head, smiling and speaking softly to him, whereupon I was affectionately mobbed by him and Matta and Tundra. Wa never challenged me again.

After our altercation, I spent some time wondering about the wolf's reasons for attacking me, eventually coming to believe that he had been prompted by an inherent need to challenge my authority in order to elevate his status. But, after learning about the results of Jim's charge against Shawano and Denali, I began to doubt the accuracy of my surmise. Wa may well have tried to attain Alpha rank when he challenged me, but now I felt that he had dared to do so because of some sign of weakness or indecision that he had detected in my behavior. Immediately after formulating this thought, however, I wondered what it was about Jim's experience that could have reminded me of my own and at the same time cast doubts upon my original conclusions. The two incidents were totally dissimilar, yet in some way they seemed to be connected. How? This question nagged me during the remainder of our stay in Michigan, and continued to do so after Sharon and I had returned home; but, try as I might, I could find no relationship between my fight with Wa and Jim's charge against his Alpha wolves. Eventually, unable to rid myself of the feeling that I was missing an important aspect of wolf behavior, I began to make a detailed comparison of the two happenings, analyzing the behavior of the wolves and of the humans involved, the age of each animal, and the events that preceded both confrontations. Afterward I drew upon my observations of wild wolves and other animals, marshaling all the behavioral data that I had gathered during half a lifetime of field study. This task has taken almost a year to accomplish, but it was well worth the doing, for it has led me to form conclusions that I believe will lead to a better understanding of the social behavior of wolves, of other animals, and, I daresay, of humans. There is no need to recount here all the laborious steps undertaken during the course of my research, many of which led me down a number of blind alleys without yielding a single clue, so I will bypass that tedium and deal only with the one factor that connected the two incidents: *aggression*, an answer that I initially rejected because it appeared to be much too simplistic, if only because no organism attacks unless it *is* aggressive. Both Wa and Jim had been similarly motivated, the wolf attacking me and the man charging the two Alphas. But because nothing else made sense, and inasmuch as I was still obsessed with the problem, I decided to review the biology of aggression and those factors that cause it to develop in animals and in my own species.

When the senses of an animal alert it to the presence of a threat, or a challenge, it will react either aggressively or fearfully, depending on circumstances and especially on the degree of self-confidence inherent in the individual. In either event, the physiological effects of aggression and fear are *identical*, because whether an individual decides to attack or elects to escape, the ensuing, stepped-up activity will demand the expenditure of high levels of energy. For this reason, when an animal (or a human) becomes aware of a challenge, its senses telegraph the news to the endocrine system, a complex of ductless glands that, during normal behavior, discharge directly into the bloodstream graduated amounts of hormones, substances without which metabolism cannot take place. When an alarm is triggered, however, the endocrine glands instantly pump out high levels of hormones, particularly epinephrine (adrenaline), which simultaneously cause the heart to beat faster, accelerate breathing, speed up blood-clotting, raise blood pressure, increase the supply of blood sugar, produce better muscle tone, and promote higher resistance to fatigue, all of which reactions enable the body to function at maximum efficiency during physical exertion.

When the metabolic rate is speeded up by the surge of endocrinological fuel, it follows that *internal* activity is accelerated; in other words, the engine is working at full power, even though the wheels have not yet begun to run. Correspondingly, the amounts of wastes normally discharged by all organisms—even when at rest—rise proportionally. Wolves and other animals are able to scent these wastes, which are discharged through the sweat glands, urine, and feces; and inasmuch as they contain high levels of endocrinological residues, a wolf's keen nose can immediately detect the change in metabolism, even across quite long distances if it is downwind of the odor trails.* Nevertheless, scent merely advertises an individual's arousal. It cannot, by itself, be used to determine whether an animal will respond aggressively or fearfully to that which has been perceived as challenging or threatening. But because wolves are exceptionally keen observers and employ all of their faculties in unison and at all times, they can tell immediately whether an animal is disposed to run or to fight by noting the way that it is behaving.

After reaching this stage of my review, I became sidetracked for a time when I confused aggression and anger, terms that are most often used synonymously, but which have completely different meanings when examined biologically. As a result, my investigations became stalled until I realized that aggression in nature is a positive arousal designed to increase the chances of an animal's survival (and, therefore, that of its species) by furnishing it with the will and the energy to defend itself, to escape danger, to secure its food, to protect its young, and to regulate its social affairs. But anger, I was forced to conclude, is a pathological emotion, signs of which I had never noted among wild animals. These things prompted me to theorize that anger is a uniquely human aberration

---

*Furred animals lose heat by panting; humans cool their bodies by perspiring. This difference has given rise to a commonly held belief that animals do not sweat. In fact, all animals have sweat glands on the skin and, particularly, on the pads of the feet. The wastes that they excrete through the pores serve at least three functions: they help to rid wastes from the body, they provide social recognition by giving to each individual its own highly distinctive odor, and, as noted, they allow animals to detect by scent the onset of aggression or of alarm.

that most probably developed after our species learned to use and make tools, especially weapons.

As soon as primitive man discovered that he could kill artificially, and that a weak individual could slay a larger, stronger opponent without engaging in hand-to-hand combat—thus ensuring a quick victory while minimizing the risks of personal injury or death—our aggressive tendencies were more easily aroused and were given freer rein. Then, too, tools and weapons allowed primitive humans to secure more food, a circumstance that must have dramatically changed our living patterns. Man could now become relatively sedentary, hunting a much smaller territory and occupying a fixed home base until he exhausted the local food supplies, at which time the family would move to a new location that was well stocked with prey, set up housekeeping in another cave, and begin the process anew.

Each human family could also afford to increase the numbers of its social unit. This rise in the birth rate—and a drop in the death rate that must have resulted when food became more plentiful and men no longer needed to engage in bare-handed fighting—probably led to the end of the small, ecologically sound, and fully independent family unit, which in due course became replaced by the tribe and eventually by the nation, or mega-family.

Although it is now impossible to trace the timing of these changes in the evolution of *Homo sapiens*, I postulate that departure from the natural social order gave rise to the many frustrations that are now endemic in all human societies. These irritants keep individuals in a constant state of stress, a condition that causes the endocrine system to pump into the blood higher levels of hormones than are needed in view of the fact that a person is not actually facing an action-provoking, life-and-death situation. The constant pressure of frustration, coupled with the chemical imbalances that result when a failure to act physically does not burn off the excess hormones, results in anger.

Wolves and other animals, conversely, dissipate the hormones of aggression by almost constantly engaging in action of one sort or another, for even when not belligerently or fearfully aroused they tend to exercise by running, playing, or mock-fighting. This activity keeps the supply of hormones in proper balance at all times and contributes to peace and conviviality within the pack. Furthermore, because wolves usually forgive a trespass or a punishment immediately after hostilities have ended, there are no grudges left to fester and to flare up later. There is no *hate* in the world of the wolf!

Thinking along these lines, it occurred to me that anger became, in effect, the bastard offspring of aggression, an antisocial, frequently self-destructive emotion that runs contrary to the natural laws of survival. Conversely, aggression, especially as typified by wolves and other wild animals, continues to instigate a positive response to social stimuli and develops within an individual at least four levels of intensity.

The first and mildest form of aggression in wolves is *passive*; it is physically advertised by the way in which an animal carries itself, its positive movements and calm manner denoting self-assurance. The second stage is *passive-active*, displayed when an individual continues to demonstrate self-assurance, but at the same time signals elevated arousal by exaggerating its behavior and movements: in this case, a wolf keeps its ears stiffly erect and forward-pointing; its hackles rise, its tail is carried high, its eyes stare fixedly, and it is likely to emit low, rumbling growls, all of these signals being directed at the object of its arousal, the intent being to intimidate and thus to preclude fighting. Stage three is *defensive*, and is most often observed in subordinate animals who feel themselves threatened. Such individuals exhibit the usual signs of submission, but at the same time, by growling, baring their teeth, and raising their hackles, they give warning that they will fight if pressed, behavior that also serves to prevent actual combat because a dominant wolf, accepting the submissive signs and noting the defensive signals, does not wish to precipitate a fight during which it may itself suffer injury, even if it emerges the victor. The fourth stage of aggression is *offensive* and will result in action if an opponent or a prey animal does not escape. Here the initial signs are the same as those exhibited during stage two *(passive-active)*, the difference being that an attack will take place.

57

Although the manifestations of aggression that occur during interactions between wolves, or even between a wolf and a predator of another species, are similar to those exhibited when the animals are hunting, during a social argument it is rare for one wolf to open hostilities with the intention of killing its opponent. That is why warnings are given and most usually heeded, for the main objective of such confrontations in the natural world is the elimination of a challenge, not the destruction of the opponent. If it were otherwise, there can be little doubt that most species of animals would have exterminated themselves long before the advent of man, who alone has earned for himself the doubtful distinction of being the only mammal that systematically makes war upon its own kind with as much dedication as it applies to the increase of its numbers.

When wolves hunt, however, they set out with the express purpose of killing their quarry as quickly as possible. They are, after all, carnivores that evolution created for the express purpose of maintaining balance among populations of their prey, just as their own numbers are kept in balance partly by their societal habits and partly by the exigencies of the hard life of the hunter. Nevertheless, and contrary to the myths propagated by those humans who fear and hate the wolf, he does not set out with the intention of torturing the animals that he must kill in order to survive. The idea that a cautious animal—who knows full well that if he is injured he will probably die as a result—would delay a kill for sadistic reasons is patently ridiculous.

Applying all of the foregoing factors to my confrontation with Wa and Jim's charge against Shawano and Denali, I realized that whereas Jim's behavior had been prompted by aggression and had therefore succeeded in intimidating the two Alphas, my attempt to punish Wa had been passive: when the wolf tried to steal the steak bone from my plate, he did so in the knowledge that he was taking a great liberty. But I did not see things from an Alpha wolf's point of view. I had finished my meal and would have given him the bone in any event, so I was not particularly disturbed when he tried to obtain the food without permission. I was not, therefore, aggressively aroused when I sought to administer a mild reproof. And Wa, detecting no change in my mood or in the odor of my body, took this to mean that I was not prepared to back up my reprimand. To his way of thinking, my action in slapping him had demonstrated aggression; on the other hand, my behavior and body odor were not signaling arousal because I was not, in fact, feeling aggressive. So, quick as wolves are to take advantage of any situation that they believe will be to their advantage, Wa attacked me, almost certainly thinking that he could defeat me and thereby gain Alpha status. My own immediate arousal and the result of our fight taught him that he could not dominate me.

In retrospect, I now realize that I profited from the experience in a subconscious way, because thereafter I reprimanded the wolves only when it was important to do so and I forced myself to become stern whenever I exercised my authority.

FOUR

During the last days of Denali's pregnancy, as her condition became clearly uncomfortable, she stopped harassing Brigit and took to spending most of her time near or actually inside the den, which was located in a fairly open area of the enclosure and almost in view of the Wuepper home. Originally dug in 1979 by Brigit and Shawano, in 1981 the tunnel had been extended by Denali and now ran a crooked course for twenty feet, past Brigit's old nesting chamber, before ending in the oval depression in which the pups would be born, a roomy, dark concavity that was approximately three feet in diameter and about two feet in height in the center.

Whenever the pregnant wolf rested underground, Shawano and Brigit, good friends again, hovered solicitously at the tunnel entrance, whining softly at intervals, scratching at the ground with their front paws and showing by their every action that they were pleasantly anticipating the arrival of the new pups. Shawano now made it his business to carry food to his mate, leaving it at the tunnel mouth if she was inside the den and whining more loudly to let Denali know that it was available. Brigit did not attempt to steal Denali's food, although she had ample opportunity to do so with impunity. Such behavior by Brigit was uncharacteristic. She is a supreme opportunist who, small as she is, eats more than big Shawano because she is hyperactive and metabolizes at a high rate. Observing the respect that she showed for Denali's unguarded food, Jim concluded that Brigit was inherently aware that the pregnant wolf was in need of sustenance, and that she shared Shawano's concern for the mother-to-be. His is an opinion with which I fully agree because it is compatible with the behavior I have often observed in wild packs, members of which are always solicitous about each other's welfare and especially so about the comfort of a pregnant female—despite any social altercations that may have taken place in the past.

On April 26, Jim noticed that Shawano and Brigit were particularly excited and had left untouched the chicken parts he had put in the enclosure. Instead, they stayed near the tunnel entrance, whining more loudly than usual, pawing, licking each other, and acting restlessly. When Jim approached them, Shawano became clearly uneasy, but tolerated his presence when he went to the tunnel entrance to listen. (The behavior of the wolves led him to think—mistakenly as it turned out—the pups might have been born during the night.) Brigit, on the other hand, raised her hackles and growled, a warning that Jim took to mean that he should not seek to crawl into the den and disturb Denali. Because all was quiet within the burrow, Jim left the enclosure, accepting Brigit's reprimand in the spirit that it had been given.

The next day, Denali gave birth to four pups. But it was not until three days later that Jim, assisted by Scott Stewart and George Wilson (whose presence outside kept Shawano and Brigit from interfering), crawled into the den to discover that Denali had given birth to three females and one male.

One of the little bitches, the smallest, was dead; she had been licked clean of the birth fluids, then pushed to one side, but because of the darkness (despite the use of a flashlight), the time delay, the confinement, and the rather rank odor given off by the residues of the birthing

61

process, it was impossible for Jim to determine whether the puppy was stillborn or had died later. Electing to leave the little corpse in the chamber so as to allow Denali to deal with it in her own way, Jim retreated by pushing himself backward along the tortuous and claustrophobic tunnel, emerging, covered with soil and soaked with perspiration, to break the news to his companions.

Two days later, Jim again crawled into the den, with Scott and George once more on guard, to check on the condition of the survivors. To the consternation of all, he found that the other two females had died. A hasty conference followed. It was decided that Jim would remove the remaining pup and would try to raise him in the house, provided that the little wolf had not already been infected by whatever disease had caused the deaths of his litter mates.

The effect that these losses had on the pack was predictable, for when any puppies are lost, wolves mourn as deeply as might a human family faced by similar tragedies. If there are survivors, the bereavement is more bearable, but if all the young wolves die, the grief is intense and, in my view, approximately equal to that sustained by our own species, although the duration and outward manifestations of the sorrow can and do vary in accordance with the emotional makeup of the family, as is also the case with humans.

Denali and Shawano expressed their grief in a controlled way, but they could not hide it from Jim's experienced eyes. The first pup's death was evidently accepted more calmly and did not cause the wolves to mourn unduly, although Denali was seen to take her little daughter's body out of the den and bury it at the far, north end of the enclosure, a grave that was never disturbed by any of the wolves, even though these animals habitually dig up old bones or the remains of animals that are encountered in their territory. But when the two females died and were likewise buried by their mother, and when Jim took the little male to his house, the three wolves seemed disconsolate. Brigit, despite having been harassed by the Alphas from mid-February until about ten days before the birth of the litter, showed by her behavior that she felt the loss as keenly as Denali and Shawano. And she joined her daughter in searching the enclosure for the missing male pup, a frantic rushing about accompanied by frequent whining that was kept up for two days and nights, after which, with the uncanny perception of their kind, they at last realized that the pup, whom Jim had by now named Thor, was still alive.

Because of their keen sense of smell, they scented the cub on Jim's clothing and person whenever he entered the den, showing their awareness by the excited way in which they sniffed him and licked at his hands. And it is probably certain that the wolves could also hear little Thor whenever he whined or uttered his plaintive baby howls. But beyond these well-documented senses, those of us who have deep empathy with wolves feel that they have ways of sensing events the manifestations of which are far beyond the reach of known perceptions and are, of course, outside the limits of human understanding. In any event, Jim felt that the way in which the wolves acted toward him suggested that they may have held him at least partially accountable for the loss of their litter. They did not show hostility toward him, but they were extremely reserved in his presence and for a time did not greet him with the same joyous exuberance they had usually demonstrated whenever he had previously entered the enclosure. The pack also became more distrustful of the student observers and were subdued in their dealings with each other. Denali and Brigit often whined softly as they trotted somewhat aimlessly through the forested section of their territory, and Shawano spent much time alone on the huge rock that is located in the southeast corner of the enclosure, within sight of the Wuepper home.

Two years later, when Jim told me about all of this, it was clear that he still harbored a sense of guilt, even though the removal of Thor from the probably contaminated den may well have saved the wolf's life. But as he told me about the pack's reaction when, after several weeks, he put Thor back into the enclosure, he positively glowed with pleasure. Even before Jim, carrying Thor against his chest, had closed his house door, the wolves rushed up to the fence and began whining and dancing, climbing over each other in their excitement. When Thor was actually placed on the ground and ran toward his mother, the wolves crowded around him, at first intimidating him, but when the pup realized that he could playfight with each one in turn with complete impunity and that every wolf allowed him to do pretty much as he liked, his happiness was complete. The wolfling was already weaned, and when he mouthed at his father's jaws and immediately caused Shawano to regurgitate a glob of partially digested deer meat, the puppy became enraptured as he devoured the offering. After this reunion, the tenor of wolf life returned to normal, except that Brigit constituted herself the personal nursemaid of little Thor, a doting babysitter who thoroughly spoiled the infant.

Once again without meaning to do so, Jim Wuepper had been responsible for an experiment that produced valuable behavioral evidence, data that, when added to what had been gathered by George Wilson, by me, and by other nonclinical investigators, amply demonstrate that wolves (and other animals) are definitely not fixed-program machines incapable of conscious thought and therefore incapable of feeling love, joy, sadness, or any other kind of emotion, as some scientists believe. Some of them go so far as to claim that even humans are incapable of conscious thought. This school, for instance, contends that when people talk to each other they are engaging in "verbal behavior." Schwartz and Lacey, in their textbook *Behaviorism, Science and Human Nature* (New York: Norton, 1982), state that if an individual wants to discover the reason for another person's given action, he or she should not ask the subject why the action was undertaken. Instead, these behaviorists propose that the subject's environment should be analyzed so as to discover the reward that, presumably, was obtained by the behavior in question. The authors then state: "Find the reward and eliminate it. The idea that people are autonomous and possess within them the power and the reason for making decisions has no place in behavior theory."

More and more of today's behaviorists are occupied with such esoteric concepts as they rush from ivory tower to laboratory to perform another series of experiments on animals, which are usually viewed as *specimens* that may be prodded, forcibly restrained for long periods, deprived of a mother's love, and eventually "sacrificed" to support some obscure and debatable "truth." There are exceptions, of course, and praise be! One of the giants among these is Konrad Lorenz. In *The Year of the Graylag Goose* (New York: Harcourt, Brace, Jovanovich, 1978), he sums up his attitude to behavioral research in this way: "The harmony inhabiting all living things is what attracts our interest, and it would be utterly unscientific, if not downright dishonest, to deny this. A strictly objective description or illustration of an animal or plant departs from the truth in one crucial respect if the beauty of the living organsim itself is not made evident."

Another notable exception is Donald R. Griffin, professor of biology at Rockefeller University, who says unequivocally: "Behaviorism should be abandoned not so much because it belittles the value of living animals, but because it leads us to a seriously incomplete and hence misleading picture of reality."*

Reality, particularly in the case of wolves, means that these animals have keen intelligence, excellent memory, and a demonstrable capacity for conscious thought. When Shawano fed his pack before keeping a piece of chicken for himself, he demonstrated not only that he could profit from experience in a thinking way, but that the other wolves could do so as well. This demonstration is alone sufficient to discredit the mechanistic theory which contends that evolution, by means of hereditary imprint, has led to the thoughtless or automatic responses of animals to any one of an enormously wide variety of natural stimuli. In the first place, such genetic programming would probably be incapable of making provision for every single experience that a wolf or any other animal might encounter during the course of its lifetime. Second, evolution, though it seemingly continues to change the biology of life in accordance with the exigencies of survival, progresses at a *very* slow rate, which means that today's animals (including man) have not had time to become inherently adapted to deal with the rapid and

*Donald R. Griffin, *Animal Thinking* (Cambridge: Harvard University Press, 1984).

65

enormous changes that our species has wrought on the planet and particularly upon its natural environment. This means also that while life on earth is still predicated on survival characteristics that were incorporated into evolutionary inheritance countless thousands of years ago, none of today's life forms could survive the changes that have taken place during the last three or four centuries (and particularly since the middle of the nineteenth century) if they were unable to think consciously—to reason, when confronted by new, basically unnatural influences. Captivity, of course, is just one of these conditions; whether man, wolf, parrot, dolphin, or any other living thing, none could survive captivity if it were not capable of adapting intelligently to its new environment. Memory, by allowing an animal to benefit from experience, plays an important role in the formulation of conscious decisions; the better its memory, the better able will the animal be to adapt to a changing environment.

When Sharon and I returned to Ishpeming in February of 1984, we did so principally to test the memory of the wolves, and especially of their leader. Would Shawano remember me? If so, how would he respond to my advances?

On this trip to the U.P., Bill and Betty Wilson, George's brother and sister-in-law, very kindly invited us to stay in their Marquette home, the top floor of which contains George's "pad."

In order to rest after the 450-mile drive from Ontario and so to be able to meet the wolves in a relaxed state, we spent our first day in Marquette more or less freewheeling, discussing the program for the coming week with George, talking with Jim Wuepper, and socializing with our obliging and friendly host and hostess. In the course of that first day, I informed both Jim and George that I wanted to meet the pack entirely on my own, and although I had to argue to some extent with Jim, who wanted to introduce me personally to the pack so as to make it easy for me, I prevailed in the end after explaining that when seeking the acceptance of wild animals (or tame ones, for that matter), I had long ago learned a technique that had proven itself many times over.

My method requires that I work alone, for a second

person invariably distracts me by his or her very presence. This means that I cannot put myself in a fully relaxed, neutral state, which I have found to be the way that works best for me when I am trying to win the confidence of a wild being. Then, too, I felt in this instance that if I were to be reintroduced to the wolves by Jim, I would not be able to determine whether they really remembered me from last year's visit. When Jim remonstrated, saying that they might not trust me at all if I showed up on my own, I rebutted, "That's fine, too. Either way, I will find out what I've come here to learn, which is whether Shawano and the others will remember me. If they don't, so be it. At least we'll have some kind of handle on the duration of their recall."

Whether or not Jim gave in to me merely to be polite, I cannot say; the fact is that he did give in, although he opined that his dog, Chico, would probably bark at me, and that in itself might cause the wolves to remain hidden within the trees at the far end of the enclosure.

The next morning, George guided me to a supermarket where I bought ten pounds of chicken parts—necks, wings, and livers. Armed with this parcel, I drove George home, then headed to Ishpeming under a clear sky and bright sun, but with the thermometer hovering at ten degrees below zero.

When I reached the Wuepper driveway, I slowed the car to a crawl, lowering the window on my side and picking up a turkey drumstick that I had bought especially for Chico. The dog stood at the end of his chain, about fifteen paces from where I parked the car. I had begun to speak to him even before stopping my vehicle and now, as I opened the door to emerge, I saw that Chico's tail was wagging gently. Before I had closed the door, quietly, the dog scented the raw turkey that was in my left hand. He began to lunge at his chain, his tail flailing the icy air, a great smile wreathing his salivating lips. Not a single bark did he utter. I gave him the offering, stood nearby as he engulfed it, and then spent a few minutes caressing the shaggy body, socializing with him until the height of his pleasurable excitement waned. Then I looked toward the wolf enclosure. Not an animal was to be seen.

I had brought an old canvas shoulder bag in which to place the partly frozen chicken parts, and now I went to the trunk, removed the various packages of meat, opened them, and poured their contents into the small haversack. Hitching this around my neck, so that it hung against my chest, I walked to the fence wire. There I called Shawano, my voice low, even, intended to be reassuring. Five times I called, then I saw him. Flanked by Denali, the big wolf stood among the trees, staring at me with that extraordinary intensity that is so typical of his kind. I called again as I returned Shawano's gaze, but at that instant Brigit scuttled up to the wire, her tail tucked between her legs, her ears flat against her head, her lips peeled back in submission. She stopped immediately opposite me. Digging in the meat bag, I gave her a chicken neck, thrusting it through the wire. In a trice, with but one offhanded crunch, she had swallowed it. I gave her another, meanwhile noting that Shawano had closed the distance between us by half, and that Denali was staring intently at Brigit, who, knowing that she was safe provided she remained close to me, continued to press against the wire, whining very softly. I gave her two more chunks of meat. As she swallowed the last piece, Shawano trotted up, ignoring his onetime mate as she retreated from him, but scenting the meat that hung from my neck. Thor and Denali came closer, but stayed about ten paces from the wire.

I fed Shawano. It was wonderful to feel the gentleness with which that great, powerful animal took each raw offering! After he had eaten six pieces of meat, I began tossing chicken parts to Denali and Thor, in this way getting the Beta to come within a yard of me, but not being able to draw Denali closer than her set distance of ten paces. Nevertheless, she watched each piece of chicken intently as it sailed over the wire, and challenged Thor for possession of two necks when the Beta darted toward her to try to get the chicken for himself.

At about this time I realized that Toivo hadn't shown himself. And knowing that six pups had been born to the Alphas in the spring of 1983, I wondered about *their* absence. Perhaps Toivo and the yearlings were too timid to come up to me. I made a note to ask Jim about the seven missing wolves, something that I should have done the previous day, but we had been busy discussing so many other matters that I had neglected to inquire about the state of the pack. I had, however, inquired about Brigit, and had learned that once again she was being harassed by the pack. Now, watching her, I had a sense of *déjà vu*, for her behavior was as submissive as it had been last year and she also showed another, perhaps slightly smaller, raw patch at the root of her tail. And Denali, even from a distance, was able to intimidate her mother.

By the time I had fed all the wolves and had squatted close to the wire to enjoy a few minutes of silent communication with Shawano, who, as he had done the first time, came right up to me, met my gaze, and again tried to steal my woolen cap, even through the wire, I had decided that I would cut short this visit and would not again approach the enclosure closely during the remainder of our stay. Denali was in estrus, breeding could begin at any time, and Brigit's harassment was at its height. I felt that my intrusion would increase the usually intense excitement of the mating time; for this reason I would content myself with watching the pack from inside Jim's house, or from the front seat of my car. In any event, I was quite satisfied that Shawano, at least, clearly remembered me and had accepted me without any trace of hostility.

Before leaving the wolves that morning, I stepped back to a position about thirty yards from the enclosure, squatted with my back to a tree, and watched. Almost immediately Denali and Thor joined Shawano, but as the two moved forward, Brigit scuttled away, her entire being advertising her total submission. Nevertheless, Denali charged her mother, growling threateningly, her ears and tail stiffly upright. Shawano merely watched, while Thor moved to a position where he would be separated from hostilities, but could observe the action. Brigit, however, was not about to be trounced by her daughter. The smaller wolf ran at full speed and soon disappeared within the trees; this appeared to satisfy Denali, who returned to the southern part of the enclosure, licked Shawano's mouth, her tail wagging, then sniffed around, licking at places where pieces of chicken had landed. Moments later the Alpha female urinated seven times, squatting to do so, this behavior signifying that she was reinforcing her status. Shawano, not to be outdone, followed suit, wetting on all those places where Denali had voided. Thor kept his distance and did not try to copy the actions of the dominant pair.

As I reflected on the pack's behavior while again comparing it to the interactions between wild wolves in the breeding season that I had witnessed in the past, it became evident to me that the Ishpeming wolves had that morning engaged in fully reasoned activity. Each animal had interpreted my arrival in a personal way and had shown itself capable of taking advantage of it. Brigit had immediately realized that my presence would allow her to come into the open without fear of Denali, and by whining at me and pressing close to the fence wire, she could also get a share of food, which she could eat in peace. Shawano, although he is almost always willing to eat, demonstrated by his general behavior, and especially by means of his body language, that he was glad to see me and that he trusted me. Thor, undoubtedly hoping for food, placed himself at a vantage point from which he could get my attention, yet far enough away from the Alphas to ensure they would understand he was being both submissive and neutral. Denali, eager for her share of food, but distrustful of humans, came closer to me than she would normally have done with a relative stranger, but I am convinced that she did so not so much because of the food, or her memory of me, as because of her concern over Brigit, who, alone by the fence with Shawano, could be expected to attempt to regain her Alpha status by wooing her ex-mate—which was precisely what she was doing! Shawano, although he showed no sexual interest in Brigit, was not hostile toward her. I interpreted this to mean that he felt fully secure in his own position and so did not need to demonstrate his authority over the subordinate female. Indeed, it appeared that Shawano did not want to get mixed up in the squabbles between his mate and her rival, whom he left in peace when Denali was not around, and whom he attacked only when he was near his mate during those times

70

when the latter became hostile toward Brigit. Pondering these things as I watched the wolves, it struck me that I was witnessing a typical example of the human triangle, the principals in this case being two female wolves competing for one male of the same species, although it could just as easily have been the other way around, an example of which I was to observe within this same pack in the near future.

Finding myself drawing comparisons between the behavior of the wolves and that of humans, I recalled the effects of the syndrome known as cabin fever, which often manifests itself after one or more individuals of our species become isolated from the mainstream for long periods. Trappers, prospectors, pioneers, miners, and others who are thrust into the wilderness and held there because of weather or other conditions today represent a minority of such sufferers, the vast majority of whom are now found as shut-ins in metropolitan centers. But whether in the wilderness or in a Manhattan high-rise, such individuals develop an *angst* that in lone people can lead to suicide or severe mental breakdown. And when two or more individuals are thus held captive by their environment, although they may have started out as close friends or as married couples, hatreds can develop that, in many instances, have been known to last entire lifetimes. In extreme cases, actual combat has occurred and murders have been committed.

Was there that much difference between wolves held in captivity, even under such optimum conditions as were available to the Ishpeming pack, and humans isolated and held in one place against their natural desires?

Examining this question at the time, it seemed to me that there was hardly any difference at all. But now, after reflecting upon the biology of aggression and linking this with my observations of wild wolves, when I had seen Alpha females drive away subordinate competitors during the breeding season, I realize that there is an enormous and most significant distinction to be made between the yearly harassment of Brigit—which has its origins in wolf hierarchy, but continues abnormally because of captivity—and the interactions between humans suffering from cabin fever, who are, of course, also held captive.

71

In the case of wolves and other wild animals, when the cause of conflict is removed, normal societal relationships are resumed. Denali, for instance, invariably accepts Brigit when the breeding season is past, and Brigit just as readily forgives her daughter, so the pack once again becomes a self-supportive, tightly knit unit.

In the case of humans, however, most people who have had serious quarrels during enforced confinement (or for any other reasons, for that matter) continue to resent and distrust each other long after the cause of the dispute has ended; in the absence of forgiveness and acceptance, the actual or supposed wrongs are kept alive in memory and are often exaggerated in the course of time. Individuals so afflicted become angry whenever they are reminded of the conflict. Thus, rancors from the past survive to influence the present negatively and, unless purged, will continue to do so in the future.

Although I had not formulated such theories while I was watching Denali and Brigit in 1984, I did detect some similarity between their condition and that of humans suffering from cabin fever, having recognized years earlier that wolves and humans are both highly social animals. There are, of course, differences to be noted in the behavior and physiology exhibited by the two species, but there are also many similarities that stem from the natural survival traits inherited during the course of evolution. These are particularly to be noted within the nervous and endocrine systems of wolf and man, which bear a close relationship to each other. In this regard, there is ample proof that many human behavioral traits are similar to those also found in wolves, not the least of which involve dominant-submissive behavior. Humans like to believe that they are truly free and not subservient to anyone, but the truth is that all of us are socially insecure and inherently ruled by the primordial "pecking order." Clearly, as in the wolf pack, dominant-submissive traits and behavior begin within the family. As wolves do, humans leave the parental fold to mate and to start their own "pack." The offspring of these unions are subjected immediately after birth to the disciplines of the dominant adults, their parents. When more than one infant is born to the human family, sibling rivalry develops and intensifies and, as the offspring approach puberty, dominance clashes result between them and their parents, although in the human condition the word *dominance* is rarely used; instead we talk about such things as disobedience, child abuse, the generation gap, wife-beating, aggressive tendencies, and parental guidance. But no matter what labels may be applied to the functions and dysfunctions of any truly social group, there is no escaping the fact that the struggle for high rank within any such group has existed since the beginnings of the first prehistoric liaisons and will no doubt continue to exist to the end of time. Even within the best regulated and most democratic human social system, there must be leaders and a subordinate hierarchy. In a wolf pack, the "top dog" is called the Alpha; in human mega-societies, he or she is called *president, prime minister*, or perhaps *der Führer*, and in human clans, the Alphas are Mom and Dad and so on, down to the newborn infant, who is loved by all— at least in the great majority of cases—but is yet ruled by all.

There are those who may feel that I am guilty of anthropomorphism when I speak of human and wolf in the same breath, but although I am comfortable about the use of human terms to describe certain aspects of animal behavior, in this instance I am not ascribing human characteristics to wolves, but rather the other way around.

Soon after coming to these conclusions, I telephoned my friend Dr. Allyn Roberts, a clinical psychologist who practices in Madison, Wisconsin, and read to him the results of my deliberations. When I had finished, he said, "As a psychologist, that feels right to me. It shows the social needs of the human and the wolf. We must learn to face our own nature, and it is hard to do, so by looking at the nature of animals, we may find it easier to understand our own."

The last part of Allyn's comment touched me personally, for I have indeed learned more about myself and about my own species by observing animals than by observing those of my kind.

After leaving the wolf pack and returning to Marquette, I called Jim at his studio to ask him about the seeming absence of Toivo and the pups, only to be told

73

that they had become infected by a virus and were all dead. Shocking though this news was, I knew that wolf-pup mortality rates can be high in the wild, so I did not find it altogether unusual that the Ishpeming pack should undergo what appeared to be regular cycles of disease leading to fatalities. I had not seen any of the newborns, of course, and their death for this reason was not quite as saddening as the death of Toivo, the carefree young comic who had made such a favorable impression on Sharon and me. Both of us were sad for the rest of our stay in Michigan, unable to forget a wolf who, although we had only known him for a short time, had nevertheless managed to affect us deeply by the grace of his be-ing, his carefree attitude, and his charming personality.

We have a photograph of the harum-scarum Toivo, hair all awry, eyes glinting with vivacity and humor. He is standing in the snow, head raised and ears erect while staring about him as though planning some new prank. Both of us like to remember him that way.

Two years ago, after noticing that very little informa-tion about the diseases of wolves was included in the books dealing with these animals, I began compiling a list of infectious agents that can cause illness in coyotes, red wolves, and timber wolves; but finding that although I had listed forty-seven different kinds of harmful orga-nisms, I nevertheless had little information on their bi-ology, their lifespans, or particularly on the ways in which they are able to infect their hosts. I turned to the U.S. Fish and Wildlife Service in Washington, D.C., mem-bers of which had already been exceptionally helpful to me in other areas of biology and conservation. Assisted by Megan Durham, a public-information specialist in the Office of Public Affairs of the Service, I was put in con-tact with Dr. Danny B. Pence, a scientist with the De-partment of Pathology at Texas Tech University Health Sciences Centers, in Lubbock, who answered my im-mediate questions and later was kind enough to send me a reprint of a study conducted by himself and Dr. J. W. Custer, also of Texas Tech, but in the Department of Range and Wildlife Management.

My conversation with Dr. Pence, and my reading of the results of the study reported by him and his colleague, revealed, to my astonishment, that North America's wild canids are parasitized by no less than 134 disease-causing agents, a number of which also affect domestic dogs and cats and other animals, such as foxes, as well as humans.

The study (entitled *Host-Parasite Relationships in the Wild Canidae of North America: Pathology of Infectious Diseases in the Genus Canis*) says at the conclusion of its abstract:

While a few case reports document diseases such as juvenile osteomalacia [a disease of the bone due to vitamin-D deficiency] in a coyote from Alaska, bilateral blindness in a coyote from Texas, osteoarthrosis [degeneration of bony joints] in a coyote X dog hybrid from Nebraska and two timber wolves from Canada, and coyotes with broken bones, missing feet, and gunshot wounds, there is little evidence that noninfectious diseases are serious problems in the morbidity and mortality of wild Canids. In contrast, many infectious disease agents are reported from these hosts. Some of these reach epizootic [of a temporary nature] proportions and occasionally affect their populations.

The present study reviews the infectious disease agents reported from coyotes *(Canis latrans)*, timber wolves *(C. lupus)*, and red wolves *(C. rufus)* and their feral and dog hybrids from North America and discusses the pathology of the more common and/or serious epizootic diseases in these hosts.

The study shows that all three species of wolves can be infected by eight viruses, four rickettsial organisms (a group of microorganisms smaller than bacteria, but larger than viruses), nine kinds of bacteria, seventeen species of cestodes (tapeworms), two species of acanthocephalan intestinal worms, twenty-five species of nematode worms, two kinds of mites, three species of lice, fifteen kinds of ticks, and thirty infections caused by fleas.

Important vital infections affecting wolves and coyotes are reported to include distemper and canine hepatitis, but it may come as a surprise to many that the most dreaded of all the animal viruses, rabies, does not appear to affect wolves or coyotes in any serious way. In this context, the study reports:

75

Finally, the enigma of wild species of the genus *Canis* and rabies virus continue to defy elucidation. Although rabies has been described as a "potential killer of coyotes" (Gier et al., 1978), only occasional cases of rabies in coyotes are reported in most western states of the United States. The coyote is listed as a highly susceptible host (*World Health Organization Chronicles*, 1974) and experimental infections indicated that strains located from coyotes have a faster rate of spread than certain fox strains (Behymer et al., 1974).

Of the 9,943 laboratory-confirmed rabies cases from the United States, Canada, and Mexico reported in 1977, there were only three cases involving timber wolves in Alaska and one case each involving coyotes from Canada and Mexico (Centers for Disease Control, Atlanta, Georgia, 1978). In rabies surveillance programs reported by Centers for Disease Control, twelve of 435 (3 percent) coyotes examined in the United States had rabies, while six wolves in Ontario and one wolf from the Northwest Territories were found positive for rabies.

Of the 8,598 reported rabies cases in Ontario, Canada, from 1961 to 1969, only thirty-five (0.41 percent) involved coyotes and/or wolves (Johnston and Beauregard, 1969). Of sixty-five coyote and twenty-nine wolf brains from wild populations trapped for pelts in Iowa and examined by fluorescent antibody procedures, none were positive for rabies (Hendricks and Seaton, 1969). Indeed, in most epidemiological reviews of wildlife rabies in North America, the coyote and timber wolf are hardly mentioned and certainly cannot be considered with anywhere near the epidemiological significance as hosts such as foxes, skunks, bats, or raccoons (McLean, 1970; Sikes, 1970). The prevalence of rabies virus and its role in the mortality of feral canids is in need of clarification.

This aspect of the study interested me greatly, for I am frequently asked by friends and acquaintances if I am not afraid of encountering rabid animals during my frequent and often lengthy stays in the wilderness. When I reply that I am not at all concerned about encountering the disease in the wild because during all the years that I have traveled the backwoods I have met only two rabid animals, one a female timber wolf and the other a male red fox, my questioners show surprise that seems to border on disbelief. (I shot and killed these animals, suspecting from their behavior that they were rabid;

76

subsequent tests proved that both had contracted the disease.)

Before Dr. Pence sent me a copy of his and his colleague's study, I had done considerable research in Europe and, later, in Canada. My findings strongly indicated that the virus is most at home in urban-rural areas where relatively large populations of domestic animals, particularly dogs and cats, are to be found. In such areas, rabies outbreaks occur on a regular basis. Yet the disease seems to be either rare or altogether absent in the true wilderness, the reason for this being that the Achilles' heel of any infectious organism is that sooner or later it runs out of hosts. It is logical to postulate, therefore, that a disease-causing agent such as the rabies virus will thrive in those locations where it can be transferred easily from host to host, particularly when many of the hosts, like dogs and cats, may well have developed seriously weakened immune systems from the continuous inbreeding to which they have been subjected during the many centuries since domesticated strains were "perfected," just as Western people are easy prey for many of the diseases found in areas of large populations where hygienic practices are not well understood, although the local inhabitants are far more resistant to the infectious agents.

Because they live as packs and usually have less frequent contact with others of their kind, and also because populations of rabies-susceptible animals, such as foxes, skunks, and raccoons, are considerably smaller in wilderness areas than they are in rural-urban districts, wolves are less likely to come into contact with rabies. And it may also be that the wild canids, exceptionally hardy to begin with, have developed strong resistance to the disease. In this context, it appears significant that wolf-dog hybrids seem to be much more susceptible to the rabies virus than are wolves. However, from studies of the available literature dealing with wolves in Europe, particularly during the seventeenth and eighteenth centuries, one gains the strong impression that the majority of attacks on humans were made by rabid animals, both fullbred wolves and wolf-dog crosses. The late Dr. C. H. D. Clarke, who for years was head of the Fish and Wildlife Division of Ontario's Ministry of Natural Resources,

77

certainly believed that rabies was the principal cause of attacks in Europe. In a manuscript entitled *Beast of Gévaudan*,* he said: "Down the long list of recorded attacks by wolves, it becomes clear that the Russian baron in his troika is folklore, but the rabid wolf is grim fact. The pattern is universal. The famous wolves of medieval song and story were all rabid."

Rabid wolves in Europe, but not in North America? The contradiction can be explained. A number of factors probably contributed to the spread of rabies among European wolves. In the first place, wolf wilderness areas that had come under the influence of large human populations had been drastically reduced, or eliminated altogether. Where the wolf packs had once lived and hunted relatively undisturbed, human villages and towns had burgeoned, forests had been cleared, domestic livestock had multiplied; so had dogs and cats. Starving wolves began feeding on cattle and sheep, pursued by hunters and their dogs; as is the case even today, every smallholder had at least one farm dog, and many of these animals were allowed to roam free and to breed with their own kind as well as with lone wolves. In such a climate, the rabies virus began to thrive, first attacking domestic dogs; then, because it is probable that no wolf is totally immune to the disease if exposed to it frequently enough, the wolves became seriously affected. Huge wolf-dog hybrids began to appear and these, rabid or not, attacked people. The two that are described in Dr. Clarke's manuscript terrorized the regions of Vivarais and Gévaudan, France, from 1764 to 1767. A history of the depredations of these animals was written in 1901 by Father François Fabre, a priest in the parish of Gévaudan who obtained the information from church records and municipal documentation. These two predators killed sixty-four humans and attacked more than a hundred. Most of the victims were children. One of these animals was killed in 1765; it weighed 130 pounds after it had been dead for some hours, so, allowing for dehydration following death, this creature in life would probably have weighed between

*Unpublished manuscript, courtesy of the Fish and Wildlife Library, Ministry of Natural Resources, Toronto, Ontario.

140 and 145 pounds. The other animal was killed about a year later. It weighed 109 pounds, but here again, it was not put on the scales until some considerable time after death. Both killers were much larger than those wolves generally found in that area of Europe. Descriptions of color and skull measurements have been preserved, and these, added to the size of the animals, caused Dr. Clarke to believe that they were not purebred wolves, but wolf-dog crosses.

Whatever doubts may still remain about the wolf situation in Europe up to the latter part of the eighteenth century, there is no doubt that in North America rabies is not a serious problem among wolves and coyotes, which is more than can be said for many of the remaining 133 infectious diseases that do affect the wolves of our continent. To give details of all the infections discussed in the study by Drs. Pence and Custer is a task beyond the scope of this narrative, but at least a few should be mentioned.

Canine parvovirus is of particular concern to me because it killed Toivo as well as Denali's newborn pups in 1983. It is also suspected of having caused Siskiwit's death in the late summer of 1982. This disease is new. It was first discovered in dogs in Texas in 1977. Soon afterward, it was reported from other areas of the United States and from Canada. Because its pathology resembles a syndrome known as feline panleukopenia, which is also caused by a parvovirus, I am tempted to speculate that the organism that now attacks dogs is a rogue, a disease agent that was confined to cats until the late seventies, and then, as viruses are known to do, mutated in order to expand its scope, invading dogs, coyotes, and wolves. Whether I am correct or not in my surmise remains to be seen, but my view is strengthened by the fact that protection from the disease is afforded by vaccinating dogs and captive wild canids with an inactivated feline panleukopenia serum.

Symptoms of this sickness include sudden onset, loss of appetite, listlessness, and bloody diarrhea caused by congestion and bleeding of the mucous linings of the intestines. Postmortems also reveal that bone marrow cells are destroyed and the lungs and liver are congested.

Distemper, a worldwide disease of dogs, cats, raccoons, and other animals, does affect wolves and coyotes and kills the majority of pups that become infected. But, here again, it seems that this virus-borne disease is not an important factor in the mortality of wild coyote and wolf populations, probably because in a free-living state they do not come into regular contact with other infected animals. In captivity, however, distemper can become a serious disease of wolves and coyotes, usually because such captives are housed in rural-urban areas where also live concentrations of domestic dogs, for the virus can travel by air and can in this way infect animals some distance from a carrier. Physical contact with nasal discharges and saliva from infected animals also transmits the disease.

Roundworms of the class Nematoda are extremely common parasites of animals and man. This group contains more than twelve thousand different species, the major of which, fortunately, are harmless. Among those that do parasitize animals, there are some that are quite nasty. Probably the best known are the dog and cat roundworms, *Toxocara canis* and *Toxocara leonina*, and although treatment is simple and effective, these parasites, some of which can be four inches long, are present in such numbers that it is practically certain that every coyote, wolf, dog, and cat will be affected by them at least once during its lifetime. Left untreated, they can seriously affect young domestic animals and it is not uncommon for puppies to be infected at birth if their mother had worms, for the organism can be transmitted to the unborn via the maternal blood. Wolves and coyotes in a free state are hosts to these organisms, which appear to have little effect on the animals, although their presence may indirectly contribute to a wolf's death if it is also burdened by other parasites or is suffering from malnutrition.

A little-known but quite common stomach worm, *Physaloptera rara*, has developed a clever way of getting inside the stomachs of wolves, dogs, cats, raccoons, and practically any other animal that enjoys eating things like crickets, grasshoppers, cockroaches, flour beetles, and ground beetles, all of which act as intermediate hosts to

80

this nematode. When an animal eats an infected insect, it gets the worms, which then adhere to the mucous linings of the stomach and cause inflammations at each site. Affected animals produce dark, slimy diarrhea that contains some blood. Treatment is readily available, however.

Wolves and domestic dogs are also infected by the giant kidney worm, a creature that may reach a length of thirty-nine inches and causes marked weight loss, frequent urination, trembling, anemia, and bloating. Fortunately, this worm rarely attacks both kidneys, because if untreated it would completely destroy the affected organ.

One of the most serious nematodal infections is produced by the dog heartworm, *Dirofilaria imitis*, which enters the right side of the heart and pulmonary arteries, affects the lungs and tissues, and causes fluids to pass into the stomach. Without treatment, death is inevitable, but because of its complicated life cycle, this worm is difficult to treat. Dr. Pence considers that prevention is definitely better than cure where this organism is concerned. Even so, preventive treatments must be administered to dogs, or to captive wolves and coyotes, *throughout* the mosquito season, for this blood-sucking insect is the intermediate host of *Dirofilaria*. A mosquito bites an infected animal, then bites a noninfected individual and passes on the condition, much in the same way that mosquitoes transmit malaria and encephalitis. Heartworm, essentially a southern-dwelling nematode, has in recent years invaded the northern United States and southern Canada, a circumstance occasioned by the increase of travel, particularly at holiday seasons (when there are hordes of mosquitoes present), by individuals who take their dogs with them. When such dogs are infected, they become instrumental in propagating the worms via mosquitoes. Humans can also be affected, although to date only one individual was found to have the worms actually inside the heart; all others suffered from invasion of their tissues. George Wilson's wolf Homer died of heartworm in Michigan. After a postmortem, a photograph was taken of the wolf's heart, which had been opened to show a great cluster of spaghetti-like worms bulging out of the right chamber.

The oldest, easiest to swallow idea was that earth was man's personal property, a combination of garden, zoo, bank vault, and energy source, placed at our disposal to be consumed, ornamented, or pulled apart as we wish.
—Lewis Thomas, *The Lives of a Cell*

FIVE

Brigit was still being harassed in mid-April of 1984, although by now Denali's aggressiveness appeared to have mellowed somewhat, an impression I formed after watching the Alpha female's behavior as well as that of her mother, who, even though she continued to signal submission, was nevertheless more active and open in her movements than she had been during February.

Watching the pack while caressing Chico on the morning after Sharon and I had once again arrived for a visit to the U.P., I detected considerable differences in the behavior of all the wolves; on this occasion they ran out of the forested portion of their enclosure as soon as my car entered the Wuepper yard. Brigit, coming alone from the northern part of the compound, rushed up to the fence and stood tight against it, watching the car as I slowed and turned into a parking place opposite Chico's kennel. Shawano, on the other hand, kept some distance from the wire, evidently interested in my arrival, but remaining on a knoll from which he had an unobstructed view of me. Denali was also watching me intently, but from farther back and partly screened by trees, while Thor, although he stood in the open, seemed to be far more interested in Denali than in my presence.

Remembering that it had been necessary to call to the wolves during our February visit, I was pleased that they had recognized the sound of my car and had evidently linked me with the vehicle, just as Chico had done; but whereas the big, shaggy dog had been pleasurably excited by my arrival and had demonstrated his recognition of automobile and human in the way he wagged both his tail and the rearmost part of his body, his mouth stretched into an enormous smile, the attention of the wolves seemed to be divided between interest in my visit and some other influence that was beyond my ability to detect.

As before, I had come alone with an enormous package of chicken parts, including a large breast for Chico, who engulfed the offering and proceeded to crunch it up with more speed than efficiency while wagging his tail and pressing his body against my leg so as to allow me to continue caressing him while he was busy eating. When the dog had swallowed his meal, he licked his lips, paws, and the still-snowy ground; then he solicited more caresses. As I stroked his head, I continued to watch the wolves, noticing at this time that Shawano seemed torn between trotting up to the fence and running back toward Denali, who remained in the same place and was still staring at me. Intrigued by the big wolf's behavior, I lingered beside Chico for some minutes, watching as Shawano ran back to Denali, turned, and immediately trotted back toward the fence. He did this eight times while I remained beside the dog.

Judging that it was time to approach the wolves, I left Chico, opened the car trunk, and emptied the meat into my carrying bag, again putting the strap around my neck and allowing the bulky haversack to hang against my chest. I began to walk toward the fence. Brigit redoubled her attempts to get my attention; Shawano moved closer to the fence, but stopped about fifteen feet from it, there to look alternately at me and at Denali. Thor also remained where I had first seen him. His interest was still fixed on Denali, who continued to look at me, her stance

84

elegant, head up, ears forward, feet well planted on the ground, the image incarnate of a very dominant wolf.

Before I was halfway to the fence, the behavior of the wolves told me that they had picked up the scent of the raw meat I carried and had probably done so the moment I opened the trunk of my car. Nevertheless, when I reached the wire, only Brigit was there to take food from my fingers. Shawano, who had been quite ready to take chicken pieces from my hand in February, would not do so now. Yet his behavior told me that he was hungry and that he expected me to toss food to him. For some moments I resisted the wolf's will, feeding Brigit instead. She, of course, was delighted to be the only one near me; she gorged, eating piece after piece of meat until her stomach began to bulge. Seeing this, I gave in to Shawano's silent pleas and tossed a chicken breast high over the wire. Brigit ran for it when it landed midway between the Alpha male and the fence, but Shawano, uttering a low growl, dashed forward and grabbed it. Now he turned, loped to his former place, and there ate the meat, ignoring Denali's soft whines and Thor's drooling stares.

Twice more I fed Shawano, and on each occasion he took the chicken and ate it. Now Denali showed signs of agitation. She was obviously hungry, but refused to approach any closer, and since her location was at least one hundred feet from where I stood, it was difficult for me to throw a piece of chicken high enough so it would clear the nine-foot-high fence and still have enough power to span the distance. But selecting a leg, I tried, heaving as hard as I could. The meat landed some thirty feet short of Denali. Shawano, Brigit, Thor, and Denali had all watched the offering's trajectory, four lifted heads that swung in unison with the flying chicken. When the leg landed, Shawano dashed up to it, went to pick it up, then dropped it as Thor started loping toward Denali.

The big Alpha ran at his subordinate, who immediately retreated. Shawano went up to Denali; she licked him, whining. Meanwhile, Brigit, opportunistic as ever, had scuttled forward, grabbed the chicken, and returned swiftly to the fence, staying close to me as she ate. While she was thus engaged, I threw a second piece of meat, trying to get it closer to Denali, but failing again. This time, however, the Alpha female dashed forward, grabbed the food, and ran back to her place. Thor stayed where he was, probably because Shawano now stood between the Beta and Denali. It was at this point that I recognized the influence I had earlier sensed, but had been unable to identify.

Even though Denali was pregnant and due to give birth within the next two weeks, Thor was very much captivated by her. Shawano, of course, was well aware of his son's interest and he was quite obviously determined to keep Thor away from Denali. This was why he dared not come up to the fence—he was afraid to do so in case the Beta should sneak in while the Alpha was eating. That part of Shawano's behavior I could readily understand, but what seemed little short of extraordinary was the fact that the Alpha male did not rush upon his subordinate so as to punish him severely.

Observing more closely, I eventually realized that Denali, far from resenting her son's quite open advances, appeared to be enjoying them. It seemed to me that the she-wolf was actually flirting with both males, that she knew perfectly well that she was occupying center stage and that she was going to continue in that position for as long as she could! When Shawano dashed up to place himself between Thor and Denali, the she-wolf whined at her mate, showed discreet submission, and licked his mouth when he got within her reach. Conversely, when Shawano left, lured to his knoll in the hope of securing more chicken, Denali's stance altered and she again showed herself to advantage, meanwhile casting glances at Thor that I can only describe as flirtatious.

Having reached these conclusions, I began to understand why Shawano refrained from attacking Thor. I had witnessed similar behavior in wild wolves, but on all those occasions, the Alpha male had unhesitatingly attacked a rival, often helped by the Alpha female. If I was reading the present situation correctly, Denali's obvious enjoyment of the attention she was receiving suggested to Shawano that she would not back him up if he attacked Thor. Furthermore, she might even take Thor's part, in which case the Alpha male would be deposed as swiftly and effectively as Brigit, his onetime mate, had been. Was this yet another love triangle in the making?

Thor has inherited qualities from both his parents and is a magnificent wolf, a calm and self-assured individual who, at the time, was already fully mature and almost as large as his father. Though he was four years younger than Shawano, who was then seven, Thor's size, youth, and determination might well allow him to defeat the larger and more experienced wolf.

As I watched the interplay between father, mother, and son, I thought back to the many times I had seen similar behavior demonstrated by wild wolves.

As with Jim's wolves, a pack in the wild begins with a breeding pair that may have grown up together and, as young adults, left the family of their own accord, perhaps because they had become pair-bonded and were prevented from breeding by their Alphas, or for any one of a variety of other reasons. More usually, however, the future progenitors of a pack are loners who have left their units voluntarily or have been chased away. Inherently social, such animals need the companionship of their own kind and will often team up upon meeting. If a lone male and a lone female come together in this way, they will breed at the proper season and form a family, although two males or two females may also become a team.

In any event, the original breeding pair constitutes a pack of two and, obviously, each wolf automatically attains Alpha rank, as was the case with Shawano and Brigit. Later, when pups are born and grow to adulthood, the expanded pack develops the age-old, complex hierarchical rituals from which a "pecking order" emerges. As a rule, the parent wolves retain their Alpha status and the strongest and most determined of their male and female offspring become the Betas. In Thor's case, however, he inherited his rank in the absence of other sibling males, although he exhibits qualities that would probably have allowed him to gain that position in any event, just as Denali became the Alpha female of the pack in competition with her mother and sister.

From the foregoing it becomes clear that Alpha rank, although it is automatically assumed by a single pair, must at some point be relinquished to a fitter challenger, or when age, injury, or illness weakens a dominant wolf. Occasionally, as in Brigit's case, a wolf becomes Alpha because of the absence of other individuals who are better able to exert leadership; it is then only a matter of time until a dominant animal, like Denali, emerges and takes over.

In the wild state, when an Alpha is forced to step down, he or she may remain within the pack and occupy a low-ranking position; or such a wolf may be chased away or may leave voluntarily to become a loner. In captivity, however, a demoted wolf has no choice but to remain as part of the pack and can be killed if its presence continues to present a challenge to its successor. If the defeated wolf happens to be a female, the real or assumed challenge she may present to her successor surfaces with the onset of the breeding season, reaching its peak during the height of the estrus cycle and thereafter slowly diminishing, disappearing altogether a week or ten days before the pups are born. But if the demoted animal happens to be a male, his presence may present a continuous threat to the leader's authority.

What I had witnessed that morning indicated that Thor was aspiring to the male leadership of the pack. Under such circumstances, a fight between him and Shawano was sure to develop. Who would win? What would happen to the loser? Only time could answer these questions. Meanwhile, all I could do was to warn Jim, so that he could keep an eye on the situation during that evening, for even if I elected to stay with the pack for the rest of the day, there would be little that I could do to break up a fight if one should develop, since I was a relative stranger to the wolves and had no authority over them. Indeed, it would be foolhardy for me to seek to intervene.

When I got back to Marquette, I telephoned Jim at his studio and alerted him to the possible developments, but I continued to worry about the wolves and I spent a restless night, waking several times to realize that I had been dreaming about a fight between Shawano and Thor.

Next morning, I hurried through breakfast with Sharon and George, keeping my own counsel but doing my best to join in the general conversation. Afterward, dashing

88

to the supermarket for a supply of chicken parts, I was aware that my anxiety had communicated itself to my wife, who guessed the cause of my worry even though I had not spoken about it to her. As she explained later, she had overheard part of my telephone conversation with Jim and had realized from my behavior that I was seriously disturbed by events in Ishpeming. As a result, she too had spent a restless night.

As I neared Jim's property at about ten o'clock that morning, I suddenly realized that I was suffering from considerable anxiety, a negative state that would be instantly detected by the wolves and might well precipitate aggressive behavior. This wouldn't do! Drawing the car off the road, I parked and got out, then I began to pace up and down on the edge of the highway, willing myself back into a tranquil state and refusing to allow imagination to disrupt my newly acquired equanimity. When I felt I was emotionally ready to proceed, I got back into the car and made myself drive slowly the rest of the way, about two miles, reminding myself that Jim had telephoned me early that morning to tell me that all had appeared to be well with the pack before he left for his studio.

Upon arriving at the Wuepper property, I parked as usual beside Chico's area, keeping my gaze fixed on the dog as I got out, walked to him, and gave him half a chicken breast. Then, as he was munching the food, I looked toward the enclosure and noticed immediately that the behavior of the wolves had altered dramatically from that of the previous day.

Shawano and Brigit were waiting beside the fence; Denali and Thor were only some ten feet from the wire, the Beta standing on his own while his mother, again regally posed, was on the knoll that Shawano had occupied yesterday. As I tarried beside Chico, the big Alpha stood upright, balancing both front paws on the wire and thrusting his muzzle through the mesh, his ears pricked forward expectantly and his piercing gaze fixed on me. When I looked more intently at Thor and Denali, it became evident to me that the Beta was no longer seeking to make contact with the female; he was also keeping his gaze away from Shawano.

Now I left Chico and prepared the food as usual, then walked slowly toward the enclosure, observing each animal in turn and noting that only Brigit showed signs of distress and even she appeared to be less tense than she had been during my last visit. None of the wolves moved until I had almost reached the wire, at which point Shawano dropped to all fours, wagged his tail, and snapped his jaws several times in quick succession, drooling and making a series of hollow sounds, rather like those produced when a person claps his hands softly. Such behavior is prompted by the anticipation of food, a sort of ritualistic mastication in celebration of the meal that will soon follow.

Brigit edged closer to me, keeping her tail between her legs and crouching submissively while whining and seeking my gaze, subdued by the presence of the Alphas, but nevertheless determined to be on hand when the food was dispensed. Thor and Denali, on the other hand, stayed where they were, but both wolves sniffed avidly in my direction, each dancing in anticipation as they absorbed the odor of raw meat, their ears pricked forward and their heads bobbing up and down.

Noting such normal behavior, I began to think that I had misread yesterday's events. There was no doubt that I had witnessed signs of conflict between Thor and Shawano, but I now wondered if I had interpreted them correctly. Preoccupied in this way, I fished out a chicken thigh for Shawano. He took it gently. While he chewed and swallowed, I gave a piece of meat to Brigit, then another to Shawano. Now I tossed a half-breast to Denali, who grabbed it in midair and began to eat. Thor was next, but my throw was off. The meat landed between him and Shawano and the latter wheeled around immediately and reached Thor just as he was about to close his jaws on the food. The Beta gave up his attempt to grasp the chicken and retreated; Shawano ate the prize. Then I noticed that the Alpha had a bloody cut on his groin, an injury about half an inch long that had turned his light fur a shade of deep pink; but from where I stood I could not tell whether the wolf had been bitten or had snagged himself on a sharp branch.

Observing each wolf as intently as possible, I continued feeding them, Shawano now taking every piece of chicken from my hand and remaining beside the wire when I threw meat to Denali and Thor. Brigit, as I had come to expect from her, remained near me, but just out of Shawano's reach, although he did not threaten her unless she tried to get the pieces of chicken that sometimes slipped out of my grasp before the Alpha had managed to close his jaws on them.

When all the food was gone, I removed the satchel and entered the enclosure, passing through a small holding pen before emerging into the main compound. Brigit scuttled up to me, but stayed out of reach. Thor and Denali retreated at first, but when Shawano came within two feet of me, reached forward to sniff my leg, then turned and sat on his haunches, offering me his back, Thor trotted forward. Denali, who hadn't gotten as much food as the others because she had refused to come close enough for me to throw to her accurately, watched me from the knoll, but Thor advanced a few more steps, working toward me from the left since Shawano was sitting on my right. I took three slow strides toward the Beta. He held his ground. At four feet I stopped, and as he was studying me, I noticed that he had a puncture on his right front leg, about three inches above his foot.

Now I knew that my interpretation of yesterday's events had been correct. The two male wolves had indeed fought for supremacy. Thor had bitten Shawano, and the latter had bitten his son. Clearly, from the way they were now behaving, Shawano had been the victor. Just as evidently, the altercation had cleared the air between them. The Alpha showed no resentment, and the Beta, apart from being careful to signal submission whenever his leader came near him, appeared to have accepted his defeat. Denali, by the same token, was no longer seeking to capture Thor's interest. Because each wolf had been so lightly injured, I surmised that the fight had been short, probably because big Shawano had quickly overwhelmed his opponent, who must have soon signaled complete submission. And Denali obviously had not taken her son's part; had she done so, it was almost certain that Shawano would have been defeated or, at the very least, more severely wounded.

91

Partly to show the wolves that I fully trusted them, and partly because I wanted to observe their behavior more closely from a comfortable position, I sat on the ground, leaning against a tree that grew between the places where Thor stood and where Shawano now sat.

The Alpha male turned his head casually in my direction, gave me one of those lupine glances of appraisal that seem to bore right into the mind of a human, then faced front again. He yawned, opening his mouth so wide that it appeared as though his jaws had become unhinged, an action that in wolves and dogs can denote either drowsiness or pleasurable excitement, the latter evidently being the reason for the wolf's present gape, for he wagged his tail, heaved a big sigh of contentment, and loped casually toward his mate.

Thor remained standing, his eyes not leaving mine until he glanced toward his leader just before taking a couple of steps in my direction. I thought that he was going to come right up to me, but as he approached, Shawano turned back, staring at the Beta aggressively while uttering a low, rumbling growl. Thor immediately backed away, tail tucked between his legs and lips peeled back in an appeasing grin. When he was about twenty paces from me, he stopped; now Shawano sat down and began to lick his injury. During this exchange, Brigit had been pacing continually along the fenceline at my back, trotting one way for a number of yards, then turning and going in the opposite direction. Denali stepped off her knoll and moved deeper into the trees, whining softly. This caused Shawano to rise. He looked at me again, then trotted after Denali, who went to meet him, her behavior showing a mixture of submission, affection, and playfulness. She grinned, arched her back, and dropped her tail; but she kept wagging the lower end of it as she pranced lightly while bowing her head.

When the two came together, Shawano stood tall, ears forward, tail high and wagging gently. Denali crouched lower, sidled up to him, and, her head turned sideways, licked at his muzzle several times before nibbling at his right cheek. She was now soliciting regurgitation, an age-old ritual among wolves, programmed in the nursery and continued throughout life. Shawano responded immediately, the first signs of his compliance emerging as he arched his back, convulsed his stomach, and dropped his head. Seconds later he opened his mouth and began to disgorge, but even before the masticated chicken parts hit the ground, Denali began to eat, taking pieces from inside his mouth. When he was done, his mate scooped up that part of the steaming offering that had actually landed on the ground. Shawano stood over her, his tail arched high, his head raised, his pose reflecting the magnificent, primordial stateliness of the lead wolf in ways that showed to advantage his grace, power, and natural beauty.

When Denali finished her meal, the two wolves became affectionate. For some moments they licked each other in the mouth, wagging their tails and dancing lightly on their front legs. Afterward, they leaned against each other and Shawano began to nibble the nape of Denali's neck while she whined and increased the speed of her tail-wagging; then, still pressed close together, the two trotted away, their movements timed so as to maintain physical contact. They disappeared among the trees.

The Alphas left about fifteen minutes after I had entered the enclosure, but Thor and Brigit did not follow them. The small bitch now lay down about three paces from my left side, resting her nose on her front paws, whining very softly, and watching me intently. I spoke to her, using her name; her ears became erect and she lifted her head to gaze into my eyes. We related silently for a few seconds, then Brigit lowered her head again, heaved a huge sigh that sent tremors rippling along her flanks, and closed her eyes. Earlier, when I sat down, I had tried to coax her to me without success; now, with the departure of the Alphas, she had come near of her own accord and seemed completely relaxed and contented.

Thor, meanwhile, was lying down about six feet away, his shoulders and head raised as he watched Brigit and me. Presently, he too lowered his head on his forepaws and closed his eyes.

We relaxed, each of us feeling the presence of the others as we related in the age-old, spiritual practice of the wild, indulging in a oneness that transcends species differences and communicates through tranquil silence. I too closed my eyes, allowing my ears and nose to keep me in tune with the environment. I could hear the soft breathing of the two wolves, and the dulcet calls of chickadees, small songs that blended with the susurrus made by the treetops in response to the caresses of a gentle breeze. The lung-healing scent of evergreens was strong in my nostrils, mixing with the slight odor of feral wolf, an unobtrusive scent unlike that of domestic dogs, which can sometimes overpower. All of these things combined to give me a sense of unutterable well-being; like the wolves, I was at peace with myself and with the world around me.

The next day I again visited the wolves on my own, fed them, entered the enclosure, and was greeted by them, each in its own way. Shawano came right up to me and sniffed my leg, his nose barely half an inch from my pants, but his eyes turned upward to meet mine. After snuffling noisily up and down the pantleg, he wagged his tail and turned away, his attention centering on Denali, who was pacing restlessly within the trees and whining insistently, with obvious intent: she wanted Shawano to come to her and to feed her. The big male joined his mate, whereupon she immediately nibbled at his muzzle, her behavior puppylike and somewhat incongruous because of her large size. Once more, Shawano disgorged for her.

I was standing near a large balsam fir when Thor walked up to me and began to sniff at the back of my hand, touching my skin with his nose and then tentatively dabbing me with his tongue, his tail wagging as he did so. I looked down and smiled and spoke to him gently. He leaned his shoulder against my leg. Slowly I raised my right hand and held it out so that he could see it before I placed it on the back of his neck, scratching him. The wolf pressed harder. I moved my hand higher, now scratching the base of an ear. We stood like that for some moments, until Brigit came scuttling up, exhibiting her usual submission, but on this occasion wagging her tail, which she carried low, but not tucked between her legs.

Thor backed away slightly and stared at the low-ranking

94

female, but he made no hostile move toward her as she trotted to within a couple of feet of me, then, as though shocked at her own daring, turned and ran toward the fence, there to take up her seemingly endless pacing. Now I sat at the base of the evergreen, knees up and clasped by my hands, waiting to see what else might happen. Of the two Alphas there was no sign, but Thor kept glancing toward the northern end of the enclosure, causing me to believe that Shawano and Denali were somewhere in the area, concealed by the trees.

Intent on watching Thor, I had not been aware that Brigit was once again approaching me until she came to stand right beside me, her lips creased by a grin as she wagged her tail. Slowly I raised a hand toward her, but she backed off a short way, so I lowered my legs, stretching them fully, and slumped against the bole of the fir, adopting a nearly supine position. Thor immediately stepped forward, stopping at my feet and lowering his head to sniff my boots; Brigit also approached, this time pointing her muzzle at my face and lowering it to within about a foot of my mouth. We looked deeply into each other's eyes and were still doing so when Shawano and Denali came into sight.

The arrival of the Alphas broke my contact with their subordinates, although the dominant wolves were not aggressive as they trotted toward us. Thor backed away, but did not seem to be intimidated; Brigit, however, scuttled into the trees, becoming hidden by the foliage. Denali had taken up a station on what appeared to be her favorite vantage point, the knoll facing the entrance to the enclosure. From there she stared hard at me as Shawano loped in my direction, stopping when he was about six feet away. Sniffing and scanning my recumbent shape, the Alpha male seemed to be preparing to approach more closely when Denali began to howl-bark, bobbing her head up and down as she stared at me. Shawano retreated immediately, going to stand near his mate, who continued to utter short, deep barks that ended in long-drawn, moaning howls, then turned to barks immediately afterward.

The Alpha female was evidently suspicious, so, intending to ease her tension, I sat up slowly. But my action added to her nervousness, causing her to retreat into the trees while she uttered one last howl-bark. Shawano followed his mate. The behavior of the Alphas caused Thor and Brigit to retreat also, but they remained in sight, the Beta male lying down in the shade and the female sitting near a downed balsam fir, the dead branches of which offered a tangled sanctuary if such should be required.

I continued to sit against the tree, thinking about the actions of the wolves during the last two days and reflecting about the personality of each animal. Presently, influenced by such thoughts, I began to make notes, comparing the behavior of the Ishpeming pack with that of the many wild wolves I had observed over the years. From these musings I later developed what may be termed a character profile of the species.

Individually, a wolf may be serious or playful, or even a prankster as fond of practical jokes as any human, but beyond these personality traits, and whether he or she is a leader or a follower, every wolf is always aware of its responsibilities and of the part that it must play in the world in which it lives.

Strong and incredibly durable, lithe, agile, and superbly coordinated, wolves could, if they so wished, emulate the humans who persecute them, and kill every prey animal that they encounter in their domain. But they do not. They know their place in the scheme of life; they are aware that feast leads to famine. They have become strong conservers, animals that fulfill an important function in the wild and, in a healthy, balanced environment that is beyond the abuses of man, exert a positive influence upon their habitats.

Of course wolves kill. They must do so to eat. But like all wild animals, they pay for what they consume, and whether they take sick, injured, young, old, or prime large prey animals, hunting wolves keep the herds moving, breaking up concentrations of moose or deer that, especially in winter, would otherwise remain sedentary and suffer malnutrition when food supplies became exhausted. By dispersing prey animals, and thus eliminating crowding, wolves also help reduce outbreaks of parasite-induced diseases. Because wolves are efficient predators, their hunting keeps prey species alert, reduces the chances of inbreeding among them, and promotes the recovery of overbrowsed or overgrazed areas of wilderness. Then, too, wolves feed a variety of other animals, such as ravens, jays, small birds, foxes, weasels, wolverines, skunks, mice, shrews, and even predominantly vegetarian animals such as hares, squirrels, and porcupines, which eat leftover meat in winter when it is available.

The wolf is both a husbandman and a policeman, in the latter role preventing his own kind from overpopulating and at the same time maintaining a balance among populations of other animals, prey and predatory species alike. It has been said that wolves take *only* sick and old animals. This is not so. Wolves take whatever they can get, and if a prime moose, deer, elk, or caribou can be taken, wolves will take it. Wolves also kill the young of large species, which is something that often horrifies people who have been raised to respond emotionally to the young, the warm, and the cuddly. The truth is that animals of all species produce annually more young than can possibly be allowed to survive; the natural reason for this seeming waste is found in a fundamental law: Nature is careful of the species and careless of the individual. This is a principle that many modern humans find difficult to understand. We obviously see ourselves as individuals and we care not at all for the idea that we are expendable; nor do we like the thought that those animals that we consider "nice" are also expendable. We think this way because our kind has more or less succeeded to date in reversing the dictum of Nature, so that we are now careful of the individual and careless of the species. Emotionally, because I am human and conditioned in this way, I approve of this shift; but clinically, as a trained observer of life, I know that humans have embarked on a dangerous course, one that, should it continue for much longer, will lead to the extermination of our own species through overpopulation, destruction of habitat, and serious depletion of our food and other resources. For millions of years Nature has been maintaining balance at the expense of the individual, a scheme that worked until the "ascent" of man, who has to date been responsible for

97

exterminating many other species while working hard at also exterminating his own.

All predatory animals have an important role within the natural scheme. Nature made all of them opportunistic, which means that they are ever ready to take what they can get most easily. It follows that sick, injured, old, or young animals are more quickly captured and killed than vigorous members of the species, so, by and large, predators take more of the former than of the latter. Here again, man has reversed the process, for the human hunter seeks the prime animals—the trophy bulls with large antlers, or prime cows or does—in this way taking out the seed stock and leaving the physically and genetically unfit to live and to procreate of their own kind. Then, too, predators kill purely in order to survive, as man used to do in ages past, but our species, because of agriculture and animal husbandry, does not, with very few exceptions, actually need the meat of the animals that are annually slaughtered in the name of recreation. And no predator ever kills an animal, rips off its hide, and carries this away while leaving the carcass to rot, as man does when trapping to supply fur for the fashion industry.

. . . In a little more than a single century (from 1820 to 1945), no less than fifty-nine million human animals were killed in inter-group clashes of one sort or another. . . . We describe these killings as men behaving "like animals," but if we could find a wild animal that showed signs of acting this way, it would be more precise to describe it as behaving like men.
—Desmond Morris, *The Human Zoo*

SIX

It was during our April 1984 trip to Michigan that I last socialized on my own with the Ishpeming wolves, again feeding them, then entering the enclosure to observe them at close quarters. Shawano again approached and sniffed my pants, after which he briefly smelled my right hand, his wet, cold nose touching my skin lightly. Done, he wagged his tail sparingly and moved about six feet away, there to stand and stare into space. Brigit remained near the fence, behind me. She whined occasionally while pacing. Thor, careful to stay clear of Shawano, sat on his haunches and watched me from about ten feet away, his expression relaxed. Denali, the wildest of the four, stared at me fixedly from a distance of about thirty feet, her expression inscrutable, showing neither aggression nor sociability. I had in the past been treated to the same kind of appraisal by wild wolves, and if maintained long enough, it always elicited mystical responses in me. There are those who find such stares intimidating. One person of my acquaintance, who was appraised in that way by Wa when the latter was only five months old, turned away, commenting, "So young and already *vicious*!" But there is nothing vicious in such looks—serious, yes, and meditative, but most of all, gloriously wild and testifying that behind the amber eyes there is an exceptionally keen intelligence. On this last occasion, Denali unlocked her gaze from mine after about one minute, then loped into the forest.

The next day, satisfied that I had obtained the confidence of the pack leader and had also been accepted by the others in one way or another, I asked Sharon to accompany me to Ishpeming, wanting to note how Shawano would react to her. But because Sharon had no real experience with wolves and might not, therefore, know how to react if approached closely by one of them, particularly in view of the lingering tensions that existed between Shawano and Thor as well as between Denali and Brigit, I decided that we would not enter the enclosure.

When we arrived, the four wolves were already waiting at the fence, and on this occasion even Denali showed some anticipatory excitement by dancing around Shawano and play-biting at his muzzle. Brigit, careful to keep a good distance from her daughter, was off to one side, crouched submissively, as usual, but watching us eagerly. Thor was rather more relaxed than he had been the day before. He stood at the fence within ten feet of the blond Alpha.

As we neared the compound, Denali retreated, taking up a position within the trees at least seventy-five feet from the wire, her action perhaps dictated by Sharon's presence. Moments later, Thor also backed away, then turned and loped to the shelter of some bushes that grew about fifty feet away. Shawano, however, remained where he was, and when we were a couple of steps from the wire he reared up on his hind legs and rested his enormous front feet against the fence. In that stance, his head was about twelve inches higher than Sharon's, who is five feet four inches tall. Looking into the big wolf's eyes from a distance of about eighteen inches, she greeted Shawano quietly, whereupon he wagged his tail and snapped his jaws, again making that distinctive, hollow sound I have come to associate with the expectation of

100

food. Afterward, still upright, the wolf sniffed at Sharon's face, inhaling and exhaling audibly and causing tiny bubbles of moisture to dance and gleam on the edges of each black nostril, his interest seemingly centered on Sharon's perfume and cosmetics, which, though mildly scented from a human standpoint, were strong in the nostrils of a wolf. Shawano's inspection was brief, probably because he was also savoring the aroma of the raw chicken I was carrying, but from the way he greeted Sharon I knew that he had accepted her immediately. I now suggested that she feed the Alpha, and she took a chicken leg and offered it to him. The wolf took it gently and ate it on the spot, and while Sharon continued feeding him, I tossed chicken parts to the others.

The next day, which was to be our last visit with the pack before we returned home, the wolves were again waiting for us as we got out of the car, watching as we fed and fussed over Chico and, later, as we collected the meat and walked toward the enclosure. The pack's behavior was much the same as it had been the day before. When we reached the fence, Shawano again stood upright, sniffed intently at Sharon's face, and immediately accepted food from her fingers, his behavior telling me that he had taken a particular liking to her.

When we had fed the pack, we stood back a few paces from the fence and watched. Brigit scuttled up and down beside the wire, Thor lay down, licking himself, and Denali, again puppylike, solicited food from her mate, who obliged by regurgitating twice for her and, after the second time, helping her eat the result.

When that was over, the leader came to the fence and we walked to meet him. Sharon squatted by the wire and the wolf again sniffed her face. After he was finished, he moved closer to me, turned sideways, lifted his leg, and urinated, managing to splash my boots and leaving me to wonder about his choice of target. Why just me? My guess is that, recognizing me as a male of my species, he was scent-marking the spot on which I stood, telling me in this way that although he was happy to welcome me to his home and glad to see me each time I arrived, he wished me to know that this was *his* range and that,

101

regardless of our relationship, he was definitely the master within the area bounded by the wire.

We left soon afterward. As we reached the car, Sharon turned, seeing that the four wolves were now standing by the fence, watching us.

"I think they know that we're not coming back," she said rather wistfully. "It looks like they're saying good-bye to us."

She was still looking out of the car window as we headed down the driveway, and she was silent as we turned on Route 41 and drove east. For that matter, so was I, for I shared her sense of loss. We were going to miss the Ishpeming wolves. After we had traveled about ten miles, Sharon turned to me and asked, "Why in the world would anyone want to kill wolves?"

"Mainly, I think, because they are afraid of them. They see them as competitors for the deer and other animals that people like to kill," I replied.

"Well . . . I just can't understand how a man can bring himself to kill *anything!*" Sharon said, expressing rare anger in her tone. "It's not as if hunters really need food. But I guess they just want to kill something. It's *horrible!*"

I agreed.

After that brief exchange we both fell silent, each thinking about the wolves. Sharon, as it later transpired, had become deeply affected by her brief contact with the pack, so much so that she could not rid herself of their memory and, indeed, began daydreaming about the possibilities of our getting wolves of our own. In this she had undoubtedly been influenced even before our first trip to Michigan, when I had talked about Matta and Wa. Later I wrote a book about them, and she read it and had been further influenced, although she had never before come into direct contact with members of the species. Our journey to the Upper Peninsula and her acquaintance with Jim's pack, particularly with Shawano, had turned Sharon into a wolf devotee, although she kept this from me at first because I had often said that I did not think I would ever want to keep wolves again. I had found the responsibilities of such a task enormous, and besides, when the time had come to part with Matta and Wa, the experience had been emotionally upsetting.

As I drove back to Marquette, my own thoughts were more clinical, centered mainly on something that George had said about the eating habits of wolves, which Jim had confirmed the evening before. Principally, what occupied me was the statement by George that "wolves do not eat bear meat." Inasmuch as I had seen wolves eating bear meat on a number of occasions and had actually used the carcass of a dead grizzly as the means of attracting a pack so that I could observe the wolves from nearby, I was startled by his remark. Upon my questioning him, it turned out that the only evidence supporting his thesis came from an incident in which a highway-killed bear had been placed in the wolf enclosure and had been rejected by the pack. Since neither of my friends had engaged in field observations of wild wolves, they had both assumed that there was something about bear meat that was unpalatable to *all* members of the species. And they were not alone in their views, for in the past I had heard others make the same claim with even less evidence to back it.

Musing in this way, my thoughts traveled back to the field research I had done in British Columbia in 1971, when, during May, June, and part of July, I had connected with the wild pack in the area of Muckaboo Creek and had been present when a young male wolf left on his solo journey, returning later to be welcomed by his family. When the five pups that had been born to the pack that year started going on trips with their parents and adult relatives, I realized that I would soon have to abandon that particular study, so I made plans to journey down the Nass River, following its course in a southeasterly direction to the junction of one of its tributaries, Damdochax Creek, a respectable stream that leads to a lake of the same name on the shores of which I had once wintered with Yukon, the part-wolf, part-Alaskan malamute who had been my wilderness companion and partner for a number of wonderful years. The distance from the wolf rendezvous to Damdochax Lake was only about thirty-five miles, a journey that, going with the current, would take about eight or nine hours.

103

I lingered in the Muckaboo Creek area for four more days without seeing the wolves, but during the last hours of my vigil, I thought a great deal about revisiting Damdochax Lake, a prospect that became more attractive the more I recalled the placid, emerald-green waters of the tarn, the rugged but beautiful mountains that surrounded it, and the two cabins that graced its shores. The idea of spending a few weeks in the place where I had experienced the rewarding and carefree life of a wilderness vagabond was irresistibly appealing. As a result, and although I might well have seen more of the Muckaboo wolves had I lingered, I began to break camp on the evening of the fourth day, sleeping that night under the stars, rising before dawn for breakfast, and leaving at first light, paddling easily and stopping occasionally beside well-remembered landmarks that rekindled affectionate memories of Yukon.

Dawdling in this way, it took me eleven hours to reach the lakeside cabins, but once there, my fond expectations were dashed when I discovered that humans had vandalized both dwellings, actually using as a toilet the one that Yukon and I had shared so comfortably. Saddened and angered, I left, paddling away from the log buildings and heading toward the southeast corner of the lake, where I knew there was a good, open area near the water that offered excellent camping facilities.

Disturbed by what I had found down the lake, but nevertheless happy to be back in a wonderfully wild region, I pitched my tent, constructed a fireplace out of rocks, cooked and ate my supper, and turned in early, somewhat fatigued after my journey. Under such circumstances, I am usually awakened by the rising sun and the singing of the birds, but this was not to be on that occasion. Instead, I was aroused during the predawn by the angry bellowing of a grizzly bear, an unmistakable and chilling sound which was coming from somewhere near my tent.

Grizzlies are not given to such outbursts unless they are seriously disturbed. And when they *do* voice their aggravation in the neighborhood of humans, they can be extremely dangerous. Beyond this, to be awakened before first light by such stentorian roars, while knowing that the thin walls of one's canvas shelter will part like

104

so much tissue paper under the onslaught of a grizzly's claws, is an experience that galvanizes an individual on the instant.

With unaccustomed alacrity, I got out of the sleeping bag and reached for my carbine, then put it down again, realizing that I wasn't dressed and that, more to the point, the gun was empty, my supply of shells buried in my duffel bag because during such wilderness trips I carry a gun only for emergencies and had never before had cause to reach for it. Scrambling into pants and putting on a thick woolen shirt to ward off the mountain chill, I slipped my feet into moccasins and started digging for the .30-30 cartridges, being serenaded all the while by the constant roaring, which appeared to be getting closer to my tent with every passing moment. At first I couldn't find the ammunition. My anxiety rose proportionately with my fumbling, until I emptied the bag, spread its contents on the tent floor, and, using my flashlight, quickly pounced on the box of twenty shells. By the time I had broken the seal and opened the carton, the roaring had come even closer; this made me fumble some more as I stuffed five cartridges into the Winchester's tubular magazine. Slipping the remaining bullets into my pocket, I unzipped the tent and went outside, my intention being to make my presence known to the bear, following which I confidently expected the animal to retreat. My optimism was based upon long acquaintance with the species, none of which had ever threatened me, much less sought to attack, although on three occasions I had retreated from bears that had also been roaring with aggravation. These experiences, however, had all taken place in daylight and none of the bears involved had been advancing in my direction.

Outside, I took time to notice that the eastern peaks were only slightly illuminated by the yet-unseen sun, their crowns glowing with greenish hues reflected downward by the snow that topped each spire. Around me I could distinguish the shapes of nearby trees and rocks, but in front of where I stood, the forest was a wall of darkness. The shoreline and the place where I had pitched the tent were about thirty yards from the forest edge. Inside that gloom was the bear. Now, besides the repeated bellowing, I could also hear intermittent crashing sounds that I knew were made when the bear swiped at bushes, or at the ground, with one of its massive front paws, sending cascades of vegetation and showers of soil sailing into the air.

Taking about half a dozen steps from the tent, I stopped in the open some fifteen yards from the forest edge, listening to the rowdy bear, seeking to determine the distance between us but unable to see more than the indistinct outlines of the nearest tree trunks. Tentatively I raised the carbine and tried to align its sights against the amorphous shape of a downed tree, wanting to know if I could see to shoot accurately, if that should become necessary. The sights were invisible. Should the bear attack, my only hope of stopping it would be to shoot by "feel," raising the Winchester to shoulder height and roughly aligning the gun with its body. Not a pleasant prospect! For a moment I considered returning to the tent to get the five-cell flashlight, but I decided against this move, because to try to position the light beside the gunstock to illuminate the sights as well as the running bear, it was necessary to hold light and barrel in one hand, the left, and during the time that it would take to align the beam, the sights, and the target, the grizzly, should it decide to charge, would close the short distance between us before my juggling act was completed. Besides, I was still confident that the animal would retreat once I made my presence known.

Slinging the gun over my right shoulder, I clapped my hands and shouted at the same time, continuing to do so for some fifteen seconds before standing silently, listening. Now the bear was quiet. I dared to hope that my plan was about to work, although the animal remained nearby, otherwise I would have heard the crashing sounds it made as it retreated within the forest. As the seconds passed and the silence continued, I began to feel concern. Knowledge of the species suggested that the grizzly should have retreated by now, if it was going to do so. Its continued presence was cause for concern.

While I was still debating these things, the bear began to bellow and to smash at the underbrush once more. Again I shouted and clapped my hands. As before, the

106

grizzly became quiet, but did not retreat. Now, definitely worried, I unslung the carbine, worked a shell into the breech, and fired a shot in the air, fully expecting that the loud and echoing report of the rifle would cause the animal to flee. It didn't. Roaring louder than before, the grizzly burst out of the forest, a huge, indistinct bulk coming directly at me. I could not escape. I had to shoot.

Ejecting the spent casing, I worked another cartridge into firing position, aimed the gun at the bear, and squeezed the trigger. The grizzly appeared to stagger, but kept coming. Feverishly, without lowering the Winchester from my shoulder, I ejected the spent casing, worked the loading lever, and rammed another bullet in place, squeezing the trigger immediately. This time, because the grizzly was only about twenty feet from me, I saw it stumble under the impact of the shot; but, roaring more loudly than ever, the enormous bear kept coming. Once more I repeated my actions—with exactly the same results: the grizzly didn't fall.

Lowering the gun, I fired from the hip. The bear crashed to the ground, the momentum of its run sliding its body forward to stop when it was only eight feet in front of me. Standing immobile, I again worked the gun's action, my gaze fixed on the sprawled bear. It didn't move. The light was now slightly better, but not yet good enough to see distinctly. I was unable to determine whether the animal was still alive.

I suppose I waited about a minute before approaching to see if it was dead. When I was no more than a step from it, I saw that the last bullet had penetrated the top of its head, about an inch above the eyes and almost equidistant from each of its ears. Holding the carbine in my right hand, my finger on the trigger, I bent down, reached out with my left hand, and searched for a heartbeat. The grizzly was dead. Only then did I realize that my gun was empty! I had loaded five shells and had fired them all—the last, fortunately for me, having found the brain.

The killing of any animal is repugnant to me, even on those occasions when I have to deliver a mercy shot to some creature that has been mortally injured by humans. My emotions run high and continue to do so for days

107

afterward, regardless of how hard I try to justify the action. On that morning, my need to kill the grizzly upset me greatly, so much so that after I had made sure the animal was dead, I could no longer stay near its corpse. Without eating breakfast, I launched the canoe and paddled into the lake, at first pushing the craft along vigorously without regard to direction; later, as the sun cleared the peaks to warm the country and to make long shadows, I adopted a more leisurely pace, seeking to bring my emotions under some semblance of control by observing the animals and plants with whom I was sharing the sunrise.

At eight o'clock, after almost four hours of aimless paddling, I felt sufficiently restored for the business of checking the grizzly to try to find out why it had been so seriously agitated and abnormally aggressive. That part of British Columbia is some three hundred miles from the nearest town or village, and I had seen no sign of human activity since I entered the region almost four months earlier, with the exception of one twin-engine Cessna that had flown low over the Muckaboo valley about eight days earlier; I therefore surmised that the bear had been accidentally injured in some way, or that it had become sick. In any event, I had to check it so that I could report the incident to the authorities when I returned to the outside.

As I approached the campsite, a flock of five ravens rose from the bear's carcass, cawing and cackling loudly, protesting my presence; but the ebony scavengers didn't leave the neighborhood, perching instead in trees adjacent to the dead bear and scolding me continuously. Torn between hunger and a desire to examine the bear, I sat outside the tent for some moments, trying to decide which should come first, food or dissection—while the ravens continued to make their fuss. In the end, I opted for food, thinking that perhaps I might not feel like eating immediately after I had finished examining the dead animal.

Then, with the sun high, its light splashing directly over the grizzly's body, I started the examination, discovering immediately that the animal had been seriously wounded by double-O buckshot, the trajectory and spread of the spheres, which measured .33 inches in diameter, telling me that the grizzly had been shot from an aircraft.

I had, at the time, wondered what the Cessna was doing in the area and why it was flying so low. Circumstantial evidence now strongly suggested that the pilot and passengers had been having some "sport," shooting at animals out of season that they had absolutely no hope of recovering, because, even if they killed any, the twin-engine wheeled aircraft could not possibly land anywhere in that country.

Closer examination of the bear's wounds revealed that they were seriously infected. One surface wound on the upper part of the left flank contained two ounces of pus; seven more slugs had lodged over the hips and back, breaking no bones, but causing horrendous lacerations. One shot was lodged against the right ilium of the pelvis, tearing and bruising the surrounding muscles over an area that measured nearly ten inches in circumference. In addition to the buckshot wounds, the bear, maddened by pain, had bitten at both of its flanks, tearing the skin and flesh and, of course, aggravating the injuries. No wonder it had behaved as it had!

Adding to the animal's trauma were literally hundreds of blowfly maggots, or screw worms, which had invaded all the wounds and from there tunneled into healthy tissue as they fed on the living flesh. When I opened the bear to examine the injured area from the inside, I found evidence of fresh, severe bleeding in the pelvic area. There was little doubt that the animal would eventually have died, had I not been forced to shoot it, but I could take no satisfaction from knowing that my bullets had ended its suffering.

When the necropsy was concluded, I was faced with the problem of disposing of the carcass, which was within twenty feet of my tent and would soon begin to smell fearfully. At first I debated cutting up the dead animal and taking the parts into the forest, away from my own area, but the labor involved and the gruesomeness of the task deterred me, so I decided it would be easier and far less traumatic to move my camp to another open location immediately across the lake. While dismantling the tent and packing my belongings, I thought that if I could devise some kind of blind from which to observe the carcass so as to study the numbers and kinds of animals that came to feed from it, the grizzly's death would yield some knowledge and would not then seem so useless and wasteful.

That same afternoon I set up camp on the far shore, temporarily leaving the bear's remains to the attention of the ravens, whose numbers had grown while I was packing and who had made the wilderness loud with their constant, impatient calls. I had hardly moved away from the shore when the birds landed and began to feed, for the openings that I had made offered them an easily accessible feast. By then, too, five gray jays had arrived and were sharing the meal with their large relatives as well as with a good number of flies and other insects.

Already the forces of nature were at work, a series of natural undertakers that would eventually see to it that all of the grizzly's protein would be used to sustain life, for even its juices, soaking into the ground, would enrich the soil and the green life that grew within the area covered by the carcass.

After eating an early supper, I recrossed the lake at about seven o'clock to reconnoiter the area, looking for a location suitable for the erection of a blind. There was none at ground level, but a group of five good-sized birches grew within twenty feet of the bear, one of those clumps that result when a number of seeds fall in close proximity to one another and take root, so that the trunks grow near each other at first, then spread out to form a sort of irregular, inverted cone above which the smaller branches intertwine to become a massive, umbrellalike canopy of green leaves.

Examining the birch cluster, I realized that it would be a simple matter to erect a watch platform about twenty feet from the ground by first securing five sturdy poles to the trunks, all at the same level to make a frame over which I would tie a series of smaller poles as a floor. From there, the line-of-sight distance to the carcass was about thirty feet. I would have an excellent view even without field glasses. The only problem was that because I would be almost too close, some of the more cautious scavengers might scent me and keep away. As I stood

110

looking at the birches, it was evident to me that twenty feet from the ground there were enough branches and leaves to offer excellent camouflage if I added a few additional leafy branches that I could cut from the local shrubbery. But what to do about my man-scent?

Anxious to start my vigil, I began constructing the platform that evening, thinking about the properties of smells as I worked. When I left the area to cross the lake, it was almost dark, but I had made the platform and I had thought of a way to cover my body odors.

The next morning, as the snow-clad peaks blushed under the influence of a great orange sun that had not quite climbed above the mountains, I paddled back across the lake and put the finishing touches to my aerial blind by cutting a bundle of leafy branches from distant-growing saplings and carrying them up to the platform, using the makeshift ladder I had fashioned the previous day. Weaving the greenery in place, I climbed down to inspect the work. Except for a two-foot observation opening that looked down on the carcass, the dense screen that now surrounded the platform offered perfect concealment.

Because I always keep a record of the lunar phases when I am out in the wilderness, I knew that the moon was then two days from full. Provided that the weather continued fine, this meant that I would be able to observe the carcass during most of the night. With this in mind, I decided to return to the campsite and go to bed, hoping to sleep until early afternoon. But first I went to the bear and probed more deeply into it, locating the bladder and taking from it about a cupful of urine, which I stored in a plastic bottle. Next I went into the stomach cavity, opening some of the intestines and collecting the already pungent fluids that these contained, adding about another cupful of juices to the bottle. The resulting "cocktail" was to form part of the scent-camouflage strategy.

Eating a large meal after I awakened at four o'clock in the afternoon, I began the business of covering up my body odors. I drew a pail of water from the lake, stripped off all my clothes, and lathered myself copiously from head to foot with the unscented soap that I always use during field work. When I was covered in thick lather, and without rinsing it off, I went to get my oldest clothing: a pair of pants, a shirt, socks, running shoes, and a sweater, taking these to a nearby beaver dam where, as is usual, there was an abundant supply of mud mixed with rotting vegetation that stinks abominably when it is stirred up. Into this soup I immersed all my apparel, soaking it thoroughly and afterward hanging it over branches to dry. Then I returned to the lake and began to pour buckets of water over myself to remove the soap lather. Finished, I stretched out on the grass in a patch of sunlight and waited for my clothing to become more or less dry, although in the end it was necessary to light a good fire to accelerate the drying process, to keep my nakedness warm, and, most important, to generate plenty of smoke to discourage the biting flies that had taken full advantage of my exposed skin.

By eight o'clock that evening my clothes were dry and extraordinarily smelly. I donned the uncomfortable garments without shaking them to remove the mud, then, taking the bottle of juices, I poured some of this over my shoes, on my hat, and on an old pair of leather gloves. The odoriferous results of this treatment are best left to the imagination! Collecting a bag of trail rations (a mixture of raw oats, nuts, raisins, and dried fruit) and a canteen of clean water, I paddled over the lake and installed myself on the observation platform, notebook, pencil, and field glasses laid out within easy reach. And I waited.

Damdochax Lake is located at a latitude of 56°35′ north; this means that at that time of year, real darkness does not arrive until nearly eleven o'clock, so that when I took up my station on the platform, visibility was excellent, allowing me to note that apart from some eighteen ravens, nine gray jays, and numerous chickadees, a number of white-footed mice and some shrews were busy dining off the dead bear. In addition, a variety of small, insect-eating birds flitted over and around the clearing, feasting on the host of flies, beetles, and butterflies that had been attracted by the carcass.

Above my hiding place, the sky was clear and the gibbous moon was hanging over the northwestern peaks, a white orb slightly highlighted by the glow of the sun, which, though itself invisible, was still daubing the western skyline with admixtures of reds, mauves, and yellows that intermingled with the sky's dark blue tones. Scanning the lake through the field glasses, I was first attracted by a beaver that was patrolling its territory, swimming lazily on the surface, its head raised, its body almost concealed by the waters. Some distance away, a loon bobbed up from a dive, then sat quietly, allowing itself to be gently propelled by the light breeze that fanned the surface. The beaver and the loon, the birds and insects, the mice and shrews distracted me while I waited for night, the time when I might expect the arrival of larger animals; but after more than an hour of quiet sitting in that peaceful setting, I became drowsy as I leaned against one of the supporting birch trunks. I fell asleep.

The calling of several loons awakened me soon after midnight, a joyous cacophony of shrieks, cackles, and wails that made loud a night wilderness bathed in moonlight and roofed by a completely clear, dark blue sky in which countless stars radiated like sun-bathed emeralds scattered on a field of dark velvet. Because years of training have taught me not to move suddenly when awakening during such conditions, I opened my eyes without moving, allowing my sight to adjust to the change of light as I listened to the sounds that surrounded me. At the same time, I resisted the urge to scratch at the mosquito bites I had received while I was dozing. Fortunately, I have been bitten so often by these insects that I have built up immunity to their poisons and no longer need to use repellent. Nevertheless, the bites do itch a little when freshly delivered.

When I was fully awake, I straightened up, moving slowly and as quietly as possible and positioning myself directly in front of the observation gap. I had an excellent view of the dead bear, which was now bathed by the moonlight.

I saw that three red foxes, all males, were feeding, each some distance away from the others. Taking up the glasses, I noted that a number of mice and voles and three short-tailed shrews were also eating scraps of meat, all of the tiny animals being aware of the presence of the foxes, their greatest natural predators, but exhibiting no concern because they knew that the hunters were fully occupied with the abundant supply of gratuitous food.

One of the foxes tore away some of the bear's intestines and immediately turned from the carcass, the sausage-like food dangling from his mouth as he trotted into the screening forest, undoubtedly taking the prize to his vixen and her young. Soon afterward, the other two foxes also left, each likewise carrying parts of the dead grizzly. As the small scavengers continued to scurry inside and on the carcass, now and then squeaking in argument over some coveted morsel, I realized that what wind there was had been blowing from the lake toward my side of the forest. This meant that although my odor was being carried toward the bear, the foxes, whose keen noses are hard to fool, had not detected man-scent; they had shown no interest in the clump of birches. It seemed that the reek of beaver mud and the smell of the grizzly's lymph and urine were doing the job I had hoped they would.

The loons were still laughing and cackling half an hour after the foxes had left, and it was because of their constant calling that I at first failed to hear the wolf howls—faint, ululating cries that appeared to be coming from a place within the forest southeast of my location and probably about two miles away. The wolves sang for almost one minute, their blended voices charged with excitement. It was the kind of singing that I had heard often while observing wild packs whose members were gathered and preparing themselves to go hunting, a ritualistic chorus voiced, perhaps, in anticipation of a successful chase. It was now 12:45 A.M. The howling stopped as abruptly as it had begun.

Shortly before one o'clock, stealthy crackling coming from the nearby forest alerted me to the approach of a good-sized animal. Could it be a member of the pack that had broken away from the group to investigate the odor of death? I waited, eyes glued to the shrouded evergreen wall. The crepitant whispers became stilled for some moments, then began again, becoming more clearly audible as the animal neared the edge of the forest, there to pause once more to inspect the terrain with nose and ears before at last emerging from concealment to be seen at first as an amorphous shape a tone or two lighter than its background and then, as it entered the spill of the moon, to resolve itself into a dog coyote, or brush wolf, as the species is called in some parts of North America. Momentarily the little wolf looked at my blind, then walked boldly to the carcass, sniffing deeply as it prowled around the stiffened body. It was as though the sheer enormity of the food had put the coyote into a state of gustatorial confusion and I almost chuckled aloud as I thought of the luxurious dilemma with which the animal was faced: *Where to start?* As it circled the mound of food one more time, the moonlight drew reflective gleams from the drool that edged its mouth and hanging tongue— a few minute, quick flashes that quickly disappeared as the coyote darted forward and thrust its head inside the open stomach, starting to eat even before it had finished dropping its body to the ground. From my observation platform I could hear the working of its jaws and the liquid sounds of its cursory mastication, a few chews that preceded a momentary silence as the mouthful was swallowed.

Engrossed in watching the display of eager appetite, I forgot to time the coyote's meal, but the animal must have fed nonstop for about twenty minutes and might well have continued to eat for longer than that if it had not become startled by some influence too faint to register on my own senses. In any event, the little wolf jumped to its feet and dashed into the forest, the sounds of its going much louder than those it had made during its arrival. Seconds later, the wilderness became a silent place of black shadows and bright moonlight; even the loons stopped laughing. And although the faint croaking of distant frogs could still be heard, nothing appeared to be moving or calling in the neighborhood of the lakeshore and the nearby forests. I too became affected by the unnatural stillness. I held my breath as I tried to hear whatever it was that had caused the change, although, after many nights of vigil in wild places, I knew it was caused by the presence in the vicinity of one or more large predators.

I had by now come to think of such abrupt, after-dark pauses as circles of silence, for the unnatural quiet keeps pace with a hunting animal—or an intruding human—

115

throughout the course of its foray. As a predator passes out of one area, normal, sound-producing movements and calls are resumed in its wake, while activity is suspended by the animals in that part of the wilderness through which the stalker continues to travel. The effect is rather like the results produced when a pebble is dropped into a still pond, except that instead of the visible rings that appear on the surface of water, circles of silence form around the hunter.

Despite the fact that I could not at first detect what had caused the change of forest tempo, I felt reasonably sure that it was triggered by wolves whose howls I had heard earlier; but I could not be at all certain that they were coming to feed off the bear's carcass, for they could just as easily be on the track of a mule deer or a moose. Still, I felt that there was a good chance they would be attracted to the grizzly if they came within the broad odor trail that it was releasing; even *I* could smell it, although the carcass was not yet decomposing.

Sitting immobile in front of the observation opening, I continued to listen. Several minutes passed while the telltale silence continued. Presently, from relatively nearby, I heard a twig snap. This was followed by the sound of rustling leaves, then by several more snapping noises, after which all was again quiet. Now I was sure it was wolves. Not daring to move to look at my watch so as to time the arrival, I began to count silently, in this way making a rough estimate of the passing seconds. Just as I reached 106, the shape of a wolf emerged from within the trees. It was a shadow almost imperceptibly lighter than the background, but it allowed me to recognize the animal for what it was and to note that it was standing broadside to me, facing the hindquarters of the dead grizzly.

Head held high, the wolf appeared to sniff for some seconds, then it moved forward and emerged into the moonlight. It was a light-colored animal, but whether gray, fawn, or dirty white I could not yet determine. Stepping cautiously and slowly, the wolf reached the carcass, lowered its muzzle to it, and remained in that stance for some moments before it lifted its broad head, turned its neck sideways, and stared at the forest. Almost immediately, four more wolves stepped into the open, all walking briskly and openly, undoubtedly reassured by the behavior of the scout, which, as I surmised then and confirmed later, was a male and the Alpha of the pack.

The five wolves ranged themselves around the bear's carcass and began to feed without so much as glancing at my hiding place, although the leader would pause every now and then to check the wilderness with nose and ears, vision being the least important of his senses under the existing light conditions. From where I sat, I could study each animal without the aid of field glasses, the use of which might have alerted the pack should the lenses cast back reflections. Now I was able to determine that the coat of the Alpha male was light gray along the head and back, tan along the flanks, and predominantly white on the legs and underparts. I judged that he weighed about ninety pounds and that he appeared to be in his prime, probably about five or six years old. A smaller wolf, of a dark gray color, crouched immediately beside the leader, suggesting that this was his mate, the Alpha female of the pack. In all probability, she had a litter of pups parked somewhere in the distant forest, no doubt being looked after by a subordinate female. Two of the other three wolves were young, perhaps the surviving offspring of last year's mating; they favored the female in looks, size, and coloring. The third wolf was appreciably larger and, although somewhat darker than the leader, was yet lighter than the others. During the next forty minutes the pack fed nonstop, allowing me to observe each animal in detail. It seemed evident that the two dark wolves were indeed yearlings; both were females. The other wolf was a male, and his behavior and the relationship he had with the Alphas indicated that he was the Beta of the pack.

The two young wolves finished eating first and withdrew from the carcass, the one to lie down near the forest edge and there to begin to lick itself clean, the other electing to sit about ten feet away and almost directly opposite my blind. She sat on her haunches, yawned prodigiously, then began to clean her front, reaching back with her long tongue to clean the gore from her chest, then working down along each leg.

117

Not long afterward, the other three wolves became sated. The Alpha male stood on all fours and stretched mightily, thrusting his back legs out and curving the upper portion of his back. He too yawned; then, recovering normal posture, he nudged his mate with his nose, nuzzling the back of her neck. She whined in response, and, from her prone position by the carcass, turned on her side, lifting a back leg, whereupon her mate licked her inguinal area while she nibbled at his face, raising her head and shoulders to do so. For some moments the two continued caressing each other; afterward they trotted into the trees. The other wolves followed.

Waiting for a time in order to allow the pack to leave undisturbed—and thus to feel free to return if they so desired—I clambered down from the platform to go and look at the grizzly's remains, anxious to get some idea of the amount of meat that the wolves had consumed. I found that they had eaten huge amounts. Almost the entire left haunch of the bear had been stripped clean of flesh, down to the bone; so had the left shoulder and part of the back, while the belly and lower chest had been similarly attacked. I estimated that the pack had collectively eaten between sixty and seventy pounds of meat, or an average of between twelve and fourteen pounds each. Nevertheless, it was almost certain that the two leaders had consumed considerably more than their subordinates, if only because they had to carry back sufficient food for the growing pups as well as for their baby-sitter.

For the next ten days I continued to watch the carcass each night, commencing the vigil at dusk and ending it just before sunrise. The wolves returned during three consecutive nights after their initial visit; never once did they realize that they were under observation. At each feeding they made great inroads into the carcass, behaving much as they had done the first night, although their arrival times varied between 11:00 P.M. and 3:00 A.M. Undoubtedly those four sightings were the most rewarding of all my observations on that occasion, although a wide variety of other animals were drawn to the dead bear and were duly recorded in my notes. Besides the usual host of small creatures, such as the mice, voles, shrews, and pack rats, I observed three wolverines on separate occasions, and two lynxes. On the tenth night, a huge male black bear arrived soon after I had taken my station and before darkness. His feeding habits were interesting, if quite revolting, for, as I already knew, his kind love rotting meats. They especially enjoy the decayed juices with their attendant host of fly maggots; they scoop these out of a carcass by using both front paws together and lifting the rancid organic soup to their mouths. This observation was my last.

Later, after I had rested for a couple of days, I backtracked the wolves and found their rendezvous in an area south of Blackwater Mountain, the six-thousand-foot peak which had been one of my favorite observation points during my stay in the area with Yukon. Because of this, I named the wolf family the Blackwater Pack, and although they had by now abandoned the summer nursery, for the pups were old enough to go hunting with their elders, I spent some time examining the terrain, seeking bones and hair so that I might identify the species of prey animals upon which the pack had fed. Among the remnants of deer, moose, beaver, and a variety of smaller animals, I found the desiccated paw of a grizzly, part of its lower jaw, and several other bones, all of them well gnawed and bereft of even the tiniest speck of meat.

Although far removed from Michigan's Upper Peninsula in distance and time, my experiences in British Columbia were pertinent to my study of Jim's wolves, particularly in view of the fact that those humans who were involved with them had mistakenly concluded that bear meat is umpalatable to all members of the species. For these reasons, as we drove back to Marquette after our last visit to Ishpeming, and while Sharon was indulging her imagination and seeing herself as foster mother to two wolf cubs, I began to make comparisons between the behavior of captive and free-roaming wolves, a task that continued to occupy me after we had returned to our Ontario home.

Many [wild] animals are so tenacious of life, so desperately flexible, that they can survive in minimal conditions. But bare survival is not enough.

—Desmond Morris

SEVEN

Anyone who has had a close relationship with wolves can never forget them. In some unexplainable way, these animals are able to give to their human friends an awareness and an understanding of life that was missing before the relationship. Perhaps this is because wolves are so extraordinarily perceptive and so joyfully eager to appraise and understand all the influences that surround them at all times. No odor, no sound, no sight ever gets by them without being investigated, either from afar and with caution, if the animals feel threatened, or from very nearby if they are relaxed and comfortable in their surroundings. Day by day, wolves teach their human friends by their own examples; or perhaps I should say that they *try* to teach us, for the truth is that we make very bad pupils because our own senses have been dulled by centuries of neglect, while our cortex has become preoccupied with logic at the expense of intuition, the inherent gift of the wild that served early humans so well and that, if given a chance to do so, can yet allow us to attain understanding without becoming lost in a maze of

120

Wolf cubs are born with their ears down, but these slowly erect and are fully upright in about six weeks. Photo shows Brigit (left) with erect ears, while Shawano's are still folded down because Shawano is ten days younger. *Courtesy of Jim Wuepper*

Showing his teeth while averting his gaze, Toivo (left) indicates submission, but advertises that he will fight if pressed too hard by older brother Thor. *Courtesy of Jim Wuepper*

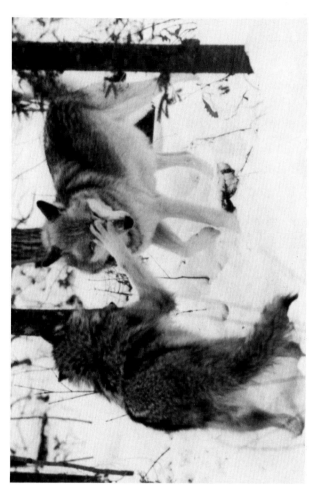

Wolves like to play. Here Thor paws at Shawano during a typical game. *Courtesy of Jim Wuepper*

TOP: The Alpha wolves at their meal.

BOTTOM: Alpha wolves usually eat first. Here, Shawano threatens Siskiwit (right) when she approaches too closely. Brigit feeds at left and Denali, still subordinate, waits her turn in the background. *Photos courtesy of Jim Wuepper*

Shawano howling. Photo shows typical posture, but wolves howl in almost any position, even lying down. *Courtesy of Jim Wuepper*

While Toivo and Thor (left) mob their leader, Brigit (far right) defers to Denali, seeking to lick the Alpha female's mouth while crouching with tail held low. *Courtesy of Jim Wuepper*

Denali during her first autumn. *Courtesy of Jim Wuepper*

Tundra and the author. Photo shows the young wolf's speculative gaze.
Courtesy of Jim Wuepper

"facts." Nevertheless, because they are such good communicators, wolves do manage to impart some of this near-mystical awareness to their human friends. As a result, we emerge the better from our contact with them. And the more we think about them afterward, when we recall the quiet times of communion that united us with the primordial wild, the more vividly we remember them.

From my work with them I have come to believe that at some time during prehistory, man and wolf were related in spirit, and traveled the forests of a younger and better world in peace. It should not be supposed, however, that a wolf can accommodate itself to life as a domestic pet. Like all wild animals, wolves are born to be free and unfettered by chains, kennels, or walls. They are too greatly influenced by heredity to accept passively the restrictions that humans impose upon their dogs and cats, themselves animals that are no longer truly natural because thousands of years of domestication and inbreeding have caused them to lose their inherent wildness and to become dependent upon their owners. Such animals are, in fact, slaves, even though many are kept in pampered luxury. The fact is, most people buy a pet in order to *own* it. Despite this, a great number of individuals sincerely love their pets, but they do so because the animals adapt to their owners. If a pet turns out to be hard to train, independent, or intractable, it is soon disposed of in one way or another.

Humans, particularly those influenced by the Judeo-Christian ethic, see themselves as rulers of the earth, an attitude stemming not from divine doctrines, but rather from human interpretation of them. Those governed by such erroneous tenets look upon animals as chattels, organisms that have been divinely created for human use and convenience. But domestic animals are the work of man. The wolf and all other wild beings are the work of nature; they are *pure wild,* gloriously so. That is why a wolf can never be owned; it cannot be mastered. This is not because it is savagely intractable, but because it will not willingly submit to any rules but those that govern its own societies.

Many people believe that the hierarchy that regulates

121

the affairs of wolf packs is predicated upon tyrannical rule exercised by leaders who severely punish their subordinates when these appear to be disrespectful. Such a view is simplistic, a man-oriented interpretation of a very complex, highly successful, and extremely ancient social order, the main intent of which is to ensure the survival of the family and therefore of the species.

High-ranking wolves are not tyrants. When they must exercise their authority, they do so with restraint and with respect for their subordinates, and when the reprimand is over, they immediately offer forgiveness and are as readily forgiven by the subordinate. Were it otherwise, the pack would not survive as a unit because lower-ranking wolves would leave, or would fight when levels of abuse could no longer be tolerated. Alpha wolves attain their status because they are best able to care for the family. Such wolves are usually the most intelligent, often the largest and strongest, and always the most determined and responsible.

Assisting the two leaders are the Betas. Usually there are two of these in a pack, a male and a female, but in small packs—as in the case of Jim's wolves—there may be only one Beta in the absence of a qualified partner of the opposite sex. These wolf-pack ''lieutenants'' may at some point in time challenge their leaders, as Thor challenged Shawano by showing undue interest in Denali, and as Denali challenged her mother. In any event, sooner or later an Alpha will be deposed by a subordinate, in most cases when he or she becomes weakened by age, disease, or accident. Then, too, an Alpha may be killed during the hunt, or by man, and it is clearly useful to have a second-in-command who can immediately take charge of the pack. In any event, those wolves who have inherited leadership qualities begin to work their way upward just as soon as they are born, when they struggle for position at one of the mother's hind teats. And as they grow older, these pups continue to strive for rank. In effect, there are two distinct hierarchical levels in every large pack: that which is to be noted among the adults, and that which quickly develops among the pups. The upper-echelon wolves, of course, govern the entire pack, while the young wolves, all of whom

122

know themselves to be subservient to the adults, duplicate the "pecking order" in their dealings with each other. But whether Alpha or Omega, every wolf exercises its full potential at all times and will unhesitatingly avail itself of any opportunity that appears to offer advantage.

For these reasons and more, no wolf can be turned into a domestic pet. Those people who would like to "own" a wolf with that idea in mind are doomed to failure at best, and may even find themselves engaged in a serious status fight with their eighty- or ninety-pound "pet" when it feels that it is time to take over the "pack." Then, too, because a wolf is so extraordinarily perceptive, it may find cause to dislike a relative, friend, or neighbor, in which case such an individual could be attacked and injured. When such attacks by captive "pet" wolves have occurred, lawsuits invariably followed, and these have always been attended by screaming headlines and very bad publicity for the wolf, though in most instances the attack was invited by human ignorance. It is one thing for a dog to bite a person; it is quite a different proposition altogether if a wolf injures a human, no matter how slightly. In such cases, the attack is taken to be proof of this animal's savage nature.

Nevertheless, wolves can be successfully kept in captivity. Under the right conditions and cared for by people who understand them and do not try to impose their will on them outside of the strictures of pack hierarchy, wolves become wonderful companions who love and respect their human associates and are delighted whenever they have close contact with them. What are the right conditions? To begin with, because these animals are highly social, no one should attempt to keep only one wolf; it will quickly become stressed, will probably try to climb out of its enclosure or dig its way to freedom, and will quite likely become intractable as it gets older. If this should happen, it will have to be disposed of, either by placing it in a zoo or some other kind of animal sanctuary, or by killing it.

A single wolf *can* be kept in the home, but humans who would raise one under such conditions must be prepared to spend most of their time with the animal; and such people should not be house-proud, for the "pet"

123

will *certainly* wreck furniture, doors, rugs, and anything else it can reach with its powerful jaws. Then, too, wolves like to play and are given to biting each other in a friendly way. With their heavy coats and tough skins, such bites are bloodless and practically painless to them, but any part of the human anatomy so treated will probably bleed, will most certainly become bruised, and will hurt a lot! And another thing: wolves greet each other by licking the face and the mouth; they always want to greet humans in the same way, but people are tall, and as a wolf must leap up to reach the face area, its great front paws, with their heavy, ever-sharp nails, can scrape and bruise. Some wolves jump up in a controlled way, giving warning of their intentions and almost *unfolding* themselves as they rise; other, more highly strung, leap suddenly, fast, aiming the muzzle at the face. If by chance the snout of the animal meets the face of a human, the front teeth, and particularly the upper canines, can punch holes in the flesh or, at the very least, deliver a blow akin to a swift, hard uppercut.

The best way to safeguard the face from such excessive love is to crouch as soon as one enters the enclosure and then, raising the face, allow it to be properly licked. This is a ritual greeting, important to wolves, and they will always seek to give it. A second, less satisfactory way of blocking the paws and mouth is to lift an arm, elbow bent, in front of the chest and about a foot away from it, so that the flailing paws and the loving but accidentally dangerous muzzle do not come into sudden, forceful contact with one's face.

When two or more wolves are kept, they should be properly and safely housed within a large, well-treed enclosure that, in my view, should not be smaller than one acre. The territory should contain a variety of natural obstacles that will challenge the ingenuity of the animals during close-contact play, or when one or another invites a companion to chase it at full speed. Such obstacles, unless very heavy and hard (such as rocks), will undoubtedly be chewed vigorously and frequently rearranged. In addition, the enclosure should contain several heights of land where wolves can stand or sit as they survey their habitat. Ideally, the terrain should also have

124

at least one scenic lookout, a knoll near a clearing where long-distance gazing can be enjoyed.

The success of Jim Wuepper's venture, now in its ninth year, is due in great measure to the fact that Shawano and his pack live in just such a habitat. They can run and romp and climb obstacles, or find solitude when they need it. And the psychology students and professors who made the experiment possible have always limited their research to observation, refraining from conducting tests that molest the wolves and cause them to become stressed. Jim, of course, deserves a lot of credit. He loves each wolf, understands its needs, plays and romps like one of them, and if Shawano on occasion growls admonition at him, Jim either ignores him completely or stares him down, for no wolf will seek to attack while its eyes are locked to those of a human.

Those individuals who are prepared to meet all of the above requirements and who might decide to keep one wolf of each sex should be aware that under normal circumstances the pair will breed annually and produce from two to as many as twelve pups per litter. Thus, after the original pair reaches sexual maturity at twenty-two months (it has been known for captive wolves to breed during their first year of life, although this is unusual), they will at least double or triple their numbers. Now hierarchical behavior is intensified and the humans involved become less important to the wolves. And if the pups are left for their parents to raise, these will never become tame enough to be handled. In such cases, it means that if any of them needs to be treated for illness or injury, they will most likely have to be tranquilized by means of a dart-gun, a dangerous procedure for the animal in question and one that causes a great deal of stress in the other wolves, who see the darting as a form of attack on the pack as a whole, for, of course, they do not know that only one animal has been selected for the treatment. Beyond these things, the increase in numbers will naturally demand the supply of more food and, most probably, an expansion of the enclosure, both of which can add up to a great deal of money on a continuing basis.

Fortunately, it is possible today to prevent mating

without separating the male and female. One way is to perform a vasectomy on the male when he is about eighteen months old. This procedure is irreversible in most cases, so if the two wolves are to be allowed to breed at some point in the future, vasectomy is clearly not recommended. A less radical option is now available in the form of birth-control pills or foods that prevent the female from going into estrus. If food is used, both wolves (or all, if more than two are involved) will probably ingest it. This will not affect the males in any way, but it is possible that the target female(s) may not get enough of it and will go into heat in any event. The pill, in my opinion, is the easiest to administer and the surest because, a week or two before estrus is due to start, one simply stuffs a pill inside a cube of raw meat or a ball of hamburger and gives this to the female, a daily treatment that must be continued until about mid-March. Both of these birth-control substances are now available from veterinarians for use on domestic dogs as well as on wolves. To date I am not aware of any harmful side effects, although experiments of some twenty years ago did cause kidney failure in test subjects.

Wolves, like human beings, are individualistic, and for this reason it is not possible to forecast the future behavior of captive animals. Some may die of old age (between seventeen and twenty years) while remaining friendly at all times to all persons. Others may be friendly to their human companions and to those individuals whom they have known for some time; yet others may show aggression toward strangers, in which case they will probably howl-bark, may even growl, and, more rarely, may snap at a hand or leg. None of these things mean that captive wolves who have been given reason to attack an individual do so with the intent to kill; such behavior would be *extremely* rare in wolves that are properly cared for and live in spacious surroundings. But wolves that have been improperly cared for, badly treated by their handlers, or kept chained up, should be considered potentially dangerous, especially to small children.

First-time visitors should never be allowed to get close to captive wolves, no matter how settled and friendly these may be, *unless such persons have had previous contact with the species and understand their ways.* A great many people, although curious to see and approach wolves, are yet inherently afraid of the animals. This creates a contradiction in the minds of the wolves. They *immediately* detect the fear by the odor and by appraising the behavior of the human who is approaching them, but such an individual, apprehensive though he or she may be, dares to advance because the wolves are safely housed behind a high fence. Now, when wolves, and indeed all other animals, recognize fear in another being, they expect such an individual to seek to escape. If the intruder continues to advance toward them, they view such behavior as threatening and they become confused, at which point they themselves become apprehensive. But because they cannot escape, and because they believe their territory is being invaded, they will most probably react aggressively. Under those circumstances, it would be folly for a visitor to seek to pat the wolves. It would be madness to allow such a person to enter the enclosure.

In some instances, a visitor may not be afraid of the wolves and may have been accepted by them, but if a person should be foolhardy enough to try to take a liberty with a wolf, he or she may well be bitten in consequence. On the other hand, by allowing the animal to make the first advances and by behaving gently toward it, a firm and lasting friendship will probably result, because wolves have a long, long memory, especially if they like or dislike a person. In the latter context, I have often been asked why a wolf, or any other animal, should dislike a person on sight, the question usually voiced in surprise and prompted by a subconscious belief that all animals should be only too glad to accept human attention. When I reply to such an egotistical question, I am careful to point out that animals are like people in that respect and, for whatever reasons, may immediately dislike a person (or may just as instantly become very attached to him or her). I am quite sure that all of us have had personal experiences of this phenomenon with others of our kind on a number of occasions. I call it "chemistry"; it is more popularly called "vibes." It happens with animals as readily as it happens with humans.

To socialize wolves to humans properly, it is necessary

127

to take the pups from the den within the first two weeks of life and to hand-raise them much as very young dogs would be reared. Proper diet is essential, and it should be noted that wolves, like dogs, are subject to cataracts in both eyes. In cases of severe inbreeding, this condition may be inherited and there is nothing much that can be done to cure it. In others, however, it manifests itself because the mother's-milk substitute being used is deficient in lactose, a particular kind of sugar found in the milk of mammals. Studies done by U.S. veterinary scientists between 1978 and 1981 show that wolf pups raised on commercial milk formulas developed cataracts, while control groups of wolf cubs raised on the same formula that also contained added lactose did not suffer from the condition. These results appear to be conclusive. Thus, those who would raise very young wolf or dog pups would be wise to add to the commercial milk substitute 15 grams of lactose to every 100 grams of formula (half an ounce equals 14.2 grams; four ounces equals 113.4 grams) in order to safeguard the vision of their charges. Then, too, wolf pups should be allowed to eat some solid food at three weeks of age, but commercial puppy food is not recommended; it goes right through them and usually causes diarrhea. Raw beef (hamburger), raw beef bones with particles of meat adhering to them, or raw chicken bits and bones will ensure healthy pups. Naturally, the older they get, the more raw meat and the less formula they will require. Healthy pups are obviously more relaxed and settled than sickly ones. This means that cubs raised on a proper diet will develop into healthy, well-adjusted adults that will be less likely to become aggressive or irritable. Many people erroneously believe that captive wild animals are less aggressive toward humans than wild ones. The opposite is actually true. This is particularly the case with wolves, who, in the wild, avoid humans at all times. Similarly, semisocialized wolves, like Jim's pack, will not approach strangers, fearing them. Conversely, wolves that have become fully imprinted on humans will readily approach visitors and may occasionally react aggressively, usually toward *men*. The fact that wolves almost always appear to feel comfortable in the presence of women, even total strangers, is in itself intriguing. It demonstrates that the animals can identify the sex of a visitor even before he or she has reached the enclosure. Such identification is made possible by the wolf's keen sense of smell, which can quickly distinguish the differences that exist in the scents of the male and female hormones, no matter how faint or how well disguised these may be. In addition, I am quite certain that wolves are able to recognize a difference in the ways that men and women move, a conclusion I formed after devoting a great deal of study to this characteristic, which is demonstrable in all mammals. During this research I noted that the gait and general carriage of most members of my own sex almost invariably reveal the more aggressive tendencies latent in males of all species; females, conversely, move more sedately and usually more rhythmically and at a somewhat slower pace.

From the foregoing, it should be clear that it is not a good practice to allow first-time visitors to enter a captive-wolf enclosure, no matter how well adjusted or how friendly the animals may be toward their handlers and toward those people whom they know well.

During the early 1960s, George Wilson kept a pack of four wolves in St. Louis, Missouri, all the members of which were well adjusted and friendly toward visitors. The leader was Homer, a large, companionable animal who was George's special friend. His mate, the Alpha female, was named Cappy, and their subordinates were Lobo and Cuddles. Although unusual in such a small pack, both females produced pups in 1964, but tragedies followed. First, a storm flooded Cappy's den and when George put both litters in an outbuilding while he sought to resettle the wolves, Cappy killed all the pups that had been born to Cuddles. Afterward, the two females fought so constantly that they had to be separated until they had settled down once more and could be reunited with the pack.

Many people went to see and play with the wolves, including large numbers of children, but in June 1965, a nine-year-old girl was bitten, her injuries requiring twenty stitches. A lawsuit followed and George was ordered by the court to get rid of his wolves. As might be expected, the case garnered a great deal of negative, antiwolf publicity within and without the community. Many of George's neighbors, including a number of the children who had become friends with the wolves, testified on behalf of the animals; other neighbors were fearful and asked the court to have the animals removed from the city, testifying that before the child was bitten, one of the wolves had escaped from the enclosure, causing an armed, unofficial posse to roam the streets, intending to shoot the wolf on sight. (George foiled them by recapturing the wolf without any difficulty.)

After the judge had listened to all the evidence presented for and against the wolves, he issued a court order requiring them to be disposed of. George sent the wolves to the Bronx Zoo, in New York, but he kept his special friend, Homer, and left Missouri, going to the Upper Peninsula rather than give up the wolf. Although Homer had to be kept in the Marquette zoo, George could still take his friend for walks along the shore of Lake Superior; the big wolf was completely free to roam at will, but he never strayed far from his human companions. Then George had a near-fatal car accident. While he was in the hospital in serious condition, Homer was parasitized by heartworms and died, aged seven years.

George still mourns his wolf companion, but he knows today that wolves as pets are not a trouble-free proposition and he actively discourages those who seek his advice about keeping wolves.

Bob and Beth Duman, who live in lower Michigan and who both have degrees in biology, had many good experiences with their female wolf, Nahani, but in the end they were forced to put her in a zoo after she attacked Bob and injured his shoulder. Before that moment, however, Nahani, though a lone wolf, had been a model of good behavior, so much so that Beth lectured to school children accompanied by the wolf. After each lecture, the youngsters were lined up, and Beth led Nahani down the line, allowing the pupils to pet her. In this way, over the years, Beth and Nahani related to nearly eighty thousand American children with but two extremely minor and controlled incidents occurring when the wolf uttered "a little growl during each occasion." Indeed, Nahani's low growls were hardly noticed by anyone but Beth, who

130

immediately pulled her away and secured her on a short lead. Later, curious about the animal's rare behavior, Beth spoke to the teachers of both children and learned that in each instance the child in question was also disliked by its classmates and was, to quote one teacher, "low in the class pecking order." Something about those two youngsters had an effect on Nahani, who, with the extreme sensitivity of her kind, detected it at once and voiced her displeasure. She did not, however, seek to bite.

The relationship between Nahani and the Dumans continued close and trouble-free until 1976, when a Michigan child was mauled by a tame lion. The resulting outcry caused Michigan authorities to ban the keeping of all wild animals by private owners, and the Dumans were ordered to keep their wolf in close confinement. The lectures with Nahani came to an abrupt end and the wolf was forced to spend her time alone in her large enclosure when the Dumans were not present. This change and the occasionally prolonged absence of the Dumans—and, no doubt, the sudden cessation of those school-trip outings— had their effect on Nahani. One day, while the Dumans were socializing with her in the enclosure, and as Bob was crouching over the wolf, petting her, she reared up suddenly, without any kind of warning, and clamped her jaws on his shoulder, holding on until Beth came to the rescue and separated the two. Bob was injured by the teeth and, as in all cases of wolf-bite, badly bruised. Regretting the need to do so, the Dumans decided that Nahani should go to a wolf sanctuary, where she lives today with a mate.

Talking about the wolf in late December of 1984, Beth told me that when she visits Nahani, the wolf is always glad to see her, rushing up to the fence and behaving in her usual friendly way. But more recently, and although Nahani was actually greeting Beth and showing every sign of affection, she backed away and growled at Beth when the male wolf approached; her action was perhaps prompted by jealousy, as though Beth were another female wolf who just might woo away Nahani's rightful mate.

I know of a number of other examples that support the

131

thesis that wolves do not make good pets. This does not mean that these animals are vicious, as some people all too readily might suppose. It simply means that wolves are wild beings and that, in most cases, they have needs that are going unanswered. Stress results from such unfulfillment, as it does among humans, and sooner or later a crisis point is reached; trouble follows. The real problem is that humans do not yet know enough about wolves, even though these animals have been intensively studied now for more than forty years. This means that there are no "wolf experts." Instead, there are some people who know a good deal about wolves, but there is no one person who knows *all* about them.

Wolves are individuals. This means that a wolf may well settle down in contentment under captive conditions, never causing any trouble for its human companions. The problem is, nobody knows which wolves are going to grow up to behave quietly and peacefully, and which are not.

Beth Duman is of the opinion that as wolves grow older they are more likely to challenge their human partners, although during the first two or three years they may have shown no signs of aggression. I agree with this view only partially. I believe Beth's conclusion is valid when only one wolf is kept in captivity and when more than one are kept in small enclosures under poor conditions. It is also valid when those who obtain wolves do not understand them and their ways. But, as Jim's pack has amply demonstrated, when wolves are properly housed and cared for by people who treat them well, understand their hierarchy, and do not seek to impose their own will on the animals, they remain tractable. Still and all, wolves like Jim's *are not pets*.

The problem of maintaining a steady state, therefore, is to counteract or to relieve stress. To do so requires, first, ability to recognize stress, and second, ability to react to stress in a self-preserving fashion. Thus, if a system is able to recognize a stimulus and can carry out an appropriate response to that stimulus, it exercises control.
                        —Paul B. Weisz, *Elements of Biology*

EIGHT

After visiting Isle Royale during the early and middle 1960s, I had maintained an interest in developments between wolves and moose on the island, although news reached me in snippets and at irregular intervals until Sharon and I took our first trip to the Upper Peninsula in 1983; then, during our second evening with George, he showed us, via videocassette, an interview with Dr. Rolf Peterson, the biologist who has been heading wolf-moose studies on the island since 1975. What Rolf had to say about the biology of both species interested me greatly, so I asked George if it would be possible to meet him.

If memory serves me, George phoned Peterson that evening and it was arranged that he would see us at Michigan Technological University, in Houghton, where he teaches biology. Our interview was to take place the next day, and since Sharon was going to accompany me, I thought it might be well to give her the biological background of the 210-square-mile island that has become perhaps the most important research locale in the world.

The primitive forests that were encountered by the first

European settlers in those areas bordering Lake Superior that were to become Michigan and Ontario were principally composed of great tracts of white pine and equally large forests of white spruce and balsam fir. These are habitats more suited to woodland caribou than to moose or deer, both of which depend in winter on the twigs and buds of woody plants, which are mostly out of reach in virgin tracts of evergreens because the crowding of trees causes the green growth to push upward, reaching for the light, and the lower branches on the trunks of such large, straight trees die and become tinder-dry.

When massive logging operations were set up and the primal trees were cut down, second-growth vegetation began to colonize the land. This included birches, poplars, small balsams, shrubs, and a variety of other plants and trees. The man-altered habitat slowly produced the kind of food reserves suitable for moose and deer. The caribou, conversely, were wiped out in the regions concerned, many of them killed by hunters, but perhaps the majority dying of starvation, or moving out of the region when their native foods disappeared, for although woodland caribou do some browsing, they depend largely on foliage, grasses, and herbs, and on lichens *(Cladonia rangiferina* and *Cladonia alpestris).*

It is currently supposed that moose first arrived on Isle Royale at about the turn of the century, colonizing the island and slowly building up their populations. Present also were coyotes, beavers, snowshoe hares, mice, and, of course, many birds, including waterfowl and grouse. In 1940 the island was declared a national park and as such became the responsibility of the National Park Service, whose biologists came to realize that moose populations were undergoing periodic highs and lows, with numbers building up beyond the point where the food resources could sustain them. Soon after attaining such peaks, moose populations crashed, after which the vegetation began to recover, and the moose numbers started to rise slowly. In due course, the cycle was repeated, a circumstance that caused much concern to men such as Victor H. Cahalane and Durward L. Allen, the former being at the time the chief biologist of the National Park

Service and the latter the assistant chief of the Wildlife Research Division of the Fish and Wildlife Service.

During the late 1940s, rumors began to reach Washington that wolves had somehow gotten to Isle Royale; their possible presence was often discussed by Cahalane and Allen, both of whom hoped that the reports were based on fact, for such an event would probably lead to a more stable moose population and would also offer a wonderful opportunity to research predator-prey relationships in a habitat undisturbed by human hunting, logging, or mining. Then, in 1951, Cahalane showed Allen the cast of a large canine footprint that had been made on the island. It was confirmed as the track of a wolf. As Durward Allen expresses it in his book, *The Wolves of Minong* (Boston: Houghton Mifflin, 1979): "Both of us were delighted, since this event introduced the greatest of all experiments in predator-prey relations. Potentially, at least, the wolves could build up, stabilize the moose herd, and bring some protection to the vegetation. It was the pattern of primitive times, now to be replayed in a world where such patterns are confused and obscured by the almost universal hunting of moose and the wiping out or heavy control of wolves."

Since the Wildlife Research Division of the FWS was the appropriate agency to initiate and take charge of research on the island, Durward Allen and his chief, Logan J. Bennett, sought to obtain funds for the program, but cutbacks were made in the financing of the Fish and Wildlife Service. Wildlife research was not at all popular at that time. Allen, however, did not give up. In 1954, he left the FWS to become executive director of the Pennsylvania Game Commission, which, a year later, he left to join the staff of Forestry and Conservation at Purdue University, in West Lafayette, Indiana. While there, as he says in his remarkable book, he had "a growing idea there was another route to follow in getting something done on Isle Royale." That something was a determined effort made by Durward Allen to raise funds for island research. His commitment and hard work produced the desired results in 1957, when he was appointed "director, fund raiser, field assistant, and chief cook in the winter camp." Since that time, research has continued on Isle Royale, spurred from its inception by the indefatigable efforts of Durward Allen, a biologist who had the foresight to anticipate the importance of this work and whose determination would not allow him to take no for an answer.

When Dr. Allen decided to step down as director of the Isle Royale research project, he handed the reins to Rolf Peterson, a young biologist who had graduated from the University of Minnesota at Duluth, and had completed his requirements for a Ph.D. with a dissertation entitled "Wolf Ecology and Prey Relationships on Isle Royale." But between the project's original director and its current head, a number of other biologists have won their doctoral or postdoctoral spurs on the historic island, including David Mech, 1958–62; Philip C. Shelton, 1960–64; Peter A. Jordan, 1966–69; Michael L. Wolfe, 1967–70; and a more recent crop of research assistants who have worked or are working under Rolf Peterson.

Although there is no actual proof available, it is generally believed that the wolves which colonized the island in the 1940s were from Ontario, probably from the area south of Thunder Bay, on the northwestern shores of Lake Superior, at which point the northwest portion of Isle Royale is only eighteen miles from the Canadian mainland. It is thought that before a breeding pair crossed over heavy ice to become established in the American national park, several lone wolves may have preceded them at different times, but whether any of these were present on Isle Royale when the colonizing pair got there is an open question. However this may be, in 1952 it was decided to release four semisocialized wolves on the island, the leader of which was Big Jim, a ninety-five pound wolf whose sire was from Michigan and whose mother had been born in Saskatchewan, Canada. The release was ill-fated. The four wolves appeared to be unable to settle and, semi-tame as they were, molested some of the few settlers that remained in the park, tearing laundry off the lines and apparently acting in a threatening manner. Three of these wolves were shot and killed by park rangers, but Big Jim escaped and may have survived to intermingle with the Canadian wolves.

In any event, wolves did become established on the

island, and as their numbers built up, they formed packs. The moose seemed to stabilize, and it was thought that a balanced predator-prey relationship had at last been attained, replacing the cycle of moose highs and lows. Nevertheless, it appears likely that the wolves could not at first increase at a rate sufficient to maintain a true balance as the moose continued to make small but significant gains during the next fifteen or so years. By 1970, 1,200 moose were clustered on the island. Food shortages occurred. As the browse dwindled, so did the moose.

By 1977, only some five hundred moose remained after a crash that was largely the result of malnutrition and stress-related ailments rather than of direct predation, although this did, of course, have some effect.

During the time in which moose numbers had been increasing, the wolf population also continued to grow, in normal response to the law of nature (and physics) which states that for every action there is an equal but opposite reaction. This is now rarely observed in most wilderness areas of the Northern Hemisphere because man's heavy hand continues to upset the balance, but in undisturbed regions—such as Isle Royale—the law maintains animal numbers at levels compatible with the food supplies.

Under what may be termed normal environmental conditions* in undisturbed environments, all animals gradually experience population increases. But when any one species increases its numbers to the point where these become a threat to the local environment, a variety of factors combine to produce die-offs—as will be noted. And if, at this time, such a population is faced by a number of severe winters, it will eventually crash dramatically.

Predators respond to periods of plenty by increasing their own numbers. They continue to prosper during and after a crash. Later, when they have picked clean all the

---

*Because the natural world is always in a state of flux—as it has been since the beginning of life—normalcy is really impossible to measure. I use the term here for convenience, in order to describe a state midway between population highs and lows, when all species are relatively prosperous, yet experience some hardships and fluctuation of numbers.

carcasses of those animals that have died, there are yet many prey animals left that have just managed to hang on to life. Many are likely to be suffering from diseases, such as arthritis, or are old and generally impaired. Thus, for some time after a major die-off, wolves and other hunters continue to live well, their numbers either remaining constant or actually increasing. Eventually, however, the predators are left with a group of survivors that came through the crash because they were the fittest and most dominant of their kind. These animals are hard to get. While the hunters have been busy cleaning up the carcasses and pulling down the unfit, these hardy individuals have enjoyed abundant forage and have become even fitter. As a result, their offspring are also strong and healthy and much more difficult to kill. The predators then face similar population reductions to those that affected their prey, and for the same reasons.

Rolf Peterson's research during the last decade strongly suggests that wolf populations crash about ten years after the prey species reaches the low point, at least on Isle Royale, while the interval between high and low numbers appears to be between twenty and thirty years.

During the 1960s, wolf numbers on the island remained remarkably stable at about two dozen animals, and moose numbers continued to rise despite predation. In the last ten years, however, major fluctuations have been noted among both species.

In 1970, wolf populations were relatively small, but moose and beaver—the latter an alternate prey animal during summer—climbed to their highest levels in twenty years. Then, in the early 1970s, a number of severe winters affected the moose, which, as noted, numbered about 1,200. At this period, there were about twenty wolves on the island.

The first die-off of moose occurred during the winter of 1971, when the population dropped to nine hundred. Two years later the animals made a small comeback, increasing by about one hundred. Wolves also increased slightly, to twenty-three. In 1974, moose numbers fell again, then climbed marginally. The wolves continued to increase.

In 1977 the moose really crashed, their numbers drop-

138

ping to about five hundred. Before this, the wolves had climbed to forty-four, then dropped to thirty-five. After the moose die-off, the hunters began to increase steadily, reaching a peak of fifty in the summer of 1980. These were divided into five packs, the members of which respected each other's territories.

The following winter, however, the wolves began to decline rapidly, falling by 72 percent, to fourteen, by the spring of 1982. In his 1981–82 Isle Royale research report, Peterson comments on the die-off. In his summary, the biologist notes:

Two years ago, the record-high wolf population of 50 included five territorial packs, with territory boundaries generally honored. Food stress was obvious, however, and pack size was steadily declining. A year later, with 30 wolves present, the food situation seemed no better and packs often trespassed into neighboring territories. In 1982, only 14 wolves remained, and the dominant pack of four wolves claimed almost the entire island. Three other breeding pairs and four single wolves were found, but these were actively tracked and likely chased by the dominant "Gang of Four." We surmise that direct killing of wolves by other wolves contributed to the rapid decline, although we found no dead wolves in 1982. We witnessed a complete turnaround in wolf food availability in 1982, and all groups of wolves had ample food.

Changes in the moose population, probably prompted by the wolf decline, were no less dramatic. Swelled by almost 200 calves, the moose population increased to over 700 in 1982. A substantial rebounding of moose is certain if subsequent cohorts of calves match that born in 1981.

If wolves exhibit a moderate rebuilding of numbers within a couple of years, as we expect, this predator-prey system should soon approximate that described 25 years ago. Accumulating evidence suggests that we are witnessing a predator-prey cycle with an extended period of fluctuation.

That was more or less the situation existing on Isle Royale when George showed us the film of Rolf's interview. As I listened to the biologist's words, I made some notes within the projection-room gloom of George's quarters, covering one small page of a notebook. The first note was prompted when Peterson told his interviewer that the island's old moose, born during the 1960s,

139

were the most numerous victims of the population crash. Practically all of these were suffering from severe arthritis, some of them so seriously that the ball of each femur and both hip sockets were badly worn. These animals, naturally, were easy prey for the wolves, for besides being incapacitated by the disease, they were also undernourished. Indeed, many of them died naturally, furnishing large amounts of food for the wolves. My interest in arthritis stemmed from the fact that my own stress research showed that this condition, if not actually caused by severe stress, was most certainly aggravated by it; then, too, there is evidence suggesting that a combination of stress and malnutrition will *considerably* speed up the deterioration of arthritic joints. Yet Rolf, with the scientist's caution, had not referred to stress during his interview. I surely wanted to talk to him about that subject! A little later, I again made a note in reference to stress. This was when Rolf described the wolf decline that followed the moose crash. This time I wrote:

"Wolves killing each other! They're at war! Stress *must* be involved. First time ever that wolves have been known to wage war like people. *Talk to Rolf!*"

When I had finished outlining the history of Isle Royale to Sharon, it was late, but I was far too excited to sleep. For more than a quarter of a century I had been amassing evidence that pointed directly at stress as the major biological factor in the decline of all species, including humans. My evidence suggested that stress was responsible for man's most unnatural habit of waging war. Now, for the first time in biological history, a nonhuman animal had evidently engaged in serious and prolonged internecine combat. I was well aware, of course, that wolves on occasion kill each other, as do most other animals, but such killings are uncommon, usually taking place during an accidental clash between a pack and a lone wolf that has strayed into forbidden territory or, more rarely, during status fights, when one wolf challenges another and the loser, for one reason or another, cannot escape after its defeat. But the wolf war on Isle Royale was the first example of what may be termed organized and prolonged hostilities.

Accompanied by George and Jim Wuepper, we left

Marquette during a snowstorm to drive the one hundred miles to Houghton in our station wagon, stopping on the way to pick up Kirsten Raisanen, a high school biology teacher who is also interested in wolves and in the Isle Royale developments. At Houghton, we met Rolf Peterson in the university cafeteria; following introductions, the biologist gave us a rundown of the developments between wolves and moose.

After Rolf had brought us up to date, he and I discussed stress, population cycles, and, above all, the incidence of arthritis in those moose born during peak populations in the 1960s, finding much common ground during our exchange. For my part, I was particularly encouraged to find in Rolf a biologist who has devoted fourteen years to *field* observations of wolves, who is not engaging in esoteric, captive-wolf experimentation, and who has broadened his outlook beyond the confines of his specialty. There are, of course, others engaged in wildlife research who also look beyond the narrow limits of their particular interests, but it appears that these are in the minority. This is a pity, for whatever major discoveries are still to be made—and I believe there are many—will not yield their truths to the singleminded specialists.

During our interview in Houghton, Rolf had not yet completed his 1982–83 Isle Royale report, but he sent me a copy some time later. It showed that the forecast he had made a year earlier was completely on target. The moose populations had continued to recover from the low level reached in the late 1970s, while the sudden crash of wolf numbers was reversing itself, with predator populations having climbed to a level comparable to that which had existed in the 1960s. These things, as the report noted, were consistent with "our hypothesis of long-term cyclicity in this island's predator-prey system."

Findings on the island up to 1985 continue to support Rolf's hypothesis, the evidence suggesting that the time span between low and crash-high levels of population averages about twenty-four years for each species, the prey animals declining first and the predators crashing eight to ten years later, a thesis that is further supported by the snowshoe hare–lynx data provided by the Hudson

141

Bay fur-cycle records, although in that situation the time span is shorter because both the prey and predatory species are smaller and, additionally, the hares are far more prolific than the moose.

In July 1985, Rolf sent me his latest research report (1984–85). It shows that the wolf population has changed little from a year earlier, but the moose have increased considerably, now numbering 1,062 individuals. This means that during the last four years, the moose population has grown by between four hundred and five hundred since its low point in 1981.

The wolf population (twenty-two individuals) remained separated into three packs, but it appeared that only two of these had young in 1984. Overall, one pack increased, one declined, and one remained the same, but the survival rate of those wolves present in the winter of 1984 was estimated at 62 percent, which Rolf Peterson believes to be low for a protected species. Beaver also increased between 1982 and 1984. These figures confirm that wildlife populations invariably return to a steady state following highs *and* lows if they are left undisturbed by humans. In my view, Peterson's report also shows that wolves are not the cause of species decline. Indeed, the wolf is a balancing factor, an animal whose numbers are also controlled by natural forces when they reach a peak.

During the years in which I have been studying stress, the evidence I have gathered leads me to postulate that there is a definite relationship between overpopulation and severe physiological-emotional stress, and that all species of animals, including our own, are affected by this syndrome. More to the point, perhaps, is that stress appears to be the principal agent by which nature reduces any population whose numbers threaten to unbalance the steady state of a climax community, whether such unbalancing occurs because of man's alteration of the habitat or because a species has in some way increased its numbers beyond the carrying capacity of the food supply. Under normal, undisturbed conditions, and within the strictures of natural economy, "bumper crops" are tolerated only after a species has undergone a major decline.

When any population begins to threaten the balance of its community, but long before its numbers have reached the crash point, the effects of even modest overcrowding cause individuals to become more than usually competitive in all aspects of their behavior. Levels of tolerance are dramatically reduced and general restlessness develops. Intraspecific aggression is heightened, social bonds are weakened (and it should be noted that *all* mammals are social to a greater or lesser degree), and each animal becomes negatively self-oriented.

All of these things occur gradually at first; they may not become readily apparent even to a trained observer during their early manifestations, but as a population continues to grow, food and shelter decline proportionally and malnutrition intensifies. Stress levels rise and create physiological and emotional changes that seriously incapacitate many members of the population. At this stage, cooperative behavior and intraspecific tolerance vanish because each individual becomes concerned solely for itself. The population is now near the crash point. If, at this stage, severe climatic changes occur in the habitat, these will almost certainly bring about a major die-off. All of these actions and reactions are common to prey and to predatory species alike, the essential difference between the two kinds of animals being that the prey crashes first and is later followed by the predators.

Invariably, because at such times animals are at low ebb, they are also highly susceptible to disease and parasitism and these, combining with malnutrition and stress-induced physiological dysfunctions, accelerate the decline of numbers. When man intrudes and alters habitat by logging, mining, exploration, and pollution, and then causes further havoc through hunting pressure, the result can be the extinction of species in large regions of wilderness. Ironically, humans then blame the predators, and especially the wolf, for the chaos.

The word *stress* has been given wide meaning in recent times and is often used outside of its natural context. For these reasons it is necessary to define the term, and if one is to understand the effects of stress, it is also necessary to know something about its biology.

Under normal conditions, stress is nothing more nor

143

less than the wear and tear of living—the process of aging. Abnormal stress results when an individual perceives threatening environmental conditions, but is unable to deal with them. If such conditions are of short duration, an animal quickly returns to normal emotional and physiological balance; but if the threat continues indefinitely and the individual is unable to counter it in any way, stress persists, intensifies, and produces emotional and physiological effects that can be extremely damaging. What occurs in such cases is that the endocrine system, a mechanism the main intent of which is to promote and coordinate physical functions, becomes upset by prolonged exposure to unnatural influences (unnatural in the sense that these do not normally occur in any habitat on a regular basis).

Things go awry, however, when animals not faced by a life-or-death situation must yet endure all the effects produced by overpopulation. Such exposure prompts what is in effect a false endocrinological response when chronic worry sets in and is interpreted as fear. This causes the endocrine system to produce more hormones than are needed in the absence of a life-threatening situation, and although the animal will be restless, it does not engage in vigorous physical activity. For these reasons, the excess hormones are not "burned off"; they are excreted slowly, but at a rate slower than they are accumulated, if chronic worry persists. Studies of humans suffering from emotional distress of this kind have shown that when the cause of such distress is eliminated, endocrine levels drop off sharply; conversely, when the distress is not relieved, hormonal output continues to be high. These findings demonstrate that emotional distress in man is clearly associated with elevated blood and urinary levels of four series of adrenal hormones. A variety of illnesses are linked to emotional stress, including cancer, arthritis, high blood pressure, stomach ulcers, cardiac disease, diabetes (caused by excess blood sugar rather than by insufficient insulin), brain hemorrhages, blood clots, gout, colitis, hemorrhoids, bloating, diarrhea, obesity, anorexia, impotence in men, and inability to conceive in women, to name some.

In early 1984, after we returned from Michigan, and

with events on Isle Royale much on my mind, I wrote a paper in which I summarized some of my thoughts on the effects of this kind of stress on animals and man. Later I sent a copy of this postulate to Allyn Roberts. His reply: "Let me share with you some thoughts from the psychologist's perspective. First, you are absolutely on target with this hypothesis. The thinking you reflect is not only timely, but essential to prod us into the next step of evolving consciousness. I have been aware that statistics show an increase in many stress-related diseases—cancer, ulcers, etc.—as opposed to other disease categories. Your material offers some interesting possible explanations for these trends. . . ."

Allyn was, of course, referring to humans, whom I had linked with mammals in my paper. He concluded: "Yes! Poor diet is a factor of unnatural tension. You are correctly pointing out that while we need to be concerned about this external symbol, we need also to become aware of the internal, or psychological effects [of stress]."

More recently, when I discussed my theories with Mike Collins, a retired biochemist who is my friend and neighbor, he drew my attention to two stress studies made on white mice, one conducted by the National Cancer Institute, in the United States, and the other by a Rockefeller grantee investigator. In both cases, the results were very similar.

The first study involved mice that were subjected to overpopulation stress for a long period. The second involved stress that was induced by frustration in solving maze pathways leading to food rewards. Their findings: Sexually, estrus was either retarded or stopped; in males there was considerable loss of libido. Physiologically, mice became anorexic; they also suffered from hemorrhages of the brain, of the gastrointestinal tract, and of the skin. In addition, they suffered from uncontrollable muscle spasms (epilepsy) and loss of digestive functions; they then became catatonic and died soon after. Social and psychological changes resulted in the spread of irrational violence, self-mutilation, killing of litters, cannabalism, withdrawal, and other conditions. Investigators noted that when stress was relieved in its early stages, recovery was rapid, but there was a point of no return after long exposure, at which time the mice could not recover.

The crash of moose and wolf populations on Isle Royale and the events preceding and following the declines of each species are of exceptional interest to all those who study the relationships of prey and predatory animals because they represent events occurring naturally in a wild habitat that is in no way disturbed by man and is, additionally, as close to the primal condition as can now be found on our continent. For these reasons alone, long-term, well-funded studies should be conducted if mankind ever hopes to understand the complex forces that govern the affairs of nature and, consequently, those of our own species. But Isle Royale, by virtue of being cut off from mainland influences, is also a *unique* habitat in which it may even be possible in the future actually to trace the processes by which evolution brings about natural selection not only in mammals, but in plants and insects as well.

The fact that Isle Royale wolves literally went to war in response to the stress created by their overpopulation, which is something that these animals have never been known to do before, is in itself of the greatest interest and importance to all those who are concerned about man's penchant for killing his own kind. It causes me to ask: Is it possible that the wolves of Isle Royale can teach us why we are continuing to kill each other and how it was that man began to make war in the first place? I believe that these questions may yield answers if major research can be developed on the island. It is already known that stress causes violent manifestations in humans, just as it causes disease. Now, for the first time, we find that a highly intelligent animal that may well, at one time, have taught man how to organize his own family units, has, because of being confined on an island, resorted to internecine combat to settle its differences. When Desmond Morris noted that if one could find an animal that made war, it would be more accurate to say that it was behaving like man, he little dreamed that one day we would, indeed, find such an animal.

There is no doubt at all in my mind that the Isle Royale wolves warred on each other because of overpopulation,

146

food shortages, stress, and their inability to disperse, as their kind will do in mainland habitats when faced by the same problems. It is true, of course, that even mainland wolves become casualties when prey species crash and overpopulation in their own ranks causes them to suffer malnutrition, illness, and emotional upsets, but the majority set off to seek new territories, leaving the strongest packs in possession of the old habitat, although the fate of the migrants is by no means certain; they may or may not make it outside of their native range, for their success or failure will depend upon a variety of factors such as availability of suitable territories not occupied by other wolves, competition from neighboring packs, and, of course, the numbers and kinds of prey animals they are encountered. Nevertheless, if given an option, the wolves will choose migration over war, and it may well be that our early ancestors made the same choice when populations grew too large for their home territories and stress began to be felt, when groups left as a matter of course until overall human numbers multiplied to the point where few suitable habitats were vacant. War may then have appeared to be the only viable alternative to the population problem. In this context it should be noted that during prehistoric times the majority of the world's habitats were probably incapable of sustaining early hominids who, primitive and relatively defenseless against such predators as lions, panthers, and other big cats, were forced into savanna-type niches on the edges of which lapped the great primal forests. There, these hunter-gatherers sustained themselves in part by using the leftovers of kills made by the far more efficient natural predators.

Isolated as they are, the wolves of Isle Royale can be compared to today's humans who, because of overpopulation, find themselves closely confined within the boundaries of their nations. They need more food and room to expand, but they have nowhere to go short of invading a neighboring country that, in all probability, is equally stuffed full of people.

Within the human experience, under such conditions trouble inevitably develops, just as it did among the packs of Isle Royale.

147

In a manner of speaking, ecosystems are what you get by mix-
ing naturalist's things in the tourist's places and letting them
cook for several millennia. . . . Environmentalists try to pre-
serve these ecosystems through political action. Yet no law will
succeed in preserving something that people know only from a
distance or do not understand at close range.

—Richard and Jacob Rabkin,
Nature in the West

NINE

The knowledge that we had traveled only one hundred miles and that there were still 3,100 more to go before we arrived home did nothing to allay our anxiety as I pulled the car over on the shoulder of the road so that we could attend to the two howling wolf puppies. The wolf-lings were just twenty-three days old, yet their reedy howls of hunger were strong and continuous as they scrabbled inside the cardboard box that housed them.

While I was guiding the car off the Alaska Highway, Sharon busily prepared two disposable diapers and un-screwed the top of the vacuum flask we had filled with blood-temperature formula before leaving Whitehorse, the capital of the Yukon Territory, where we had been staying until that morning. It was May 1984, and we were returning home two weeks earlier than I had planned, because of the need to care for the wolf pups that had quite unexpectedly come into our care.

We had undertaken such a long and trying journey from our home in Ontario as a result of my concern over the wolf killings that were taking place in British Columbia and the Yukon. Because of the very subjective reports that had filtered through the media, and also because information that I had gathered by telephone invariably reflected the partisan views and emotions of both the proponents and the opponents of the wolf kills, I felt that I should go to the locales and conduct my own investigation. At first, because the Alaska Highway presents some horrendous difficulties in the spring of the year, I had intended to go on my own, meaning to spare Sharon the discomforts of such a journey. But Sharon elected to join me, although she knew from past experience that our journey would involve driving some 1,500 miles of grueling roadway "paved" with gravel and heavy clay, which begins at Dawson Creek, British Columbia, and ends in Fairbanks, Alaska. Because our time was limited, we drove nonstop through Ontario, Manitoba, Saskatchewan, and Alberta, entered British Columbia, and overnighted at Dawson Creek (not to be confused with Dawson *City*, Yukon), a trip of somewhat more than two thousand miles. In the morning, tired but determined to reach the first wolf-kill area as soon as possible, we set off early, plodding northward through a vast and thawing wilderness until we reached Fort Nelson, the "capital" of the wolf killers. Here we spent three days gathering information and speaking to those on both sides of the issue.

Horrified by what the government of British Columbia was doing to its wolves in the name of conservation, we left Fort Nelson on day four en route to Whitehorse, with 635 miles of the Alaska Highway still to negotiate, a journey that we completed in stages as we stopped along the route to visit friends whom we had not seen since 1978. In this way, it took us three days to reach the Yukon's capital, where we settled into a hotel in the center of that city of twelve thousand people.

The next day, I went to the government building and sought some of the biologists whom I had known in the past, but we didn't seek to survey the local people until that evening, when we both went down to the bar after dinner. Soon we got into conversation with several people sitting at adjoining tables. One of them, a young man

149

who was slightly inebriated, was loudly critical of the Yukon's program of wolf control.

Since he appeared to be most interested in wolves and exceptionally concerned over the government's plans to kill them, I asked him to join us at our table, little realizing as I did so that by morning we were to become the guardians of two wolf puppies whose needs would cause us to abandon any further research and to make for home the next day, immediately after breakfast.

The tipsy young man introduced himself as Pete King and told us that he had spent three years in the Yukon and northern British Columbia, working at whatever jobs he could find, at times laboring in mining camps, on other occasions as a logger or in lumber mills. He was between jobs when we met him, but was due to start work the next week in a mining town north of Whitehorse. Having explained these things to us, he leaned toward me suddenly, lowered his voice, and told me that he had "a real bad problem." Now, when a stranger whom I have just met in a bar tells me that he has a problem, I always expect him to ask me for a "loan" to enable him to buy a few more rounds of drinks; for that reason, I do not usually ask the nature of the problem, knowing that if my surmise is correct, I will be told in any event.

Pete turned out to be the exception. His problem, as he related it to us in a near whisper, involved a female wolf.

"I got this bitch wolf, you know. Had her for more'n three years now an' she's just great, follows me everywhere and don't chew up much stuff, you know . . . but last February . . . I was livin' in Carcross . . . Elsa— that's her name—she was tied out at night an' I guess she made out with a wolf. I'd heard 'em howlin' near the shack I live in, an' come mornin' I saw all the big tracks, one set right around Elsa's place. But I didn't think nothin' then, figurin' mebbe the wolves'd just come to visit . . . they'll do that sometimes, you know . . ."

It turned out that one wolf had done more than visit, for Elsa had become pregnant and had produced six pups on April 27, a circumstance that created some real problems for Pete, who, migrating from job to job and often having to stay in motels and cheap hotels, had problems enough with *one* wolf. Suddenly he had seven of them!

The young man was evidently very fond of Elsa and had a great admiration for wolves in general. He knew something about their general habits, but little about their biology, for, as he told us, he had left school at sixteen and had not gone beyond the eighth grade. But he was inherently attuned to nature and he was a kind person. He had never hunted or fished and disapproved of those who did, although, because he was of mild disposition, he did not often voice his disapproval. But when the government of the Yukon announced its plans to shoot and poison wolves, Pete became angry. He protested by writing letters to the government and to local newspapers; and he got into many arguments with those who favored the wolf slaughter. He had even been involved in several fistfights.

When Elsa gave birth, he realized that he could not keep the wolf pups and he tried to give them away, a tactical mistake in an antiwolf country where news travels fast. Hitherto, he had claimed that Elsa was a German shepherd dog, but now it became generally known that he had a wolf. Threats were made. He disregarded them, thinking that no one would dare hurt Elsa. But when the puppies were seventeen days old, and while the wolf was taking a rest outside Pete's little rented cabin, a pickup truck drew up on the gravel road in front of the building and a man sitting in the passenger seat of the vehicle rolled down the window and fired at Elsa with a shotgun. Most of the pellets hit her right thigh, but a number of them glanced off and lodged in her belly, injuring her teats. The wolf was not mortally wounded, but she could no longer nurse her pups.

Pete did his best to bottle-feed the six cubs, but four of them died. Elsa, meanwhile, became seriously ill, for Pete did not have enough money to take her to a veterinarian. Depressed, he had decided to "get me a few drinks," and had thus been in the hotel bar when we entered it. When he finished his story, he looked at us and asked, "You guys wouldn't want to take them pups, would you?"

Sharon and I looked at each other. I saw deep sym-

151

pathy in her eyes, but at that moment, although I was angry over the spiteful shooting of the wolf, I wasn't prepared to accept the responsibility that wolf-keeping entails. Instead of replying to Pete's question, I suggested that having the animals killed painlessly might be the kindest thing to do. This got me in trouble with Sharon and caused Pete to exclaim loudly, "No way, man! No bloody way!" Since my wife was looking at me crossly and because Pete, fueled by rye whiskey, was becoming very agitated, I compromised by asking him to lead us to his cabin so I could look at Elsa and the two surviving pups, to see what could be done for the mother and to try to judge the condition of the cubs.

We followed Pete's dilapidated car to the Carcross area, which is about forty miles from Whitehorse, and we saw the wolves. Elsa's wounds were badly infected and she appeared to be suffering from mastitis—inflammation of her breasts caused by the fact that she was still lactating, but had no way of eliminating the milk. The wolf, docile and friendly despite her injuries, allowed me to examine her, but would not let me touch her nipples to try to relieve the pressure. Each dug was red and swollen and pockmarked by birdshot. Her leg was very badly festered. After I had finished examining the wolf, Pete led us into his rather bleak little dwelling and showed us the two pups.

One, a female, was brown; the other was a black male with a white star on his chest. They reminded us of Shawano and Denali. Both had the blue eyes of very young wolves, and their ears were not yet fully erect. When Pete uncovered the rather stained and messy cardboard box he had been using as a nursery, the female was sucking on the male's left foot and he was sucking on her groin, both of them mouthing avidly as they sought to nurse. When I picked them up, holding them against my chest, they mouthed at my hands, searching desperately for milk. Well, that did it! My reluctance vanished! With its departure came decision. I agreed to take the pups and I gave Pete enough money to take Elsa to a vet and have her properly looked after. Then, before we left, I asked Pete what he had been feeding the pups, and how. He produced two eight-ounce feeding bottles equipped

152

with nipples, which were adequate, but he had been giving the wolflings full-strength cow's milk four times a day. As patiently as I could, I explained to him that cow's milk is no proper substitute for wolf's milk, and furthermore, very young pups must be fed every four hours, not four times a day. Indeed, it seemed like a miracle that the survivors had lasted as long as they had!

In our hotel room that night, we did the best we could for the pups, using cow's milk because we had nothing else and there were no drugstores open where we could buy prepared human infant formula at that time of night. But we diluted the milk by 50 percent, using boiled water that I scrounged from the kitchen on the excuse that I wanted to make myself instant coffee.

That turned out to be quite a night! Half-starved as they were, and because the diluted milk could not sustain them for long, we had to feed those two little howlers every two hours, hoping that nobody in the hotel would want to investigate the strange sounds coming from our room.

In the morning, Sharon went to breakfast alone while I wolf-sat; when she came to relieve me, I had a quick meal, then went out to buy baby formula, some lactose to add to it, two more bottles, and a large vacuum jug. I also got a bottle of multiple vitamins. By ten o'clock we were on our way, the pups now housed in a clean cardboard box that we had scrounged from the grocery store in which Sharon had bought a huge box of disposable diapers and four rolls of paper towels. By the time we had traveled one hundred miles, the pups had screamed for food three times, meanwhile wetting copiously and, during the second and third food stops, producing some very thin, yellowish diarrhea.

When we had fed the two waifs the third time and they were again settled in their box, which we kept on the back seat, we had a cup of coffee from our own vacuum flask and started off again, thinking that the pups could not possibly survive and wondering when they would actually die. Some four hours later, as we were preparing to stop for something to eat at Rancheria, a tiny community thirty-five miles from Watson Lake, the pups were still silent after their last feeding. We were reluctant to open the box to look at them, fearing that they were dead. But no . . . as soon as the box was moved, the whelps began to whimper. We fed them, cleaned them off with a sponge dampened in warm water, waited till each had urinated and defecated on our paper-towel-covered laps, and then put them back in their newly diapered bedroom, whereupon they immediately went to sleep. Now we felt better, convinced that the two would survive. During a brief lunch, we discussed names for them and settled on Tundra for the male and Taiga for the female.

Those who have read my books *Secret Go the Wolves* and *The Zoo That Never Was* will doubtless recall that I had a wonderful Alaskan malamute called Tundra, but although I was happy that the little male wolf would bear the name of the dog, it was not chosen especially in his honor, but rather because it represents the treeless tundra region of the north, just as the word *taiga* (pronounced "tie-gah") has been given to the broad band of evergreen forests that almost ring the northern parts of North America, Europe, and Asia. We felt that the two wolflings fully represented these habitats; besides, we liked the alliteration!

Back in the car, Tundra and Taiga were still fast asleep. From then on, the only stops until we reached home were made in order to feed the pups or ourselves. Since Sharon was acting as chief nursemaid, I drove all the way, mile after mile of gravel and mud and rain and potholes, until at last we reached the blessed asphalt one hundred miles from Dawson Creek. Then it was blacktop, wide expressways, and buffeting truck transports, a day-and-night marathon of driving punctuated by periodic, fifteen-minute catnaps. Two days later, exhausted, but triumphant because by now we had two very healthy and vigorous pups, we marched into our home and surprised our housesitter, Murray Palmer, a young graduate biologist who is also an excellent photographer. Murray's camera went into immediate action as Sharon and I sat on the floor of my study and fed Tundra and Taiga. That date was May 20.

For the next five days, Tundra and Taiga continued to occupy their cardboard-box den, partly because I had no

154

better accommodation for them and partly because I felt that they might react negatively if they were forced to acquaint themselves with yet another nursery before they had an opportunity to get used to us. At night we took pups and box upstairs to our bedroom, to make it easier for us to feed them every four hours as well as to be near enough to them to hear their cries, should they become distressed for any reason. Their days were spent in my office, where, between feedings, they slept soundly despite the clacking of my typewriter and the frequent ringing of the telephone that was, of course, followed by the sound of my voice.

Although the pups did not appear to react badly to the noises I had to make during the course of my work, I worried about them, wondering if they were being disturbed at the subconscious level; but since there was no help for it, I tried to ignore my concerns. In fact, as we would learn later, they were affected by the experience in good ways, the exposure to the normal sounds and odors of our home becoming imprinted on them and causing them to feel comfortable in our surroundings as well as to respond positively to my voice.

By May 25, the pups had settled nicely. They had gained weight and size, measuring seventeen inches overall, their tails being four inches long. And their teeth were just starting to grow, showing as tiny, needle-sharp points that barely protruded from gums which were rather inflamed and red. On contact with our fingers, the minute fangs hurt! In order to ease the discomfort of teething, I took the two thigh bones of some chicken we'd had for supper, to which bits of meat and gelatin still adhered, and put them in the nesting box. By morning, the porous ends of the bones had been chewed off and the harder parts were devoid of even the smallest bit of meat. From then on, Tundra and Taiga were given cooked chicken bones every second day, the offerings containing a little more meat each time. This helped ease the pain caused by the sprouting teeth, gave them some extra nourishment, and amused them, for after the meat had been eaten off the bones, the pups continued to chew for hours, occasionally fighting over one of the pieces amid much baby

155

growling and whining when one or the other was bitten too hard.

At this stage, Tundra and Taiga were already starting to look more like wolves and less like the little bear cubs they had originally resembled. Their ears were beginning to straighten, and although their eyes continued to have a somewhat unfocused look, their vision had greatly improved; so had their hearing and sense of smell. They were now twenty-eight days old and taking six ounces of formula every four hours. Feeding times, however, were somewhat chaotic. Tundra, who from the beginning had been a difficult customer, invariably losing the nipple and spattering formula over himself and whoever was holding him, continued to display the same lack of coordination, but to this trait he had added a worrisome habit: he often refused to feed entirely. Taiga, conversely, was a frantic feeder. She scrabbled with all four paws, scratching her handler with cat-sharp nails, lunging, grasping the nipple with tenacity, and sucking like a small pump, often breathing and swallowing at the same time and actually squirting formula out of her nostrils. She had an enormous appetite, and because she invariably finished before Tundra, she would then seek to push him away from his own bottle so as to get a second helping. Tundra, showing even then the calm and generous disposition he was to demonstrate later, would often relinquish his bottle in his sister's favor, but we would not allow her to overeat.

Although both pups appeared to be in excellent condition, I continued to be concerned about Tundra. Whereas Taiga moved her bowels regularly and the condition of her stools was always good, Tundra alternated between constipation and diarrhea. He also whined a great deal, although he played a lot with his sister and displayed a good deal of energy. Taiga was clearly a very high-strung animal, bursting with energy, self-confident, and at that stage, appearing to dominate her larger sibling. She growled at Tundra a great deal during play, wrinkled the upper part of her muzzle in a seemingly ferocious manner, baring her little teeth, and would never pass up a chance to bite our fingers playfully. The trouble was that her minute fangs, now about an eighth of an inch long, were astonishingly sharp and could cut our flesh on contact. We started wearing leather gloves when playing with either of them.

On May 30 we began to take the two outside, allowing them to play in the grass near the house for ten to fifteen minutes, but unable to let them linger much longer because the blackflies, those tiny, ferocious, blood-sucking pests common to many areas of the north during the spring of the year, vectored on them by the dozen, biting each pup in the groin and ears, and also biting their human companions. To protect them from the flies, I now began to "mantle" them—to crouch on all fours and so cover them with my body—and to lick them and nibble their ears and necks. Both responded to these mouthings by remaining under my body and pushing their noses into my face, sometimes licking me, at other times nicking my skin with their scalpellike fangs, especially Tundra, who seemed to enjoy play-fighting with me and nibbling in his uncontrolled way at my chin, neck, cheeks, and lips. Taiga, of course, always tried to push her way in, but in these instances Tundra became dominant, using his greater weight and strength to push her out of the way. At about this time I made a mental note to end the practice when their teeth grew longer!

When the pups had been in our care for eight days, their Yukon box was both too small to hold them and too soiled to endure in our bedroom, so, on May 29, I went shopping for lumber and artificial turf to make a good den and a collapsible playpen for them, tasks that were completed by late afternoon of that same day. The den, made of pine lumber, was twenty-four inches square by sixteen inches high. It had a removable lid and an entrance hole large enough to allow for their future growth. The pen was six feet long, four feet wide, and two feet high, each of its four sections fastened to the others by hooks and eyes. The synthetic turf served as a floor, its grasslike surface rough enough to allow the pups to have good traction and its waterproof backing preventing their urine from staining the floor of my office, where they were to be kept from now on. We were still feeding them every four hours and would have to get up and go downstairs during the night, but because they continued to be active after dark, we felt it would be better for their development to have the space in which to romp. Then, too, we hoped that they would soil outside of their den rather than in it, as they were forced to do when confined by the cardboard box.

The inside of their new den was lined with disposable diapers, as their box had been, three of them being needed to cover the entire area. Before transferring the pups into their nursery, I collected some small logs and finger-thick, green branches six inches long on which they could chew. We also bought a small dog-food bowl that we filled with water.

Tundra and Taiga became immediately apprehensive when we placed them on the artificial turf, but because I had put one of their soiled diapers inside the den, they quickly scented it and took refuge in the boxlike structure. From there, hesitantly, they made short forays to the outside, each time advancing a little farther, checking the objects near them, then scurrying back when some new scent, sight, or sound alarmed them. By the next morning, however, they had become accustomed to their surroundings and were clearly enjoying the space and the "toys" we had put in for them. And we were pleased to note that although they wet inside the den, they had moved their bowels outside of it.

At five-thirty in the morning of June 2, Tundra and Taiga awakened us by howling, their calls louder and more wolflike than before. Our initial reaction was to believe that they were hungry, although their next feeding was not due until 6:00 A.M., but on going downstairs we found that they were merely having a sing-song, standing in the center of the pen, heads close together and muzzles uplifted, howling in earnest. When we approached the pen, they turned to look at us and wagged their tails in greeting, but they continued to call until we leaned over and picked them up, Taiga in Sharon's arms and Tundra in mine. After we had caressed them for a time and they had licked us in customary fashion, I held them both in my lap while Sharon went to get their formula, now strengthened with Pablum.

They fed as usual, Tundra spilling a good deal, Taiga sucking like a small and frantic pump while scrabbling on Sharon's leg with her back feet and leaving a series of scratches on her flesh, a painful experience, but one to which Sharon had become quite accustomed, although her legs, from ankle to knee, were by now looking as though she had been walking through brambles. Before this I had offered to feed both pups, to save my wife's legs, but she would not relinquish the intense pleasure that she derived from feeding Taiga, whom she preferred to handle over Tundra at this stage because, despite her ebullience and extreme enthusiasm, the female pup was easier to feed and always finished before her brother, who, in any case, also scrabbled with his back feet.

At noon of that same day we offered the cubs some cooked chicken meat, shredded, which they thoroughly enjoyed. Afterward they spent some moments licking themselves clean. Tundra confined his attention to his front paws, lips, and lower chest, but Taiga tried to lick herself all over, a laudable attempt that caused her to fall down repeatedly, especially when she tried to reach the inguinal areas.

Although both were still quite wobbly, their coordination was improving daily, even if they often missed a target when seeking to play. And their ears were now fully erect. Both could move them, pricking them forward, from side to side, or up and down. Their eyes continued to be blue and myopic and could not focus properly on any object that was more than six feet away. This caused them to exercise considerable caution, even within the by now fully explored area of their pen. If one of them moved a stick, or pushed the water dish away from its accustomed place, the other would immediately back up, stop, sniff, then advance cautiously, ready to retreat on the instant, but continuing forward nonetheless. When satisfied that the object was familiar, they would immediately relax and ignore it.

At noon on June 3, we took them out of the pen and allowed them to explore the downstairs part of our house, a big event in their lives! A first they stayed close to us, their little bodies held erect, their bottle-brush tails tucked between their legs, but step by step they advanced, most often side by side, but at times separating as each became interested in some particular object. If

159

one of them became startled and stumbled back toward us, the other would react in the same way, and since I was moving along the floor on hands and knees, they would get beneath me, whereupon I would caress them and lick their heads. Seconds later they would go again, explore a little, come back to the shelter of my body, and so on. It took them an hour and a half to explore the entire living room and to determine that a good place to go and hide when they became nervous was under the couch, a low-slung affair with a high back that stood against one wall. Within this always-shadowy hiding place, the pups felt secure while they assessed the situation, seeking to understand the sound, movement, or object that had made them nervous.

Watching them as they explored, retreated, advanced, and sniffed and mouthed things, I was fascinated by the total commitment that each displayed and by the speed with which they learned. Sharon, who had spent sixteen years teaching young children, became greatly intrigued when she noted many similarities between the behavior of the pups and that of kindergarten tots during their first day in the classroom. Like our two young wolves, first-day-at-school human children showed themselves to be apprehensive and interested at the same time; some even took to hiding, and Sharon had soon learned that it was best to allow such youngsters to emerge in their own time, coaxed out of concealment by an intense, inherent need to know and to explore.

Day by day the little wolves became more confident, playful, and affectionate toward us. On one occasion, while I was talking with a visitor, Sharon mothered the pups on her own, discovering that each wanted to have her undivided attention, a fact that they advertised by fighting, the one that was getting petted being attacked by the other. When Sharon tried to caress both of them at once, the fighting persisted, each trying to drive the other away, a clear display of sibling rivalry that was accompanied by much growling and whining as each sought to dominate the other without success, although the biting was controlled and bloodless. Hitherto we had each played with one pup, alternating between them haphazardly so that each was given a turn with Sharon and with me, this arrangement tending to prevent them from individually imprinting too strongly on one or the other of us.

By now, Tundra and Taiga looked upon Sharon as the Alpha female and upon me as the Alpha male. Now, too, Taiga began to demonstrate in earnest the high-strung nature that she had inherited from one or both of her parents, signs of which she had frequently given from the first day she came into our care. But Tundra continued to be calm and gentle. He was a *thoughtful* pup, given to looking at us seriously, as though appraising each of us, his eyes serene, yet deeply probing, at times even speculative. On other occasions he would be aloof, refusing to be petted and going about his own affairs in a dedicated way, only to change his mind a short time later and come up to one of us, whine softly, and ask to be caressed. Then, too, he often had spells when his sense of humor was uppermost, whether playing with Taiga or with one of us. His eyes would twinkle and he would smile, then he would dance in a wobbly way, raising a front paw to bat at his sister, at Sharon, or at me. Taiga's own sense of humor was almost always present, her eyes shining with mischief, her face, when she wasn't wrinkling her nose in mock aggression, wreathed by an impish grin. She was definitely a tease, small as she was; and whereas her stolid, easygoing brother was often slow to react to food or to some prized plaything, Taiga was always quick to gobble up meat or to grab some new toy. We continued to worry about Tundra. Although he was definitely larger than his sister, he ate about a third less than she did. He was also plagued with bouts of diarrhea, even though both cubs were given the same food.

I fretted over Tundra for another reason: He seemed to be too good! Whereas I had already needed to discipline Taiga on several occasions, leaning over her, fastening my teeth on her scruff, and shaking her, whereupon she would whine loudly, wet herself, and become instantly contrite, Tundra was a model of deportment. Such calm and responsible behavior was highly unusual in a wolf pup.

Each evening, after we had settled the two in their den, I would sit at my desk and make notes on their behavior,

161

the condition of bowels and bladder, the amount of food ingested, and whatever other details appeared pertinent to the development of both pups. Looking back on those notes, I find that I questioned Tundra's state of health every second or third evening, but the next day's entry tells me that he appeared to be perfectly fit again.

On June 4, when they were thirty-eight days old, Tundra and Taiga simultaneously weaned themselves. We got up at 5:30 A.M., as usual, prepared their formula, and went to my study to find that they were up and eager to be taken out of their pen. Each of us carrying one of them into the kitchen, we settled on the floor, Taiga on Sharon's lap, Tundra on mine. We offered the bottles. Tundra refused his immediately, no matter how hard I tried to coax him, but Taiga began to feed. Was Tundra ill? Before we had time to do more than phrase the question, Taiga released the rubber nipple and scrambled off Sharon's lap. From that moment on, they would have nothing more to do with formula, preferring to drink water from their bowl, which was something they had taught themselves to do on the first day that we put the dish in their pen.

Having rejected their bottles, however, the pups showed by their behavior that they were nevertheless hungry, so Sharon gave them some cooked chicken. When they had finished that, she offered them some raw hamburger. This too was quickly dispatched; more was demanded and given. Now, fully satisfied, the two began to play and to explore the house, their movements still quite uncoordinated. They had not yet attempted to run and they wobbled a good deal when they walked, their large paws causing them to stumble whenever they tried to accelerate their pace.

One afternoon, as I was working in my office and the cubs were napping, Tundra inside the den and Taiga lying on her back in one corner of the pen, I happened to need a large book that was in the bookcase above my desk. The volume was on the top shelf and I had to stand up to reach it. I took hold of the volume and pulled it toward me; it made a slithering sound that the wolves had not heard before. Taiga was galvanized into swift action. From lying fast asleep on her back, she righted herself

162

and *streaked* into the den. I was not surprised that she had been panicked by the alien sound, but I was astounded by the way in which she reacted to alarm, for in the literal seconds that it took her to awaken, right herself, and rush into her shelter, her actions were perfectly coordinated! Yet, when I called and she and Tundra came outside again, relaxed by my reassurance, her movements were once again clumsy; they were to remain so until she attained full command of herself in the weeks ahead.

When an animal is alarmed, its system is immediately prepared for action by endocrine hormones, particularly by adrenaline, which helps to coordinate movement while effecting a series of other physiological changes. It had never occurred to me, however, that adrenaline could actually produce immediate and perfect coordination in a young animal that was still particularly clumsy in all its movements, or that it could increase speed so dramatically. By themselves, these things were biologically significant, but I was also interested in the fact that when Taiga's alarm had passed, she had so quickly reverted to puppy clumsiness. This suggested that the rate at which the elevated levels of endocrine "fuel" is used must be exceptionally high. Furthermore, when the reaction is caused by inherent caution (which dictates that any unknown influence is suspect until it turns out to be harmless), realization that the originally fearful stimulus poses no threat immediately relaxes the animal and causes its hormonal output to return to normal control levels. As I thought about the little wolf's behavior, it occurred to me that I had just witnessed a perfect example of what Dr. Hans Selye called positive stress, an emotional-physiological reaction that, when functioning properly, is designed to increase an individual's life span.

Discussing this with Sharon later that day, I began comparing the behavior of Tundra and Taiga with that of Matta and Wa, only then realizing the futility of such comparisons. When I said as much to Sharon, she was surprised, believing that my experience with the first two wolf pups should qualify me to prejudge the actions and reactions of our present wards. Earlier I would have agreed with my wife's views, but now I knew that beyond

163

those general traits shared by all wolves, individual behavior could not be assessed in advance. As matters have turned out, I am glad that I formed that conclusion as early as I did, for Tundra and Taiga are uniquely different from each other and just as different from Matta and Wa, and indeed from all other wolves that I have known. When I explained this to Sharon, she was still somewhat puzzled.

"But surely they're wolves, aren't they?" she said.

"Yes, they're wolves all right, and they eat meat and they howl and they share many things with other wolves," I answered. "But each is unique, one of a kind."

I long ago concluded that the only trait universally shared by all life forms is uniqueness and that all animals are distinct and separate entities with personalities wholly their own. Because of these things, and although they have been genetically structured to behave in accordance with the general norms that govern the biology of each species, all of them express themselves in highly individualistic ways, a characteristic that is also to be noted in their physical shapes.

On August 7, when the pups were thirteen weeks old, Tundra weighed thirty-four pounds and Taiga thirty pounds. This meant that the male had attained an average gain of 2.53 pounds per week since birth, while the female had gained 2.23 pounds a week, these calculations based upon the assumption that each had weighed about one pound immediately postpartum. At this date they looked more like wolves, although their ears still seemed too large for their heads, and their huge paws persisted in getting in their way. Nevertheless, their coordination had improved dramatically and so had their speed, facts that were frequently drawn to our attention when we tried to catch them during those regular occasions when they were loose in the house and had managed to get hold of some item that was fragile and not designed for the jaws of wolf puppies. At such times, they would dash under the couch, squeeze themselves tightly against the wall, and continue chewing their forbidden prize, all the while looking at whichever one of us was flat on her or his tummy, seeking to reach them with one extended arm.

164

Soon, however, I discovered that what was almost impossible to accomplish by direct action could be done by guile, an awareness that came about when, unable to reach either of the two, who were sharing one of my slippers, which Taiga had stolen, I began to whine, my poor imitation of lupine distress causing both pups to dash out of their hiding place and rush to me as I remained on all fours, each frantic to lick my face. This ruse worked as long as the pups had not taken refuge under the couch because one of us was cross with them. Under those circumstances they stayed hidden, coming out only when they detected that affairs had returned to normal. In this regard, the two gave us a wonderful example of their ability to pick up our emotional signals when, while we were entertaining visitors, Tundra moved his bowels on the rug. Sharon, who is quite sensitive about mess or untidiness in the house—especially when we have company—became dismayed when she suddenly detected an odor that was not usually present in our living room. Investigating, she discovered its source and noted that, as was usual with him, Tundra was standing by, tail erect, front quarters slightly crouched and bottom presented for wiping, a habit he had developed when, during bouts of diarrhea, Sharon used a soft tissue to clean him. Unlike his sister, who did her business and strolled away casually, Tundra always presented himself for wiping, but on this occasion Sharon, without realizing the effect that her reaction would have on the pups, paused, looked down at the mess, and exclaimed, "Oh . . . *Tundra*!"

The offender instantly dropped his tail and, in unison with his equally alarmed sister, streaked for shelter under the sofa. It took Sharon some minutes to coax them out again, but when they did emerge, they both mobbed her, fussing and licking until my wife began to laugh, then the two began to play with her, grabbing at her clothing, fingers, or any other part of her that was handy.

I knew from past experience that wolves and many dogs can tune in to human emotions; I had already explained this to Sharon, but that one demonstration by Taiga and Tundra did more for her understanding of wolves than anything I had said. Our visitors, who had

165

never seen wolves outside of a zoo, were quite astonished, and were hardly able to credit that the animals could pick up emotion from just one exclamation. And there was more to come.

About a week after Tundra messed on our carpet and caused Sharon's distress, I decided the time had come to make a suitable outdoors enclosure for our two delightful ruffians. They were developing so quickly that they could hardly squeeze under the sofa; besides, there just was not enough room for them in the house. We could not allow them to run loose, and although we took them on long walks on their leads, the task of guiding two rambunctious wolf puppies through a forest that had not been touched by axe or saw for some sixty years was an exhausting and frustrating experience, at least for the humans. Tundra and Taiga loved these jaunts, of course, but were unaware that humans could not squeeze through tight, low, and narrow interstices between sharp branches, under downed tree trunks, and through blackmire swamps.

Busy as I already was with many other projects, I realized that I needed help. Mike Collins, whose willingness to help a neighbor knows no bounds, immediately offered to assist me. So did Murray Palmer, who came to stay with us for a week and helped me dig a trench around the perimeter of the pen and further aided me in the cutting of cedar posts from our property. When these chores were accomplished and the postholes had been dug, Mike arrived full of his usual enthusiasm and we put in the posts and stapled the fence wire to them. Two days later, the job was done, and as I walked the inside boundaries of the 50-by-150-foot enclosure, the south end of which was anchored to our century-old log barn— which was to shelter Tundra and Taiga at night in case a wandering black bear decided to drop in and dine on wolf cub—I was satisfied that this miniature ''territory'' would do for the time being. Later, when time permitted, I planned to extend the enclosure to incorporate about an acre of forested land that slopes down to the stream that runs through our property.

Putting the two pups into their new home was an event attended by Sharon, Mike, and myself, a festive occasion during which we watched with delight and fascination as the young wolves began to explore their new range, exercising that supreme caution that is the hallmark of their kind as they ventured farther and farther afield, interrupting their adventures frequently to dash back to us so that they could be patted and reassured. By that same afternoon, however, the two had definitely taken possession of their territory and showed that they knew practically every inch of it. The land involved is studded with seedling larches, a few small cedars, and some young spruces as well as clumps of black poplars that were then about seven feet tall. Grasses, wildflowers, and wild clematis vine added to the vegetation. To the north, the pups had a view of about five acres of lowland on which grow alders and willows and through which our stream meanders. Beaver can be seen on occasion, and birds in the hundreds, including seven large ravens that soon got into the habit of paying their respects to the pups every afternoon at about four o'clock.

Later, assisted by Tundra and Taiga, I dug a small den, roofing it with old cedar logs and rocks. In no time the pups, especially Tundra, had deepened and widened it so that the two could curl up inside, protected in some measure from flies and enjoying the coolness of damp earth.

TEN

Before we moved Tundra and Taiga to their outdoor enclosure, I had always fed them raw meat without having a barrier between us, taking a cube of beef in each hand and simultaneously offering a piece to each of them, in this way preventing them from trying to snatch at the same prize. This habit came to an abrupt end, however, when I entered their enclosure the morning after they had been settled in it, carrying the meat in my left hand and offering one cube to Tundra with my right. I should have known better, of course. Before I had lowered the beef close enough for Tundra to take it, Taiga leaped at it, snapping it out of my fingers and in the process gashing my index finger. Tundra, having been deprived of the snack, began to leap also, but not before Taiga had swallowed the meat and joined her brother. Now I had two wolves jumping at the dish and at my freed hand, their gleaming fangs flashing mere millimeters from my flesh. I ended the melee by dumping the meat on the ground and letting them scramble for it. Taiga got the biggest share.

168

From then on we fed the cubs through the wire, Sharon giving meat to Tundra and I to Taiga, coordinating our movements so that the pups got their share at the same time. Within two days, the young wolves learned of their own accord to position themselves so that Tundra stood opposite Sharon and Taiga opposite me, a habit that they continue to maintain, for we still give them a snack each morning, their main meal being carried into the enclosure in two huge dog bowls during late afternoon or early evening. Interestingly, although they leap around me excitedly when I enter with the food, they have never tried to get at it until I have placed both bowls on the floor of the barn, at which time Taiga usually stands on my right and Tundra on my left, the same position that they adopt when we give them their morning tidbits.

At the time of this writing, the wolves are more than a year old, but they have never once quarreled over food. They are always willing to share, although Taiga continues to eat quickly and usually manages to get more food than Tundra, but it is now clear that she needs to eat more because of her heightened metabolism, while Tundra, who continues to be calm and easygoing, attains more growth and weight than his sister on considerably less food.

If the wolves are given a bone, however, or if they find a favorite piece of meat of some kind, they immediately take it outside the barn and settle down to eat it in the shelter of the forest and will protect it by growling if the other sibling goes too close to the one that is eating. Most often the growl is purely ritualistic and is recognized as such by the interloper, who approaches until his or her nose is an inch or two from the food, yet does not try to take it. But if the rightful owner is really hungry, the resulting growl is deep, rumbling, and definitely threatening, whereupon the approaching wolf turns away immediately, its manner suggesting that it had no intention of trying to steal the meat or bone.

Nevertheless, on occasion, Taiga manages to take food away from Tundra by guile when the latter is not truly hungry. She will approach, ignore the ritual growls, sniff at the food and whine, then lie down very close to Tundra. He continues growling as he eats and as Taiga rolls

169

closer to him. Little by little she continues to roll and sidle until she turns herself over, her weight pushing Tundra's head away from the food. Wriggling further, she covers the prize with her shoulders, then, giving one more heave, she snatches the meat or bone and springs away. Sometimes Tundra chases her, whereupon the two run at full speed through the enclosure, leaping obstacles and dodging trees with wonderful agility, but after a time he gives up and allows his sister to eat the food. Tundra has never resorted to such tactics and he does not appear to resent his sister when she employs them.

After the wolves were moved into the enclosure, we made it a practice to stay away from them while they were eating their main meal of the day or when they were chewing on a bone, but when they were six months old, one or the other of them would elect to carry food over to us and to eat it at our feet, showing that they knew we would not try to take it from them. We appreciated the trust.

Occasionally, when not particularly hungry, Tundra or Taiga will come out of the barn ostentatiously dangling a piece of meat while looking at us with a grin and a twinkle in the eyes. This is an invitation to play. If we don't immediately respond, they will bounce in front of us, toss the food in the air, and deliberately allow it to fall on the ground a yard or two from where we are standing; then they will bow over it, stretching their front legs forward and lowering their heads, then lifting them to look us in the eyes. If we make a move toward the offering, whichever one is soliciting our attention will grab the meat, usually a chicken wing, and dash away in high glee, chased by us and by its sibling. The object of this is the *game*, not the prize, for if the one being chased drops the food, or even a stick, the other does not try to pick it up. If one of us reaches for it, however, we are allowed to take it, but we are then expected to dangle it above the heads of both wolves, who leap repeatedly for it. After some moments, we allow one to snatch it from us (they are always careful to avoid closing their jaws on our hands now), and the chase resumes anew. The wolves will keep up the play so long as we are willing to chase them, but inasmuch as they can attain a rate of about

170

twenty-five miles an hour when going at full speed, we clumsy humans can never catch up. Indeed, when we are too greatly outdistanced, the one carrying the prize will stop and wait for us, sometimes even running up to us, dropping the prize, and quickly snatching it up again before we can take it.

During our first summer together, the four of us gradually became a close-knit family, our relationship based on love, trust, understanding, and respect, each giving wholeheartedly and taking as amply from the others. During our walks through the forest that surround our home, the zest for life that Tundra and Taiga always demonstrate, the curiosity they display, and the intelligence they apply to their explorations of the wilderness never fails to elicit similar feelings from us. No matter how trying a day either one of us may have had, or how depressing has been news of the outside world, our boisterous, often fatiguing walk (which Sharon calls "our daily *drag!*") invariably renews us. And afterward, back in the enclosure, during the quiet times of loving and communion in which our civilized barriers are swept aside by the primordial essence of the wolves, our physical contact with them puts us back in touch with the wildness that is latent in all humans. Each evening, Sharon and I leave the enclosure renewed and tranquil.

In early September our local veterinarian, Dr. Laurie Brown, came to give the pups a vaccination against rabies, parvovirus, and distemper, a precaution taken because we did not want to run the risk of disease, which had killed Toivo, Siskiwit, and the various pups in Ishpeming. Of the three diseases, parvo and distemper were of the most concern, and I only consented to the rabies vaccine when Laurie assured us that it was made from a killed virus, which ensures that an animal will not become a carrier of the disease, as has occasionally occurred when some dogs and wolves have been injected with a live-virus vaccine.

Laurie Brown is a slight young woman who more than makes up for her lack of size by dexterity, excellent qualifications, and—a thing that I prize above all in a veterinarian—a deep concern for all animals. She had not previously had anything to do with wolves, but when I

171

telephoned her a few days after we returned home with the pups, she unhesitatingly came to examine them. (Not all veterinarians will treat wild animals.) The way in which she handled the wolflings, and the immediate, positive response that she elicited from them, told me that I had chosen our veterinarian wisely. She immediately discovered that Tundra had a small umbilical hernia and that Taiga had a vaginal infection. Both are common in very young canids, and she felt that Taiga's problem would clear up on its own accord—which it did—and that in all likelihood Tundra's hernia would also correct itself as he grew older. Otherwise, she found them in excellent health. Later, when I realized that they had roundworms, Laurie supplied medication for them.

When it came time to vaccinate them, since she had by then visited them a number of times, she had no scruples about entering the enclosure. Wisely, she immediately leaned against the barn wall so as to stay on her feet while being effusively greeted by her patients, who could both now put their paws on her shoulders. When the joyous lupine hellos had been delivered, she injected each one while I held the patient as a precaution. We need not have worried. Tundra, the biggest, who then weighed forty-nine pounds, whined a little, but this was because I held his scruff too tightly, as though I were reprimanding him. He took no notice of the needle prick. Taiga, who is always eager to be fussed over and lies down at any excuse, was too busy licking and mouthing my hand to notice that she had been given an injection. Indeed, even though I have the experience gained with Matta and Wa, I am still astonished at the toughness of our two wolves. They bite each other quite hard during play, they smack heads together with loud *thunks*, and they bang into things, but no matter how hard they strike an object, which at times is the leg or knee of one of us, they don't even pause in their stride. We do, however! The head of a wolf, I am sure, is made of cannonball iron!

A few days after the vaccination, my daughter Alison arrived from England to spend two weeks with us. Alison, a policewoman with the Surrey Constabulary, had never seen a wolf, but having read my books and talked with me by telephone about Tundra and Taiga, she had no hesitation about entering the enclosure the morning after her arrival. Beforehand, however, I explained that the pups would mob her, as they had mobbed every one of the eighty-seven visitors they had received since their arrival at our property.

They would stand upright so as to give her face a few licks, I predicted, so she should use her arms to ward off their large and heavy paws, which are capable of scratching if they come into contact with bare skin. I also told my daughter that I would intervene once the two had been allowed to welcome her in proper wolf fashion, after which they would certainly want to get to know her personal odor.

Usually, whenever we take a visitor down to the enclosure, the pups gather at the fence and wait, exhibiting excitement by dancing and climbing over one another. As we get close to them, they stand upright and stick their heads through the large mesh wire that is joined to the small aperture fencing four feet above the ground. At this point, I will allow a visitor to pat them and to accept a lick or two if I am sure that the newcomer is not nervous.

I was somewhat surprised, therefore, when Tundra and Taiga exhibited calm behavior as Alison and I approached them. Indeed, they were acting as though I were coming on my own, treating our joint arrival as a routine visit from their Alpha human male. When we got to the wire they stood up and licked me as they usually do, but without the exuberance they reserve for Sharon, and certainly without the *super*-exuberance with which they greet strangers. Alison patted the two heads; the wolves responded by licking her hand and wagging their tails, then they dropped back to all fours. Alison asked to be let inside.

When I take a visitor into the enclosure, I usually let him or her go first if the wolves show that they have accepted the newcomer. My reason for this is that they are so anxious to get to a visitor that if I enter first, they are liable to slip past me and get out so as to greet the stranger in proper style. Thus I bring up the rear and close the gate while Tundra and Taiga are mobbing their

173

guest. By the time I have done this, the visitor has been well and truly licked and I bring the mobbing to an end, whereupon the wolves start to sniff their new friend, eager to become more intimate with the person's scent, in the process causing some individuals considerable embarrassment when they stick their noses in very private places. But when Alison preceded me into the enclosure, neither wolf leaped up to lick her. Instead, they behaved exactly as they behave toward me. I was astonished, especially when each of them flopped down at my daughter's feet and assumed the submissive pose, ears back, tail between the legs, one rear leg lifted and urine dribbling freely. These are signs of respect, recognition that they are in the presence of an Alpha and are happy to offer homage. Seeing their behavior, I told my daughter to squat down and stroke them. What followed left no doubt in my mind that Tundra and Taiga looked upon Alison as an Alpha female. They treated her in exactly the same way that they treat me.

Until that moment, I had not devoted much thought to my relationship with Tundra and Taiga. I realized, of course, that they looked upon me as the Alpha male of our human-wolf pack, but my automatic appointment to this "office" had developed so naturally that I had simply accepted the role and its attendant responsibilities in much the same way that, many years earlier, I had accepted fatherhood. Indeed, if I thought about the matter at all, I suppose that I considered myself the surrogate male parent of the wolves, who, just as they looked upon Sharon as they would have viewed their natural mother, showed by their behavior that they considered me to be their lupine progenitor. Because of these things, they came to me for protection when startled, they solicited my affection when they felt in need of it, they accepted me as a referee when one was necessary to settle those disputes that arose between them, and they showed that they were aware of my pack standing by according me the same level of respect that they would have given an Alpha of their own species. As a human child looks to its father in these matters, so Tundra and Taiga looked to me, and for my part, I behaved toward them as though they were, indeed, by own issue. I still do. So does

Sharon. The fact that between ourselves we refer to them matter-of-factly as "our kids" is, I believe, sufficient indication of our feelings toward them.

Just as human children need the point and counterpoint of a mother-father relationship, so it is with wolf children. Similarly, when the young of either species begin to mature, the bonds that have been formed by family ties strengthen if they have been tempered by mutual respect, fairness, and understanding. From the start, Sharon and I loved our adopted wolf children, and they returned our love. We played with them, laughed with them, worried about them, made sure they were properly cared for, and, when necessary, disciplined them, a role that fell mostly to me, but one that Sharon also accepted when necessary, although as a human female of a most gentle disposition, my wife was never quite able to bring to her reprimands the level of sternness exhibited by a mother wolf. Nevertheless, Sharon's gentle ways have always had great influence with Tundra and Taiga; they may at times take liberties with her that they would not take with me, but they surely love her deeply, a fact they demonstrate without fail every time Sharon enters the enclosure. Taiga, the high-strung, mischievous extrovert, always leaps up to lick Sharon's face and will not be satisfied until my wife crouches and presents her face so that it can be properly tongued, an action that Sharon recently described this way: "When Taiga licks you, it's like you're a car going through a car wash! Her tongue feels like it's two feet long. Tundra is the dainty one!"

My wife has an inherent wit that invariably demonstrates deep insight. When I am bright enough to see beyond the comic aspects of her impromptu quips, I invariably discover that Sharon has managed to sum up in a single joking sentence a series of truths that I have been searching for in vain, her comment here being a case in point. Sharon made the remark after I had typed a rather disjointed account of the ways in which our wolves lick us. I rejected what I had written and went to discuss my problem with Sharon. Her reply put matters into perspective, because the way in which each wolf licks also demonstrates the differences in their personalities.

Of the two, Taiga is the one that must be disciplined

175

on a regular basis, while Tundra rarely needs to be reprimanded. Taiga continues to be exuberant and mischievous, whereas Tundra is deeply thoughtful, controlled, and exceptionally calm. He, too, has a sense of humor and enjoys a prank, but he never allows himself to be carried away by excitement and he is almost always self-controlled. Taiga is *always* ready to play, a trait reflected in her twinkling gaze, but all too frequently she does not know when to stop. Similarly, when she licks, she does indeed give one a "car wash." When she howls, she gapes wide and her voice is shrill, unmodulated, and downright discordant; she is guileful, eager, loving, and very beautiful.

Tundra, although he plays readily enough, seems to spend a lot of time in thought. Unlike his sister's definitely slanting eyes, his are round and capable of directing extremely penetrating stares at whatever individual or object attracts his attention. They are remarkable eyes, serene yet quizzical, direct but not threatening, and when they change and show the latent humor that is never too far below the wolf's consciousness, they sparkle to such an extent that I must always chuckle. When Tundra licks, he does so with the very tip of his tongue—little, moist dabs that are repeated three or four times in quick succession and are then abruptly stopped, after which he sniffs at us, his nose often resting on chin or cheek, while he gazes into our eyes. Unlike his sister's voice, Tundra's is deep, well modulated, long drawn, and emerges from a mouth that is tunneled, his lips forming an almost perfect circle that has a diameter of probably two inches.

Taiga is easily excited, but she is also quite sensitive; she demonstrates this whenever I must discipline her and she tells me most clearly that she is sorry. Her entire demeanor suggests that she will never trespass again, but minutes later she will probably do just that. So I must discipline her, my tone of voice being generally sufficient to control her behavior, but at times I must scruff-shake her, or even bite her muzzle. Then she is most contrite and wants to be loved; so I love her, stroking her body, scratching her neck and ears, and, cupping her face in both hands, kissing her gently on the lips. After that, up she bounces, joyful and probably triumphant! And the

176

chances are that the whole scene will have to be replayed again . . . and again. In fact, I am beginning to suspect that she transgresses in order to get the extra loving that always follows the reprimand.

Tundra is, I believe, even more sensitive than his sister. On one occasion, when I had to slap his nose and speak sternly to him, he refused to approach me for two whole days! Indeed, I had to go out of my way to get him to forgive me, but when he did, his behavior told me that he was very glad to be friends again. He pressed himself against me, took my hand gently in his mouth, wetted himself a few times, then lay down so I could rub his body, his eyes half-closed in ecstasy. Some days later, after Taiga had been trying to steal a bone that he was chewing and he had finally warned her off by emitting one of his deep growls, I went to walk past him and he growled at me and actually made a threatening motion with his mouth, aiming at my leg, though he "pulled his punch." My reaction was quick and positive, if exceptionally mild. I took off my old, well-traveled, and much-prized bush hat and hit him with it, thereby ending the headgear's long life, for the brim and the crown parted company. Tundra had clearly realized his trespass, for he abandoned his bone and beat a very hasty retreat, his tail tucked between his legs, his ears pasted to his head. Aware that his threat reaction had been prompted by Taiga's pestering rather than by my accidental approach, I squatted and called him to me. On this occasion he responded immediately, running up, giving me several dab-licks, and then lying down so I could fuss over him. Since then, I have not had to discipline him again, and nowadays, whenever I have occasion to scold Taiga, Tundra dashes up and joins me, roughing up his sister until she whines in submission.

These things characterized Tundra and Taiga and our relationship with them even at the time that Alison came to visit and was greeted by the wolves in the manner I have described, a pattern of behavior so different from that which they had always exhibited to all other visitors that I at first believed it was coincidental, that for some reason they had not been in their usual boisterous mood when confronted by yet another stranger. But after somewhat more than an hour, during which I removed myself from the immediate vicinity of my daughter and the two wolves, their behavior remained constant—there was no doubt that they were treating her as an Alpha. Was it possible, I wondered, that the wolves were actually able to detect the bloodline that Alison and I shared? I rejected this at first; it just seemed too incredible. Then I reconstructed my behavior as I had walked alongside my daughter toward the enclosure. Had I, in some way, signaled our special status to the wolves? I pondered this all morning and through lunch, and decided in the end that I had treated Alison exactly as I treated other visitors prior to introducing them to the wolves: I had talked about their differences, explained their behavior, and told her how she should react to them, which was precisely what I had done on eighty-seven previous occasions.

When it was time to walk the wolves, I suggested that Alison might like to lead one of them, replacing Sharon for the first time. But I did not discuss with either my wife or my daughter the unusual way in which Tundra and Taiga had reacted to Alison, feeling that to do so would prejudice Alison's future behavior and, frankly, not really accepting the possibility that the wolves could indeed sense the genetic lineage that my daughter and I shared. Pretending that I had something to do in my office before we went for the walk with the wolves, I asked Sharon to instruct Alison in the proper way to handle Taiga, who was usually led by my wife; my reason for making the request was that I did not want to risk influencing Alison in any way. The leads that we use are spring-loaded, extending to a maximum of sixteen feet, but retracting automatically when they go slack. Each is also fitted with a brake so a dog—or wolf, in our case— can be held at any distance from two feet up to maximum extension. They are easy to use, but given the nature and exuberance of the wolves, there are some tricks that a beginner should know.

After Sharon had explained these things to Alison, we walked down to the enclosure. Alison, who had greatly enjoyed her contact with Tundra and Taiga, strode out, anxious to get to them again. I held back, pacing myself so that I remained about eight feet behind my daughter, who therefore arrived at the wolf pen ahead of me, allowing me to take careful note of the ways in which the wolves greeted her. Again, they behaved as though she were I! They continued to show her the same respect after we had both entered the enclosure. Taiga, who usually danced around Sharon in her excitement to go for a walk, was always difficult to collar at first, but she submitted quickly when Alison went to put the chain around her neck. During our walk, Taiga behaved as if I were holding the lead, which I do on those occasions when she plagues Sharon and we swap—Tundra, who pulls more strongly, but is easier to control, is then led by my wife, and the irrepressible Taiga, responding to my sterner handling, settles down as soon as the exchange is completed.

An hour later, when we had returned from our forest walk and the wolves were back in the enclosure, there remained no doubt in my mind that Tundra and Taiga had detected the blood ties between Alison and me. And they had done so even before we reached the outside of their territory. How did they know? I immediately dismissed hearing, for my voice bears absolutely no resemblance to my daughter's, and even our manner of speech and our accents are quite different. I also dismissed sight, for the wolves do not use vision to recognize Sharon or me, or anyone else that they know, until we are almost at the fenceline. So, I decided, the answer had to do with scent, with hormones, particularly with *pheromones*, which are chemical substances known to be used in communication between members of the same species, and are also thought to be the ancestors of endocrine hormones.

These chemical attractants are produced by plants, by invertebrates, and by vertebrates, including primates and humans. They are highly volatile and emit extremely detectable odors that can be scented across distances of up to several kilometers, even though they are released only in minute quantities. Because man's olfactory system has, through disuse, become so ineffective, we humans live in an odor-deprived world as compared with that of other animals. For this reason, our knowledge of pheromones is still very limited, although in recent years biologists

179

and biochemists have been hard at work researching pheromones and trying to understand the roles played by these hormonal chemicals. And it seems that the more pheromones are studied, the more complicated they appear to be, although it is now known that their transport through space is linked to certain sulphur molecules, to which they are harnessed. Inasmuch as they continue to be found with great regularity in all species wherever a determined scientific search is made, it appears certain that chemical communication by means of scent is universally distributed in all living organisms.

Simply stated, pheromones are discharged by animals at all times as part of endocrinological metabolism. But there appear to be many different kinds of these chemical messengers present in every organism, each type probably conveying very specific information, the odors of each being used by animals to recognize each other, to recognize an enemy, or to identify a prey animal. Pheromones also advertise the sexual readiness of males and females, as well as aggression and friendliness.

In this context, Sharon became aware early on that Tundra and Taiga were able to sense the hormonal changes that took place in her body prior to her menses, the wolves being capable of doing so four to five days before Sharon was aware of these things herself. At such times, the wolves are especially interested in scenting her in ways that might be considered embarrassing were it not that they behave so naturally. It seems that just as soon as Sharon's hormonal metabolism begins to alter in response to the timing of her cycle, Tundra and Taiga immediately detect the changes. Then, too, I have become aware that during those occasions when my emotions are being affected by work stress, no matter how slightly, our wildlings can sense the increase in hormonal output, nosing at me as intensely as they scent-examine Sharon.

On two different occasions during November 1984, the wolves detected severe stress in two of our visitors (both men) long before either of them had come near the enclosure. Taiga showed her awareness by tucking her tail between her legs and retreating, but Tundra displayed open aggression, which was something that he had never

180

done before. His hackles became erect from the root of his tail to the top of his head, his ears were pricked forward, his tail was held high, and he charged the fence while emitting deep growls and barking intermittently. Since we knew that both individuals were quite seriously distressed at the time, it was not difficult to understand that Tundra and Taiga had been able to "tune in" to their emotions by sensing elevated hormonal levels. And Tundra, though only seven months old, made it quite clear that if either man approached the fence he would attack.

Both episodes interested me because of the very opposite reactions that the wolves had displayed toward Alison and the friendly ways in which they had greeted all other visitors. And although I was concerned that Tundra had shown so much aggression, I was also pleased that he had advertised it so early and so unequivocally, thereby alerting me ahead of our arrival in each instance and allowing me to lead the men away from the enclosure.

I knew the first man well and was aware that he was undergoing serious emotional problems; though we knew little of the second individual's circumstances, by the ways in which he talked and carried himself, it was obvious that he too was distraught. Thus I concluded that because both men were disturbed by factors that were beyond their abilities to control, each was reacting angrily to his own individual problems.

Anger, as I have noted, is invariably interpreted as aggression by all animals. As a result, Taiga, more timid in such circumstances than her brother, became afraid, while Tundra, already showing Beta-male qualities, responded by exhibiting defensive aggression.

For several weeks, I pondered these matters at considerable length, at the same time searching the literature on pheromones and learning that although much has been written about these chemical messengers, much research remains to be done before it will be possible to understand their composition and the manner in which they facilitate communication. Nevertheless, findings to date confirm those theories that I formed by observing our wolves and noting the various ways in which they react to olfactory stimuli. I don't think, though, that I would have so readily formed my conclusion if Tundra and Taiga had not demonstrated that they were able to detect my relationship with Alison.

More recently, I sought Mike Collins's opinion, showing him my notes and discussing my ideas with him. To my relief, he entirely agreed with me, the more so, perhaps, because he knows Tundra and Taiga and often pops in to visit them unaccompanied by Sharon or me. Always he is greeted effusively. Mike has known the wolves since a few days after we returned with them from the Yukon, and he has had many opportunities to observe them. As he has expressed it to me a number of times, he is convinced that they are endowed with acute olfactory perceptions that are quite beyond the reach of human noses.

When a human sets out to track an animal, he relies entirely on vision; but when a wolf or other predator picks up a spoor, it relies entirely on its sense of smell, the pawprints or hoofmarks themselves being meaningless to the predator. Indeed, wild hunters do not even look at the tracks, their eyes being focused instead on the way ahead while their ultrasensitive noses, held some inches above the trail, can detect whether a spoor has been made recently or whether it is old and of no interest.

In this way, a wolf trots along at a fair clip, its nose probing the ground or snow, as well as its general environment. If it so happens that it gets started on a fresh track in the wrong direction, it reverses itself the instant it realizes that the scent is getting weaker rather than stronger. Sharon and I have seen Tundra and Taiga behave in this way countless times. What is more, if either of us has strolled in our yard before we take them for a walk, they are not satisfied until they have sniffed our old trail, dragging us along those routes that we have taken earlier. They do this regardless of season or weather. Whether the ground is bare or dry, whether it is wet or covered with snow, they track us, never satisfied until they have examined every one of our previous footsteps.

We, of course, know when they are tracking either one of us, but we rarely know when they are following the spoor of a visiting animal, such as a squirrel or a fox. On September 30, for instance, as we were leading them toward the forest, Tundra swung off course and dragged me back toward a small pond that lies between their enclosure and our garage. On this occasion the grass was wet following a heavy rain the previous night, but Tundra, nose aimed at the ground, insisted on sticking to his course, Sharon and Taiga following us.

When we reached the edge of the pond, which is bordered by smooth Cambrian granite, Tundra hesitated a moment or two, casting about with his nose, then turned right, followed the edge of the water, and led me to a place where a narrow drainage ditch had been dug in the distant past to prevent overflows during flood times. Here there is some mud. Tundra dragged me along, sniffing intently at the mud, all the while staring at the distant trees, and then he marched on. As I was about to step over the ditch, I saw the track of an adult wolf; some six inches ahead of it was Tundra's smaller track. We, or rather our pups, had been visited by a wild wolf! Later I returned and measured the single paw mark, which was $4\frac{7}{8}$ inches long by $3\frac{3}{4}$ inches wide. Tundra's front paw track, in contrast, measured $3\frac{3}{4}$ inches long by $3\frac{1}{4}$ inches wide. The adult wolf had visited sometime between the previous evening and three o'clock in the afternoon, and in view of the fact that neither pup showed any further interest in tracking the animal once its course had been traced as far as the pond, it seemed clear that the lone wolf and our two had related in our absence.

I have witnessed a great many almost uncanny demonstrations of the olfactory abilities of wild animals, but Sharon had not been so privileged until Tundra and Taiga came into our care. Since then, however, she has seen how keen are the noses of our wolves; it was the first time that Taiga stopped dead in her tracks, thrust her nose into some grasses, and came out with an old mouse nest that Sharon realized fully just how sensitive they were. What at first puzzled my wife, however, was the undeniable fact that the wolves could track our steps no matter what kind of shoes we had been wearing at the time.

"How can they smell us through our shoes?" she asked me.

I can only guess at the answer to this question. They

obviously can, but whether the scent "soaks" right through the soles of the footwear or adheres to the outside of the shoe or boot is more than I can say. Sharon is also puzzled about the ability of our wolves to track in snow, but this is perhaps easier to explain, for it appears that when a track is imposed on fresh snow, the moisture in the crystals accentuates the odor; and when the track is covered by a topping of fresh snow, the fact that the subsurface temperature is higher also accentuates the odor.

In any event, whether a wolf is sniffing at paw marks or sensing any one of literally hundreds of airborne aromas, there can be no doubt at all that those seemingly ubiquitous but hard-to-fathom pheromones really do exist. In his book *Lives of a Cell*, Lewis Thomas ponders the possible presence of pheromones in humans:

"What are we going to do if it turns out that we have pheromones? What on earth would we be doing with such things? With the richness of speech, and all our new devices for communication, why would we want to release odors into the air to convey information about anything? We can send notes, telephone, whisper cryptic invitations, announce the giving of parties, even bounce words off the moon and make them carom around the planets. Why a gas, or droplets of moisture made to be deposited on fence posts?"

Commenting on a paper written by Dr. Alex Comfort and published in *Nature* magazine in 1971 under the title "The Likelihood of Human Pheromones," Thomas writes: "Comfort has recently reviewed the reasons for believing that we are, in fact, in possession of anatomic structures for which there is no rational explanation except as sources of pheromones—tufts of hair, strategically located apocrine glands, unaccountable areas of moisture. We even have folds of skin here and there designed for the controlled nurture of bacteria, and it is known that certain microbes eke out a living, like eighteenth-century musicians, producing chemical signals by ornamenting the products of their hosts."

Thomas's book was published ten years ago. Since then, more information has come to light that will help answer this eminent biologist's questions, but I believe that Lewis Thomas might well be as interested as I am in the way Tundra and Taiga were able to determine that Alison was my daughter and that she should be respected because she smelled like me. As for me, I now know that paw marks are not the only things that leave discernible spoor.

ELEVEN

As the autumn grew older and painted colorful panoramas on the canvases of the forest, Tundra and Taiga responded to the change of seasons by howling with greater frequency at night and during the afternoons when the ravens flew in and perched themselves on trees near the enclosure, there to chatter excitedly while looking down on the wolves. We had a flock of seven ravens that year, large, coal-black birds that arrived daily between 4:00 and 4:30 P.M. to spend about half an hour talking to each other and to our rangy cubs.

On the afternoon of October 12, while I was socializing with Tundra and Taiga, they turned away from me and ran to the north end of the pen, their noses raised and their ears pricked forward as they detected an influence hidden from my senses. Standing side by side, they remained immobile and stared at the sky, but although I followed their line of sight while I listened intently, I failed to see or hear whatever had so suddenly attracted them, even after I walked to where they were and placed myself immediately behind them. The pups were so intent on what they were attuned to that they barely acknowledged my presence by halfheartedly wagging their tails for a few seconds.

After some moments of fruitless vigil, I was about to turn away and leave the enclosure when I heard the faint cawing of ravens. Now Taiga whined softly and Tundra pawed at the fence wire. The raucous calls grew louder but were still distant, and the sky remained empty. I waited, alternately watching the wolves and the sky; presently I saw the first raven as it flapped over the trees. It was followed by the other six.

As the birds neared the enclosure, they started to call more frequently. The wolves began to dance, whining to each other and rising on their hind legs, one sometimes climbing on the other so that the passenger's back legs were off the ground and its front legs had to move at twice the normal rate to keep up with the haphazard pacing of its companion. This behavior always denoted excitement. It was practiced every time we walked toward their quarters. At one moment, Tundra was giving a piggyback ride to Taiga, and at the next, the positions were reversed and the rider became the carrier, a performance that was kept up until their excitement dissipated.

The wolves separated when the ravens dropped below the treetops and approached us. Now the cubs sat on their haunches and watched the birds until they flew over our heads in disorderly formation, losing height rapidly just before they alighted on nearby trees. Tundra and Taiga trotted toward the landing area, arriving there just as the ravens started to call, at which the young wolves began to howl rather discordantly and to pace back and forth.

I was no stranger to such interspecies communion, having learned soon after I encountered the North American wilderness that ravens could lead me to wolf kills, sometimes after the hunters had eaten and left the scene, on other occasions while the wolves were actually feeding. The first time this happened, I was surprised to see that the birds were sharing the meat with the hunters and were tolerated by the adult wolves, but charged by the untutored yearlings, who were eventually to learn that their tactics were never rewarded by success. Quite the contrary! Ravens are hardy, daring, and highly intelligent birds, always ready to steal anything edible that is not actually inside the mouth of a predator or hidden in a metal garbage container equipped with a locked lid. Although these voracious members of the crow family will steal from one another when opportunity presents itself, they cooperate magnificently in filching bones or meat from inexperienced wolves and dogs. Beyond this, as I have observed a number of times, ravens appear to act as scouts for wolves by congregating near prey animals, calling loudly and excitedly. It may be that the birds have learned that there are times when an old or injured deer or moose is dying, or has already died, and will thus offer them a sumptuous meal; or it may be that the birds are deliberately advertising the presence of prey in the hope that the wolves will respond and make a kill, after which the ravens drop down from the trees to take their share. However this may be, just as *I* learned that the birds could lead me to the wolves, the latter have also learned that when ravens congregate in a given area, they may well be signaling the presence of potential prey animals.

Sooner or later, all wolves learn to accept the ravens when these are sharing a kill, but during their first year of life, the young hunters acquire wisdom the hard way after the wily birds have stolen many choice morsels from them. Ravens employ tactics that are simple but effective. Two or three will drop down to the ground and begin to strut within seemingly easy reach of the jaws of a feeding young wolf, who, jealous of its food and at the same time unable to resist the urge to pounce on such a tempting target, charges at the nearest bird, snapping audibly and futilely at the air as the ravens spring upward and find safety in the trees. Meanwhile, long before the wolf can turn around, a raven that has been waiting nearby, but out of sight of the hunter, darts in, grabs the food, and flies off with it, after which it is itself chased by its erstwhile partners, each of which will steal the prize if it can. After three or four such experiences, adolescent wolves usually learn to ignore the ravens, which then wait until all pack members have become nearly sated, then alight on the carcass to peck off pieces of meat.

Just when the raven and the wolf developed their relationship is impossible to determine, but the fact is, each appears to be at least equally fascinated by the other, even when food is not the issue. I have often seen wolves following the chattering black scavengers as they fly-hopped from tree to tree, talking in their many voices or uttering their harsh *kwaawk*. And the raven appears to be at least equally fascinated by the wolf.

The Indians and Eskimos of North America certainly recognized this strange affinity, for their legends often couple the bird and the mammal, both of which were also endowed with spiritual or even godlike qualities. More than a few clans adopted either the wolf or the raven, or sometimes both, as their special totems; individuals saw one or both animals in dreams induced by sweat-baths and fasting, and then accepted them as alter egos.

After my years of experience with the animals and birds of the North American wilderness, during which I have had many encounters with raven and wolf, I can sense the mystical aura that emanates from both, and I am always strangely moved after each encounter that I have with them, individually or collectively. Nothing is more haunting, spiritual, and primitive than the calls of ravens and wolves coming at the same time from the same location, a wild concert not infrequently heard during the breeding season of wolves and after a pack has made a kill. On the ground, lying, sitting, or standing, the wolves begin to howl, the throbbing, sweetly melancholy calls seeming to fill the entire evergreen forest. In the trees, the ravens respond, perhaps a dozen or more of them spread around the pack, each uttering its own particular repertoire of gurgling notes, bell-like sounds, and slurred chatter that to my ears is akin to human language. At such times the wolves seem to be spurred by the ravens and the birds appear to be stimulated by the lupine voices. I have been privileged to attend seven such concerts, the most recent being in the southern region of the Yukon Territory, in 1978, during a January morning when the temperature was sixty degrees below zero and the air was laden with ice fog, a magnificent northern phenomenon that occurs when the moisture in the air freezes. Experienced from within the cloister of a forest of black spruce during the fleeting time that the winter sun runs its flat race across the hidden horizon, and even though the sun does not show its orange face above the treeline, the display is truly magnificent; the ice fog glistens ethereally, each minute crystal casting off red, green, blue, and orange flashes as the weak sunlight sheds its evanescent glow over the deep-frozen land; not a whisper of breeze can be felt and the evergreens stand proudly and beautifully, each mantled in white, each showing pure green clusters of needles that peek from within sculpted, niveous adornments. To be in such a place at such a time, and then to hear the emotional outpouring of the ravens and the wolves that one has been quietly observing from a distance of some fifty yards, is an experience that awakens the primal emotions each of us carries deep within his being. And then, when it is all over and the wraithlike shapes of the wolves disappear into the forest on whispering pads, the ever-curious ravens come to examine the human observer; and they talk to him as they peer with one jet-black eye, head held sideways the better to see, and the great black beak, shutting and clacking softly. Unforgettable!

Tundra and Taiga sang with the ravens for about three minutes on that autumn afternoon, such timing being about average for wolves everywhere, which, unlike coyotes, rarely call for prolonged periods. Afterward, the pups came to me to be petted, then went to lie down within their favorite stand of poplars. The ravens continued talking to each other for the next half hour, then flew away, heading in the direction from which they had come. But as they passed overhead, I, wondering if they would return if I induced the pups to howl again, gave my poor imitation of a wolf's call—a rendering that, despite its definite shortcomings, invariably elicits a reply from the cubs. On this occasion, however, Tundra and Taiga merely screamed, uttering a few shrill calls from where they lay before falling silent. The ravens took no notice at all.

Unlike Matta and Wa, who refused to sing until they were about two months old and were unusual in that respect, Tundra and Taiga have always been great howlers. At first, if I whistled, however softly, they would call; then, when, without thinking about them, I began to sing

190

to myself as I was picking up their droppings inside the pen, they howled in response. Now, often they will howl if we talk to them in an only slightly raised voice, but their best performances are given in response to my imitation howl, which stimulates them so greatly that they continue calling after I stop. If I howl while standing upright, the wolves go close together and howl either face to face or side by side, but if I call while crouching, they come up to me and get their muzzles as close to my face as possible. At such close quarters, their voices have the power to cause uncomfortable vibrations in my ears. Frequently, and especially at night, Tundra and Taiga enjoy sing-songs during which they may call for a minute or two, remain silent for several minutes, then call again. And when a wild wolf or a coyote calls from within the forest, our wolves always reply, but if a neighbor's dog barks from its location a mile away, they ignore the sound. Likewise, when Mike brings his dog, Moose, to visit us and ties him near our entrance gate, Tundra and Taiga show very little interest in him; when he barks, which he does often, they pay no attention.

The howl of the wolf is for me the most haunting of all wilderness sounds, a deep, wonderfully primordial, and long-drawn song uttered for any one of many reasons, its cadence altered in response to whatever stimulus has triggered the call. No one, to my knowledge, has yet compiled a catalogue of these lupine variations.

It has been suggested recently that wolves howl to confuse neighboring packs that may have hostile intentions, a theory stemming from the fact that when a pack calls in unison, the varying pitch of their voices may deceive a listener into believing that the number of wolves in the group is greater than it actually is. This argument also proposes that when pups call on their own during the time that they spend in a summer rendezvous, they deliberately deepen their voices to give the impression that adults are actually doing the howling, thus deceiving neighboring wolves that might be tempted to kill them.

These theories are farfetched. They imply that wolves are always at war with one another, which is not the case, and they fail to take into account that lone pups would be much safer if they kept quiet. Most important, the theorists are interpreting the calls of wolves from a purely human standpoint. It is true that to the human ear the combined voices of wolves often make it extremely difficult for a person to determine the number of animals in the pack. But the hearing of wolves is capable of fine acoustical discrimination, and for this reason I do not believe that they would fail to recognize the calls of cubs, no matter how modulated these might be, for the voices of adults.

Wolves sing when they are happy and when they are sad. They howl when they are excited, especially during the breeding season; they do so together, as humans do around a piano. Wolves almost always howl before they set out on a hunt, probably because they are excited at the prospect of the chase, which I believe is as important to them as the actual kill. Then, too, wolves call to each other to keep in touch and to communicate with neighboring packs; and lone wolves howl to attract a mate, or merely to "talk" to other loners or packs that may be within sound of their voices. An important reason for howling is to advertise their presence in a given locale, in this way reinforcing the messages left on the many scent stations upon which wolves urinate, such as particular logs, stumps, trees, clumps of grass, or rocks that are scattered within the boundaries of the land they occupy. Wolves probably howl for a variety of other reasons, one of which, I am convinced, is that they *enjoy* doing so.

There are doubtless times when the very volume of pack howling may serve to inhibit neighboring wolves that might have hostile intentions, but such occasions are probably the exception rather than the rule and are most likely to occur during periods of heightened stress, as was the case with the wolves of Isle Royale. I base these conclusions on the data that I have so far gathered, which strongly suggest that at least three different kinds of interaction may take place between wolf packs: the first is friendly coexistence; the second, which may be termed a state of armed neutrality, occurs when neighboring wolves merely tolerate each other; the third is characterized by out-and-out aggression because of scarcity of food or disruption of the environment by human abuses and probably by other, unknown causes.

Ten days after I had heard Tundra and Taiga sing with the ravens, the moon became full and hung overhead at about midnight, bathing our property and the surrounding forest with light, and coaxing me outside. As I walked toward their enclosure, the young wolves ignored me, their attention centered on the north, an area of dense wilderness that comes within one hundred yards of the enclosure. Because the yearlings never ignored our presence unless they were particularly interested in matters of their own, I stopped walking. As I stood, I heard the call of a wild wolf, its volume suggesting that the animal was about a mile away. Tundra and Taiga replied immediately, their voices rising and falling in unison with the call of their relative. The three wolves continued to howl for about one minute, then became silent.

I walked to the enclosure and entered it as Tundra and Taiga came to greet me, but when the wolf called again a few minutes later, somewhat closer now, they dashed to the bottom end of the enclosure, howling as they went. This time the calls were sustained for a longer time, perhaps three minutes, before the stranger became quiet. As I waited for more, it suddenly occurred to me that if it was possible for wolves to recognize bloodlines in humans, it must also be possible for them to recognize these among members of their own kind. If this should turn out to be the case, it would explain why some packs are friendly toward their neighbors and why others are merely tolerant or actually hostile.

Lone wolves often leave a pack to seek mates elsewhere; if it so happens that a male of one pack should meet a female of another pack and form a third group in the same general region, these two will probably be welcomed by both of their parental groups inasmuch as the pheromones emitted by at least one of the animals will be recognized by each neighboring pack. It would also follow that any issue of the newly mated pair would carry a combination of pheromones that would make them acceptable to their related groups. Such a genetic scheme may well account for the fact that wolves do not normally make war on each other.

193

The more I thought about this, the more convinced I became that my conclusions were correct, at which point my musings were interrupted by the realization that I had been standing in the enclosure for some ten minutes, though the wild wolf was no longer calling. Taiga and Tundra had changed position and were now looking toward the northwest, but were not sniffing as eagerly as before. I gathered from this behavior that the wolf had moved away and was even then traveling through the most heavily forested section of our land, behind the northern boundaries of which lie many thousands of acres of government wilderness in which live deer, moose, coyotes, and a variety of other animals and birds.

Bearing in mind the tenor of my earlier thoughts, I wondered whether the wild wolf that had been howling was a loner and might be searching for a mate, which would account for the fact that his visit appeared to be motivated by interest rather than by aggression. On the other hand, the animal might be a member of a local pack that was initially attracted by the odor of the pheromones discharged by our wolves.

Such speculation returned me to my original postulate because it suddenly occurred to me that there might be a flaw in my reasoning. If bloodlines are chemically advertised and kinship proclaimed by them, thereby encouraging friendly interaction between related packs, how could I explain the hostilities that had taken such a toll among the wolves of Isle Royale, which were almost certainly interrelated? This question seemed to blow a hole right through my theory. But then I recalled the exceptionally negative effects of stress that my own species has repeatedly demonstrated. Apart from having waged war on one another for many thousands of years, some of today's emotionally distraught humans continue to make headlines by killing their immediate relatives, including their own children. If stress can cause people to commit such dreadful acts, why should the condition not affect wolves in similar ways?

By the time I left the wolf enclosure that night, I was once again convinced that my pheromone theory was eminently defensible and that it furnished one more reason why Isle Royale research should be better funded.

During the following week, a number of events occurred that so occupied my attention that they caused me to set aside further pheromone inquiry. The first involved Tundra, who had buried a four-inch-long piece of flank meat and, after we returned from our daily walk, proceeded to dig it up, an action that hardly merited more than a casual glance from me at first because it occurs with such regularity. But then I noticed that he was walking about the enclosure, holding one end of the meat with his incisors and simultaneously shaking his head abruptly up and down and then to left and right. I wondered why he was behaving in such a way and then realized he was offering me a wonderful example of applied intelligence. The damp meat had been buried in the ground, so it was covered with earth; Tundra was shaking it to get rid of the adhering soil, and I could actually see the bits of earth flying off each time the wolf shook the strip of meat. There was absolutely no doubt that Tundra was demonstrating conscious behavior, for when he and Taiga were younger and had buried pieces of meat, they had later eaten them without shaking them first. As a result, they had always sought to clean their mouths afterward, spitting out bits of dirt and grass, moving their tongues around their mouths, and drooling brown spittle. Now the wolf was cleaning the meat before eating it, and he was doing it remarkably well, for by the time he settled down to chew, very little earth was sticking to his food. Later, I was to see Taiga do the same thing, a practice they both stopped when snow fell and they could bury food in that natural refrigerator, where it remained clean until it was reclaimed later.

On November 10, Murray Palmer came to help me enlarge the wolf enclosure, our project having been too long delayed and now being most urgent, for winter was already upon us and the ground would soon be too hard for digging. Busy with a variety of jobs, I was not able to help Murray as much as I would have liked and I am most grateful to him for the way in which he tackled a hard, wet, and very muddy job. But I did spend time with pick and shovel, and between us, in pouring rain mixed with sleet, we completed the digging. When Murray returned home, I hired two workmen to help me complete the job, which we managed to do by November 19. By now, the snow was on the ground and the temperature had fallen to twenty degrees. When the last section of fence wire was stapled in place, I breathed a sigh of relief, for the wolves now had a large section of forest in which to play and shelter, a total of 52,000 square feet of territory.

The next morning, I opened several sections of the original fence and allowed Tundra and Taiga to enter their new range, which was something that they did with their usual caution, exploring new ground a little at a time, although by that same afternoon they had already started to remodel it in places by removing branches, chewing logs, digging under roots, and making a new entrance to a structure of cut trunks and evergreen boughs that I had asked Murray to make in the center of the wooded part of the enclosure so that the yearlings could find sanctuary inside it during winter storms.

The next morning, Sharon and I were greeted by two very active and enthusiastic young wolves when we arrived with their breakfast snack. Later, as we entered the pen and bent down to greet them, each kissed us on the mouth, causing me to realize for the first time that only wolves and Western humans love each other in this way. I also wondered: Who taught whom? This was later to remind me of the many other social similarities that exist between humans and wolves. And it caused me to wonder why those who seek to understand the nature of man do not study the wolf and compare their findings with the results of those researches into the behavior of humans and primates that have already been conducted. It appears that because primates are the animals most like us physically, students of the antecedents of mankind have become infatuated with these distant "cousins" of ours to the almost total exclusion of all other species.

There is probably much still to be learned by continuing to observe the behavior of apes, but those who concern themselves with the social interactions of humans cannot do better than to study the wolf, whose family system is more like our own than are the loosely knit group relationships of the primates. To the best of my knowledge, wolves have not yet been studied with this aim in mind. Jane Goodall and Hugo van Lawick did study hunting dogs, hyenas, and jackals in Africa, but it seems that they failed to seek, and thus to make, comparisons between the social regulations of these animals and those of chimpanzees, the study of which Goodall has pioneered. In any event, although the behavior of the hunting dog can be compared with that of the wolf, that of hyenas and jackals is notable more for its dissimilarities than for its affinities.

There is no doubt that wolves are united by humanlike family ties. Most usually, the Alpha male and female enter into a relationship during which they will mate only with each other, and although an occasional "divorce" is to be noted among them—as was the case with Shawano and Brigit—these are the exceptions rather than the rule, occurring with far less frequency than is the case in human societies today. Among primates, male-female relationships are quite different. Chimpanzees are notoriously promiscuous. When a female comes into estrus, she is mated by any and all males that can reach her. This means that when an infant is born, the identity of its natural father can never be determined. Perhaps this accounts for the fact that although males are generally protective of the infants, they have little to do with their upbringing; when males engage in their frantic and quite regular dominance displays, they may kill an infant chimpanzee if it gets in their way.

Gorillas are different again; they live in bands in which a dominant male mates with all the females in his harem and leaves the mothers to look after the infants. Vegetarian-insectivores, gorillas are, however, much more peaceful than the unpredictable chimpanzees, which practice cannibalism. Another of man's primate relatives, the orangutan, is a predominantly solitary creature when fully adult, a female mating with any male she happens to encounter during the period of estrus and continuing alone during her pregnancy and after the infant is born until the next mating period occurs, five or six years later, when the young orangutan is able to care for itself.

Conversely, wolves are extremely solicitous of their young. The fathers take an active part in their rearing

197

and education; they feed them, groom them, and protect them. Certainly no wolf would ever be guilty of harming one of its own pups, nor would any member of the family. Then, too, all members of a pack are closely united, even the lowest in rank, although, as has been noted, there are occasions when a subordinate wolf leaves the family of its own accord or because it is in the interest of the unit to banish it.

I am not suggesting here that comparative studies of primates and humans should not be made, but I would point out to those who engage in such research that the social relationships so far recorded for these animals are quite different from those that have been observed in humans and wolves.

Besides being the two most social species of terrestrial mammals, man and wolf are also the most adaptable. But primates have been unable to adapt to the many changes that have taken place in their environments from prehistoric times.

Although I have never encouraged our pups to hunt (as I did Matta and Wa, whom I raised with the intention of returning them to their natural environment), Tundra and Taiga demonstrated at an early age that they were inherently prepared for the life of the predator, at first stalking each other or lying in ambush, the one who was playing the part of hunter lying flat on its stomach, its haunches drawn up, ready to pounce on the one that was the supposed prey. After we began taking them for walks, they hunted in earnest, Tundra being the first to score when, despite being on a lead, he charged into a bush and caught a young sparrow. Taiga was next when she caught a snake, then a mouse. They were not yet three months old at this time.

After the large enclosure was completed, the pups hunted whenever opportunity presented itself, catching mice, voles, shrews, and occasionally birds. During the next spring they snapped up flies, mosquitoes, and dragonflies. Tundra, until he learned that he could not actually fly, frequently leaped at birds that were much too high for him to reach, and Taiga spent many hours digging at mouse and mole tunnels. Watching them carefully, I was able to note that although their genetic programming did not at first allow them to attain a high rate of success, they gradually built upon their innate skills, exercising their intelligence and showing themselves eminently able to learn from experience.

By January 1985, they had become experts. And although they did not eat what they killed, they could not resist the temptation to hunt, the contradiction rising from the fact that, although they were well fed, they were not responsible for the "kills" that supplied them with their daily rations and were therefore not expending the abundant energy with which they had been endowed. All predators *must* earn their own living. To do so, they must work hard on an almost full-time basis if they are to be adequately sustained. This means that when a predator is held captive, even from birth, its metabolic rate and energy levels will not allow it to become sedentary: *Mind and body must be continually challenged*, otherwise boredom will set in and on its heels will come stress, which will soon be followed by aberrant behavior, and, if not relieved in time, will result in death from metabolic breakdown.

In their natural world, and as soon as the pups are moved to their rendezvous, they hunt constantly, at first using each other as surrogate prey, as Tundra and Taiga did, then hunting clumsily, seeking mice and other small animals. The difference betweeen such cubs and our own is that wild pups eat what they catch because, despite the care lavished on them by the pack, they frequently must go hungry.

By the time the cubs begin to go hunting with the pack, usually in late August or early September, they have already become adept at finding and catching small animals, acquiring their skills in the nursery without benefit of adult tutelage. But when they set out with the pack on their first hunt for large prey, the young wolves are little more than spectators during the actual kill, although they actively participate in the chase. Gradually, as they grow older, stronger, and more sure of themselves, they learn how to attack the various prey animals upon which the pack subsists.

In North America, wolves prey on moose, caribou,

elk, deer, sheep, goats, bison (in a few locations, principally in Wood Buffalo National Park, which is located in northern Alberta and the southern Northwest Territories), beaver, birds such as grouse, ducks, and geese, and on a variety of small animals. In the far north, their principal prey is the caribou; in the boreal forest regions, moose will probably form their major prey, although in some locations moose, deer, and sometimes elk are found together, thus offering wider selection and opportunity.

Since wolves are supreme opportunists, they will take whatever they can get most easily, including domestic stock, but nature designed them for running and equipped them with the size and stamina most suited for killing large prey. Indeed, it can be said that the wolf taught the moose how to run—or, conversely, that the moose taught the wolf how to chase! However this may be, large animals that are in good condition can always run faster than wolves, which might suggest that the predators are at a disadvantage. Nevertheless, although a wolf may attain an all-out speed of about thirty miles an hour—which is about ten miles an hour slower than a moose or a deer—it has the stamina to trot after its prey for hours on end, tiring the quarry and eventually slowing it down, when it may then be killed.

When the quarry is moose, it has been calculated that wolves must chase between eleven and thirteen animals before they manage to kill one. For deer, the estimate is between eight and eleven; the odds are similar for caribou and elk, but far higher for bison.

When hunting such quarry, wolves usually stay together, but occasionally, because of terrain, a pack may split around a natural barrier. When this happens, it is possible that some of the wolves will accidentally outflank the prey and will thus be in a position to make a quick kill, although this is the exception rather than the rule. But when hunting small prey, such as beaver, hares, birds, and the like, wolves resort to stalking and ambushing, sometimes working alone, and sometimes in concert with one or more other members of the pack.

In suitable habitats, wolves spend most of their time hunting the large prey animals, for though such quarry is more difficult to bring down, the prize yields enough food to keep the pack satisfied for several days.

Large, adult members of the deer family must be attacked on the run, for they are too powerful and dangerous to be seized if they stand at bay. Moose, caribou, and even deer use either of their front feet as weapons, stab-kicking at a wolf and often killing it with one slash of the pointed hoof. If a quarry so engaged is attacked from the rear by another wolf, it will kick with a back hoof, much as a horse will do; and if such a blow connects it will send an attacker flying, perhaps killing the hunter or injuring it so severely that it will die later. In this regard, it has been claimed by some authors that wolves always kill an injured companion. This is pure nonsense! There are more than enough sighting records to prove that wolves will feed wounded pack members until they are either well enough to resume their place in the pack, or until they die from their injuries.

If a moose, elk, or caribou stands at bay, a pack will surround it, testing it occasionally by making bluff charges in the hope of stampeding it. If such an animal refuses to run, and many of them do, the pack will give up after about twenty minutes, leaving in quest of easier prey. When they encounter an animal that will run and they can eventually attack it, the wolves always aim for the rump or flank in an attempt to make the quarry stumble and fall. Because wolves have very powerful jaws, and teeth that interlock following a bite (rather like the jaws of a closed trap), the hunters can hang on to their target and bring it down sooner or later, at which point the entire pack piles in and the kill is made quickly. Sometimes, however, a wolf may miss the rear of the animal and secure a hold on its neck or shoulder; if it cannot unlock its jaws in time, the quarry may dash it against a tree, almost certainly killing it.

Tundra and Taiga will never have to earn their living in this way, but I have little doubt that they could now do so if necessary, although at first they would probably go hungry quite frequently and would spend most of their time hunting smaller animals. Sooner or later, however, they would learn through trial and error and would then

201

be capable of killing large prey, provided that they stayed together. A lone wolf is always at a disadvantage when trying to bring down a big, *healthy* animal, but it can kill the old, sick, injured, and young.

Through nature, through the evolutionary continuum and ecological relatedness and interdependence of all things, we are as much a part of the wolf as the wolf is a part of us. And as we destroy or demean nature, wolves, or any creature, great or small, we do no less to ourselves.
—Michael W. Fox, *The Soul of the Wolf*

TWELVE

The winter of 1984–85 was long and severe in our part of Ontario. Temperatures fell in December to thirty-five degrees below zero, and the snows piled higher and higher as the nights lengthened; but although the business of splitting stove wood and clearing pathways through the white blanket that insulated the land considerably increased my workload, the beauty of our forests and the high glee with which Tundra and Taiga greeted the hibernal changes more than made up for the additional tasks that were imposed on me.

I remember the way that the wolves reacted to the first really heavy fall of snow during a morning in early December. There was no wind. The flakes, each as large as a fingernail, descended lazily, fluttering like small and aimless butterflies and landing as gently as thistledown, every one individually noticeable, all of them together forming a white screen that softened the outlines of the entire landscape.

The moment we left the house, carrying their morning snack, Tundra and Taiga rushed to the fence, their fur covered in snow that flew off in small clouds as they danced excitedly while waiting for us to arrive.

Entering the enclosure after we had fed them, we were greeted briefly but exuberantly before the cubs began running and leaping aimlessly, pausing now and again to nose into the snow, then rolling in it, all four legs in the air and kicking frantically, only to jump up and start the whole process all over again, as exuberantly as before. Presently, Tundra stopped dashing about and began to catch snowflakes, snapping to left and right with head slightly raised, evidently surprised when each snow-star that he caught disappeared the instant his jaws closed on it. Taiga immediately copied his actions; but whereas Tundra became thoughtfully puzzled when the flakes vanished, Taiga showed herself to be completely exasperated by her inability to *bite* a single one of those elusive targets. Impatient as she is, she quickly gave vent to her frustrations, leaping upward frantically, snapping rapidly, and yapping, her voice shrill and discordant.

Meanwhile, Tundra appeared to realize that the flakes were related to the snow upon which he and his sister had been quenching their thirst. Having formed this conclusion, he came trotting toward us, now and then catching a flake or two as he traveled and demonstrating that he was tasting each droplet of melt by the way he moved his mouth and licked his lips. Upon arriving at my side, he flopped down, lifting a back leg and soliciting my attention. This caused Taiga to abandon her fruitless assaults on the snowflakes in favor of dashing up to Sharon so as to leap at her affectionately; she did this with far too much abandon, in the process scratching my wife with her sharp claws.

Seeing that Sharon's face had been rather badly scraped and that blood was flowing from her bottom lip, I grabbed Taiga by the scruff and forced her to lie on her side, whereupon the overenthusiastic young wolf became instantly contrite; but because I wanted her to understand that she had taken too much of a liberty with the Alpha female of our pack, I shook her scruff and scolded her sternly. Taiga whined pitifully, wet herself, and sought to lick me; but before I could release her so that we all might "kiss and make up," Tundra rushed over and fastened his jaws on her neck, his great fangs brushing my fingers as he sought to reinforce my authority by pinning her head to the snowy ground while emitting a low growl.

When Sharon noticed what was going on, she forgot her pain and interceded on Taiga's behalf, scolding Tundra and me and telling us that Taiga had not meant to be so rough, a fact of which I was well aware. In any event, having disciplined the recalcitrant young wolf, I forgave her. So did Tundra. The four of us then had a "love-in" during which Taiga, perforce, had to lick Sharon's face in her inimitable style. While his sister was thus engaged, Tundra positioned himself behind Sharon's crouching form, raised himself slowly and carefully on his back legs, and settled both his great paws on her shoulders, holding that stance as he dab-licked my wife's forehead. A few minutes later, the young wolves ran off to play in the snow and we left the enclosure. Sharon watched the cubs as I closed the gate, then turned to me.

"They look as if they are in their element," my wife remarked.

"They *are* in their element," I replied. Walking toward the house, I reminded Sharon that wolves thrive in winter, provided they can get enough to eat. Indeed, they actually enjoy the cold and play in it even when fully adult.

In the early autumn, wolves begin to grow their thick, woolly underfur, and their long, rather coarse guard hairs become glossy. Soon afterward, they are garbed in coats so thick that they add about a third to their bulk, raiment that makes them impervious to the cold and keeps them dry even when they must enter water, for the underfur is made impermeable by natural oils.

Our cubs were no exception. By October they had started to grow their new finery, and they appeared deceptively large in it. Tundra showed areas of coppery brown on his back and sides; Taiga lost most of the attractive russet tones that had decorated her face, flanks, and legs; she was now light fawn, almost white in places. But because young wolves do not get their permanent colors until they begin to molt in May and June of the following spring, the tones they acquire during their first winter make it impossible to determine what their adult

205

coloration is going to be. Despite the browns that showed up in Tundra's coat, I felt fairly sure that he would revert to black during the spring molt, for this is usual in pups that are born black. In Taiga's case, however, although I thought that she might return to at least some of the colors that she had exhibited as a pup, I was far less certain.

The heavy snowfall that had so delighted the cubs was the harbinger of true winter, ushering in temperatures that caused the thermometer to plunge well below zero two days after the skies had cleared and allowed the sun to shine again upon the wilderness. During daylight, the differences between sun and shade temperatures were enormous. On one occasion, at noon, while the thermometer on the north side of our log house registered ten degrees below zero, I hung a spare thermometer in the direct sunlight striking the south side of the barn. The mercury climbed to sixty-seven degrees *above* zero within three minutes.

At night, of course, it was a different story. Under clear skies, the temperature dived as soon as the sun fell behind the trees; it continued to drop until it reached its lowest point at about 3:00 or 4:00 A.M. Between times, the blue-black heavens were filled with numberless stars, the constant sparkling of which was periodically complemented by the phosphorescent displays of the northern lights.

During those nights, I would often go outside, enter the enclosure, and squat in the snow, flanked by the wolves. Silently, communicating through body contact, we would watch the red-green stars and the coruscating aurora borealis and we would become as one under the blazing heavens. Sometimes I would be compelled to howl; and even as I prepared to do so, Tundra and Taiga would be equally urged, their ululating songs rising above my puny voice and echoing throughout the wilderness.

Regardless of the cold, the wolves slept in the open, disdaining the barn and the brush shelter that Murray Palmer had made for them; their bedding places were easy for us to find when we entered the enclosure every morning, because their body heat always melted the snow and ice, creating saucerlike depressions about three feet in diameter. The pups never slept in the same place twice in succession, although when an old depression had been properly covered by new snow, it would be used again, the reason being that by the time they awakened in the morning the melted area had turned to ice, its hard surface preventing the wolves from settling themselves comfortably on it again the following night. Like dogs, wolves trample down a sleep area by circling over it a few times, then they lie down and shuffle themselves into position, their hips and shoulders pressing on the snow or ground and creating slight indentations that fit the contours of these bony parts. Curled up, their noses covered by their bushy tails, they then sleep comfortably.

Tundra and Taiga often slept so close together that the two saucers they melted took the shape of a figure eight; but even when their bodies were not actually touching, no more than a foot separated their bedding places. Usually, the presence of only two saucers made it evident that the cubs had slept undisturbed in the same location, but some mornings we would find four depressions, two in one part of the enclosure and two in another. Such evidence told us that the wolves had been awakened and had evidently investigated the cause of their disturbance.

On Christmas day, Sharon prepared a special meal for Tundra and Taiga, arranging the food so artistically in their bowls that I was prompted to ask if it was for us or for the cubs. This reminded us of an evening in September during Alison's visit when we had eaten the meat intended for the wolves and they had dined on our freshly ground sirloin of beef that was supposed to have been made into hamburgers and grilled outdoors. The error was not discovered until after we had enjoyed the "wolf burgers," when Sharon remarked that she had been surprised to notice that the ground beef bought that day for our use had turned very dark by late afternoon. My daughter then realized that she had unwittingly taken the wolf meat out of the refrigerator and handed it to my wife, who had used it to prepare the hamburgers. None of us experienced any bad aftereffects, however. In fact, Tundra and Taiga most often eat the same meats that we ourselves consume, the only difference being that they usually eat theirs raw.

In February, the cubs showed signs of restlessness and

207

howled frequently at night, which suggested that although they were not yet sexually mature, they were experiencing some preadolescent hormonal changes in concert with the breeding season. Then, too, wild wolves and coyotes often howled from within the surrounding forests, and their cries, no matter how faint, invariably elicited replies from our wards.

During February's full moon and under clear skies, the cubs became especially restless, at first playing excitedly while uttering high-pitched barks that were punctuated by companionable growls, but soon after midnight they began to howl repeatedly. We were in bed, but I got up, dressed, and went outside, using the side door of our house, which is not visible from the enclosure. I wanted to watch and listen, if possible, undetected by the cubs.

The moonlight was considerably enhanced by the snow, offering excellent visibility as I walked quietly to stand in the shadow of the garage, from there watching through field glasses. Tundra and Taiga were sitting side by side at the far end of the open part of the enclosure. They were staring intently toward the northwest, their bodies rigid, their ears pricked forward. At first the night was utterly silent, but after a few moments the howl of a wolf rose above the forest. In near unison, our wolves responded, their calls harmonizing with the more distant song of their wild relative. I timed the performance. It lasted one minute and forty-seven seconds and ended as abruptly as it had begun, the three wolves becoming silent almost simultaneously, as though by prearrangement, although our two lagged fractionally behind the forest-dweller.

I had thought that the cubs were completely unaware of my presence, for they had not even glanced briefly in my direction when I stationed myself close to one corner of the garage. But now they both turned and trotted toward the gate; upon reaching it, they stood and stared directly at me, or at least into the shadows in which I stood. Then they whined and began to dance expectantly, so I left my shelter and walked down to them, entering the enclosure and squatting between them, stroking them and being licked in turn. Ten minutes later I returned home, glad to be back in the warmth. The temperature outside had fallen to thirty-two degrees below zero. Back in bed, I read for a time before turning out the light, but as I began to doze, the wolves howled again. If there is a better way to go to sleep, I don't know it.

Spring was late arriving in 1985. And it was a wet season, a period during which temperatures rose and fell repeatedly at first, one day showing the promise of melting snow and new plant growth, the next bringing fresh avalanches of white. But if the humans started to get a bit fed up when April was ushered in with a snowstorm, Tundra and Taiga welcomed the changeable weather. They especially enjoyed the new, wet snow, rolling in it, play-fighting, and generally having a wonderful time, quite oblivious of the fact that they greeted us every morning soaking wet and shockingly covered in mud, much of which they shook on us as we squatted outside the fence while giving them their morning snack. After such encounters, we would return to the house spattered by nearly black mire and soaked to the skin, although the pleasure we derived from being with the yearling wolves and watching the enthusiasm with which they greeted the change in seasons could not be dispelled by dirt or moisture.

On April 27, the cubs were one year old. Sharon prepared them each a birthday dish consisting of such delicacies as slices of boiled ham, salami, liver pâté, and freshly ground hamburger, the whole enhanced by tastefully arrayed raw chicken wings and decorated by sprigs of parsley! As though wishing to celebrate the birth of two such wonderful beings, the day dawned sunny and warm and two robins appeared on the lawn. Then the ravens came, six of them settling in the trees within the enclosure, there to whistle and coo and croak with great abandon. I accused Sharon of being overly imaginative when she maintained that the birds were singing "Happy Birthday" to our wolves.

The weather continued to improve. When May arrived, new buds showed on the trees; wildflowers started to appear. So did *hordes* of blackflies. Fortunately, the birds had also arrived by this time: tree and barn swallows, warblers, sparrows, and flycatchers, all of them feasting on the bloodsuckers; but they left more than enough to pester the wolves and their human companions.

Now Tundra and Taiga spent most of the day inside the barn, having soon learned that blackflies infrequently bite in semidarkness. At night, when the pestiferous gnats quelled their bloodthirsty desires in favor of sheltering on plants and grasses, the cubs busied themselves outside, playing, digging, chewing up old logs, and frequently interrupting their activities in order to howl.

Toward the middle of the month, Taiga began to molt, her thick underfur coming out in handfuls when Sharon brushed her, a task that my wife performed with dedication because she saved the woolly fur, which she intended to spin and to weave on her floor loom so that it would eventually become a part of some mysterious garment, the design of which was not to be divulged to me.

Taiga greatly enjoyed the grooming. She would lie on her side, eyes closed, while Sharon plied the wire brush assiduously, clearing the fur off after four or five strokes and stuffing each little bundle into a pocket. Tundra, whose coat was still tight, would often try to eat the brush, or would otherwise interfere by biting Taiga, who, not unnaturally, would become annoyed and snarl at her brother. I don't know just how much wool Sharon got from Taiga, except that it gradually filled two shopping bags while the wolf became sleeker and looked appreciably smaller. In due course, she emerged wearing a coat that was the color of butterscotch on the back, sides, and flanks, and russet behind the ears, forehead, and legs. Most attractive.

Tundra began to molt three weeks after his sister. He, too, was brushed by Sharon, although much of his wool was rejected because, being a male, his guard hairs were more numerous, longer, and coarser and they became inextricably mixed with the wool. Guard hairs, I am told, have to be removed from the fur if this is to be spun; this intelligence may have gladdened Tundra's heart, for he appeared to think that being brushed was beneath his dignity; he demonstrated this by seeking to bite the brush.

At this time we again began to get visitors. Some

were repeaters and known to Tundra and Taiga, who always remembered them and greeted them profusely. Others were strangers. Most of these were also given enthusiastic welcomes. But one afternoon the arrival of a married couple elicited a surprising reaction from Taiga.

At first, both wolves rushed up to the fence, demonstrating their usual eagerness to greet the newcomers, but when we arrived at the wire and Tundra leaped up to greet the female visitor, Taiga began to growl at him. As the male wolf persisted, his sister became more and more aggressive, biting him, pushing him down with her front paws, and even causing him to flop on his side and whine submissively while seeking to lick her. Unlike the two men whose stress had caused Tundra to react aggressively, Taiga clearly objected to the attention that her brother was trying to lavish on the woman. Although the wolf was directing her aggression at her brother, I thought it best to bring the visit to an end. Thinking about Taiga's behavior, I could only conclude that for some reason she had become jealous of the visitor.

Two weeks later, another couple arrived. They, too, were strangers to the wolves. On this occasion, it was Tundra who reacted aggressively toward Taiga when she sought to greet the man. Once again I had to interrupt the visit.

To date, the wolves have reacted in this way toward six visitors whom they have never seen before. Tundra has become aggressive toward Taiga on four occasions when she has sought to jump up and lick a male's extended hand; Taiga has twice been aggressive toward Tundra when he has tried to greet a female visitor.

I hold my initial conclusion: the wolves become jealous and direct their aggression toward each other rather than toward the object of their jealousy. But why is it that only certain individuals produce this reaction? If the wolves continue to demonstrate such selective jealousy, I hope that it will be possible to question the visitors without causing them embarrassment, for I am convinced that individual hormonal metabolism *during the time of contact* is responsible for the negative behavior that both wolves have demonstrated. Meanwhile, I am encouraging

211

those visitors who have already been made welcome by Tundra and Taiga to return periodically so that we may see if the behavior of the wolves changes at any particular time. In this regard, talking with Mike Collins about the matter, we decided that since his wife, Lou, had not seen the wolves since they were two months old, he would bring her to visit them so that we might monitor their behavior.

When Mike and Lou arrived, they walked down to the enclosure, but although almost a full year had elapsed since the cubs had seen Lou—and then on one occasion only—they immediately remembered her and made a great fuss over her. There the matter rests.

I have no doubt that jealousy is responsible for the other reactions and I feel confident that an individual's hormonal activity at the time of arrival furnishes the scent that causes the jealousy, but there is much yet to be investigated. Beth Duman's experience with Nahani supports the jealousy theory.

To this writing, Tundra and Taiga have received 109 visitors; only eight of them have produced negative behavior. Significantly, when Tundra reacted aggressively upon detecting stress in the two male visitors mentioned earlier, Taiga retreated from them, ears back and tail between her legs, leaving Tundra to deal with them on his own. Furthermore, both wolves become mildly jealous of each other when Sharon and I are with them and we stop to caress one or the other. This is a twice-daily occurrence that has been taking place since they were only two months old; it demonstrates sibling rivalry. Usually, as soon as one of us bends to pat one wolf, the other wolf rushes up and seeks our attention, at the same time growling at its sibling and biting it in a controlled fashion. But if only one of us is in the enclosure, there is no rivalry between them; they are then quite likely to station themselves on either side of Sharon or me so as to be petted simultaneously. Often under such circumstances, after the initial greeting, one wolf will go and lie down, perhaps ten feet away, content to rest while the other is getting attention. This is something that neither of them will do when we are both in the enclosure. Yet, at feeding times, neither is the least bit jealous of the other. In the morning, they still maintain their positions, Taiga in front of me and Tundra in front of Sharon. During the afternoon feed, they continue to trade bowls, or to feed out of the same one. At this time, also, if one comes to us to be caressed, the other doesn't seem to object. And during the frequent play periods that we enjoy daily, neither of them exhibits rivalry and will often take turns at chasing and being chased.

Our wolves are now fourteen months old, and although each has strengthened the early characteristics that we observed in them, their individual personalities remain the same. There are occasions when both are stimulated at the same time regardless of weather, hour of the day, or any other influence that we can detect. In such a mood, they leap joyfully at us, nose into our clothing, lick us, and play-bite our fingers, but do so softly. Then they dash away, chasing one another, only to return to us, smiling and exuberant. On other occasions, especially after they have been particularly active during the night, they are sleepy and very loving, inviting caresses and refraining from competing with each other. Then there are the times when they are seriously preoccupied with their own affairs. It may be that a squirrel has perched itself high up in a tree within their enclosure and sits there shrieking at the wolves while eating spruce-cone seeds; or they may have found a fresh mole tunnel and are attempting to capture the animal. They become very interested when ducks land on our stream, or when they see one of our beavers swimming on the surface. Once, last spring, a large beaver surfaced within ten feet of the enclosure while we were walking with the cubs, and although the big rodent submerged quickly, Tundra and Taiga remained near the spot, waiting for it to reappear with the kind of patience that only a predator demonstrates. The beaver wisely kept away.

Apart from those occasions when they are so stimulated that nothing seems able to dampen their enthusiasm, I have noticed that they are as much affected by the weather as we are. On high-pressure days when the sun is strong and a cool breeze is present, they become extremely active and playful. Conversely, during periods of low pressure they are quiet, gentle, and seemingly lazy, and they yawn a lot, gaping wide and stretching their bodies at the same time. On really hot days they sleep a good deal, seeking out shady locations or retreating into the barn. The heat also depresses their appetites and they are more inclined to be solitary.

Daily, the wolves demonstrate some new behavioral trait the reason for which is often impossible to determine, even though I have been studying the species for so long; and although I am always intrigued *and* frustrated when I can't understand their motives, I am not surprised. In fact, at those times when we cannot detect the underlying motives that prompt a particular kind of behavior, I do not consider that we have failed, but rather that we have once again established that wolves are as individualistic as humans and that it is folly to ascribe to all members of the species those personal traits observed only in some of them. It is not so much the ways in which wolves act, but the reasons for their actions. It is easy to tell when a wolf is content, happy, excited, afraid, or aggressive, for they all demonstrate these emotions in more or less similar ways. The challenge is to be able to know why they are so motivated. Many behaviorists have all too readily formed hard-and-fast conclusions that purport to explain fully the behavioral motives of all wolves, but if it is borne in mind that sociologists and psychologists are still unable to understand all the personal motivations that prompt behavior in humans, the reason for our failure to properly understand wolves (or any other species of animal) soon becomes apparent. Western man has for too long thought of himself as a super-being who is in no way to be compared with the "brute beasts" with whom he must share the world environment. As a result, he has persistently denied that animals think, have emotions, and are capable of making individual decisions.

Such egotistic bias has caused many biologists and especially behaviorists to think of animals as purely mechanical creatures to be studied and described in clinical ways. These people consider as odious any attempt to compare the habits and behavior of their "subjects" with those of humans, an attitude manifested in the contempt in which they hold those who dare to make such com-

214

parisons, accusing them of anthropomorphism. The term is borrowed from two Greek words, *anthropos*, meaning "man," and *morphos*, meaning "shape." Translated into plain language, anthropomorphism ascribes human form or attributes to a being or thing that is not human, especially to a deity; it is therefore largely misused when it is applied to those of us who discuss animals in proper English.

When an investigator painstakingly avoids using human terms in order to describe the deportment of animals, such a person most often produces scientific papers that are almost incomprehensible to laymen and can only partially be understood by a colleague, even after several readings. At the same time, the champions of abstract description frequently confuse the perceptual abilities of humans with the perceptual capabilities of animals, which are much greater than our own. Thus they find it impossible to measure the total reality of life.

We cannot smell the world of the wolf, we cannot hear it, we certainly do not see it in its proper perspective, we cannot taste it, and we do not know how to come to terms with it. Instead, we blunder through it, believing that we are the masters of creation and refusing to accept that the "lower animals" are constantly in touch with the realities of the universe. If such an approach persists, humankind will continue to defy nature and will surely fail to secure the peace that it so desperately needs. But the wolf can teach us. With its uncanny perceptions and a social system that closely resembles our own, this much-persecuted animal can put us back in touch with our own realities, once we begin to understand and respect it.

Sharon and I live with Tundra and Taiga in this awareness. We know that in teaching us about themselves, they are also teaching us about ourselves and about our own kind. We share life with them in full trust. We love them, and we know that they love us; we *try* to understand them, and they most definitely understand us.

Sometimes we are asked, "What are you going to do with your wolves?"

We reply that we do not intend to *do* anything with

them. We are simply going to live with them. And we hope that they will continue to teach us about the realities of life.

AFTERWORD

Killing for sport, for fur, or to increase a hunter's success by slaughtering predators is totally abhorrent to me. I deem such behavior to be barbaric, a symptom of the social sickness that causes our species to make war against itself at regular intervals with weapons whose killing capacities have increased horrendously since man first made use of the club—weapons that today are continuing to be "improved."

When I think of these things, I cannot help but compare the behavior of wolves with that of my own kind, inevitably finding that the social interactions of humans suffer greatly by comparison.

As I complete the writing of this book, biologists, politicians, and bureaucrats in Minnesota, British Columbia, the Yukon Territory, and Alaska are working with hunters and hunting outfitters to bring about the destruction of a very large number of wolves, animals that for the most part inhabit wilderness areas and whose only "crime" is that they are living as nature intended them to live. Since I am quite sure that the killing of wolves

217

in all those regions will not have been brought to a complete halt by the time this book is published, I shall now review the programs that are either already in force or are about to be instituted in the areas in question.

MINNESOTA

This is the only one of the lower forty-eight states to have a major wolf population, the numbers of which have been estimated at about 1,200. In 1973 the United States passed an Endangered Species Act in which the wolf was included; as a result, the animal was afforded federal protection. This did not, however, satisfy the state. Through its Department of Natural Resources, it began to pressure the U.S. Fish and Wildlife Service of the Department of the Interior, asking that wolf management be turned over to Minnesota to allow the DNR to implement wolf-control programs, for which hunters, trappers, ranchers, and some politicians were clamoring.

Until 1983, the Department of the Interior turned down all the DNR's requests, but in August of that year, during the tenure of Secretary of the Interior James Watt, the U.S. Fish and Wildlife Service proposed to change the regulations governing the conservation of wolves in Minnesota as follows:

> In certain areas of the state the amendment will allow a carefully controlled taking of wolves by the public and by designated State and Federal employees. The taking will be allowed primarily in areas of recurring wolf depredation of livestock, and will not be permitted in areas where it might affect wolf recolonization of Wisconsin. The wolf population in the affected zones of Minnesota will be maintained at or above the level recommended in the Eastern Timber Wolf Recovery Plan.

Before 1983, however, the FWS had proposed amendments to the Endangered Species Act as it applied to Minnesota wolves, and it had announced that comments would be accepted for or against these changes. Many protests were made, and the service modified its proposals. Even so, conservationists took the matter to court.

Federal district judge Miles Lord ruled in favor of the plaintiffs in January 1984, finding that allowing trapping of a threatened species that has not overpopulated its range violated the Endangered Species Act:

> *Excerpt from Endangered Species Act: Background of the law:*
> The Endangered Species Act of 1974 (Title 15, U.S. Code, Sections 1531–1543) is the legal embodiment of popular and congressional concern with this Nation's and the world's natural environment. Congress has recognized that various species of our fauna and flora have been rendered extinct as a consequence of economical and population growth and a corresponding encroachment on wildlife and its habitat untempered by adequate concern for conservation. Congress has further recognized that other species are so few in number that they are on the verge of extinction. The Act, then, is the legal recognition of this sad state of affairs and represents the people's desire to provide a way to reverse the situation.

The first round went to the conservationists. But on October 10, 1984, the U.S. Department of the Interior petitioned a panel of three Eighth Circuit Court of Appeals judges to overturn Judge Lord's decision. Interior's attorney, Dianne H. Kelly of the Justice Department, claimed that Judge Lord had misinterpreted the law. Kelly told the panel of justices that the U.S. Government did not seek the changes "because it's fun to go out and kill wolves." Rather, she claimed, the institution of a sport trapping season, commercializing the animal's fur, and turning over the management of Minnesota wolves to the state's Department of Natural Resources were *conservation measures* designed to help the wolves! The appeals court ruled two to one in favor of upholding Judge Lord's decision, and Minneapolis lawyer Brian O'Neill, who handled the case on behalf of a coalition of fourteen conservation and environmental organizations, called the verdict "a victory for wolves," an opinion not shared by Joseph Alexander, commissioner of the Minnesota Department of Natural Resources. "I think the wolf is the loser in this decision," said Mr. Alexander. "Wolves are being indiscriminately killed now without control."

This comment, coming from the chief of an agency that is responsible for the control and protection of the state's natural resources, led Brian O'Neill to say that he was unable to understand the argument. "They [the DNR] won't manage the [wolf] population unless they can have sport trapping. If they were honestly interested in the wolf, they would control poaching. That Minnesota does nothing about it is a national disgrace," Mr. O'Neill concluded.

Conservationists believed that the Department of the Interior might appeal the decision before the U.S. Supreme Court, but in July 1985, I telephoned the U.S. Fish and Wildlife Service in Washington and was told that no appeal would be launched.

In Minnesota the wolf is actually listed as *threatened*, a category that the Endangered Species Act defines as "any species which is likely to become an endangered species within the foreseeable future throughout all or a significant portion of its range." But neither federal nor state authorities have so far been able to protect wolves in the state from being illegally killed by hunters, trappers, and ranchers. The state occupies 90,009 square miles of land, of which 57,227 square miles are open to hunting and trapping. It has been estimated that at least 250 wolves are illegally killed each year, many of them being shot during the hunting season. This is not surprising when it is considered that in 1982 alone, the state licensed 451,000 hunters, or an average of eight gunners per square mile of available land.

Wolves are not curtailing deer numbers in the state. In 1980, Minnesota hunters killed 77,097 deer. I have no figures for 1982 or 1983, but in the latter year, a reported total of 12,344 deer were killed on state highways (something in the order of 50 percent of highway kills are not reported and the animals die unnoticed in the forest). These statistics tell me that there is room for both hunters and wolves in Minnesota, especially now that deer populations are definitely on the increase, a fact that was noted by *Sports Afield* magazine in its July 1981 issue in a regular feature entitled "Worldwild Hunter." In a four-and-a-half-inch story, the magazine notes that Minnesota white-tailed deer populations have been making a "striking" comeback since 1971, a time when hunting was stopped because deer populations had crashed. The magazine suggests that out-of-state hunters should consider Minnesota as a source of trophy animals.

Why, then, should Washington have wished to alter the rules of its own Endangered Species Act? On the face of it, the official reason is that wolves are killing domestic stock, but according to one Fish and Wildlife Service biologist, only about thirty to thirty-five wolves attack livestock each year and, says this official, many cases of livestock depredation occur because of poor farming practices. In other words, the problem of wolves killing cattle is not serious. This was confirmed by the Fish and Wildlife Service in the very proposal that sought to change the wolf rules in Minnesota. The *Federal Register*, volume 48, number 155, published August 10, 1983, states: "Plainly, wolf depredation of livestock—sheep, poultry and cattle—does occur, but it is uncommon enough behavior in the species as a whole to be called aberrant." To return to my earlier questions: Why change the rules in order to be able to kill wolves? There can be only one answer: political pressure exerted by those who hate wolves and who want to shoot more and more deer.

BRITISH COLUMBIA

The war on wolves that was declared in British Columbia by that province's Minister of the Environment shocked conservationists in Canada, the United States, and Europe, and drew severe criticism from professional biologists. Here again, politics and lobbying are at the root of the matter, and inasmuch as Anthony Brummet, the British Columbia government's choice as environment minister, was elected by voters in the region where the wolves are being killed, it seems clear that this man responded to pressure from these interests.

Events in the province were set in motion in 1983, when, out of the blue, the government announced a "predator management program" aimed at killing 80 percent of the wolves living in the Peace River–Omineca region of the province, an area of deep wilderness that lies on the northwest flank of the Rocky Mountains and extends westward to the border of the Yukon Territory

221

and northeastward to the boundary of the Northwest Territories. None of the wolves that were killed in early 1984 ranged anywhere near any community. Indeed, the region has few towns and villages, and anyone who sought to ranch in that wilderness would be doomed to failure, for the land, the weather, and the vegetation are totally unsuitable for the proper rearing of domestic stock.

To save money, the British Columbia government became a party to a scheme that must surely be unique in the history of wildlife management when it agreed to accept wolf-killing money raised by a lottery that urged people to buy a ticket, and help to kill wolves by doing so, and perhaps win a trip to Zimbabwe, a proper white *bwana makubwa* hunting safari! The raffle was sponsored by the British Columbia Wildlife Federation and by northern guide outfitters. In addition, the Foundation for North American Wild Sheep—whose members helped to kill almost 1,500 sheep in the United States in 1980—donated $100,000 to help the British Columbia government's wolf-kill fund, the three sponsoring groups contributing a minimum of $200,000 to the ill-conceived plan.

Protests were sent to Minister Brummet and to the British Columbia Government by a great many individuals and organizations. The Canadian Nature Federation protested and urged its members to do the same, commenting publicly in its magazine, *Nature Canada*:

BUY A TICKET; KILL A WOLF; WIN A TRIP: WILDLIFE MANAGEMENT, B.C. STYLE We were amazed to learn of a raffle to raise funds for a massive wolf kill north of Fort St. John, British Columbia. The B.C. Wildlife Federation and the Northern B.C. Guides Association have sponsored a raffle to pay some $100,000 to the B.C. Environment Department to shoot as many as 400 wolves from helicopters. The intent is to increase numbers of elk, moose and caribou.

The Wildlife Society of Canada and the Wildlife Biologists' Section of the Canadian Society of Biologists then wrote to Brummet asking him to "provide any documentation upon which your Ministry's program has been developed. Be aware of our concern that the role of biology in this controversy be accurately presented.''

After receiving a news release from Brummet's department and some documentation of the British Columbia government's claims, the biologists reviewed the facts and sent the following to the environment minister:

WOLF CONTROL PROGRAMS IN
NORTHEASTERN BRITISH COLUMBIA
POSITION STATEMENT

There is no *biological* basis or *biological* justification for the wolf control programs currently being conducted in northeastern British Columbia.

This is the major conclusion of an assessment conducted by an *ad hoc* committee comprising representatives from the Wildlife Society of Canada and the Wildlife Biologists' Section of the Canadian Society of Zoologists, and endorsed by a majority of their respective Executives. . . . The assessment of available research reports found no evidence that the decline in ungulate populations "corresponded to increased numbers of wolves" nor "that a reduction in the numbers of wolves can reverse the decline in numbers of prey animals." Similarly, the Committee found no indication of increased mortality in wolves associated with the current declines in prey populations. Nor was it apparent "that other measures to protect and enhance wildlife populations . . . will fail unless predator control is also included."

The research reports provided by the Minister provided evidence which is consistent with a decline in ungulate populations since 1975, a decline which is correlated with a succession of winters of above average severity. It cannot be concluded, therefore, that the effects of factors such as severe winters have been minimal, as stated in the News Release. In fact, a 1981 report from the same ministry . . . attributed the decline in ungulate numbers specifically to habitat changes, hunting pressure [by humans] and severe winters.

The position statement concludes with the comment: "Our concern as professional wildlife biologists is that the science of wildlife biology has been misrepresented in the Minister's News Release, i.e., that documents provided with the News Release do not support the Minister's statements. Such misrepresentation compromises the role of wildlife biologists in the management process.''

223

The clear-cut, amply documented rebuttal of Brummet's statements, which the biologists sent to the minister, was dated February 1984. It did not stop the killing. Committed, fearful of losing face, the British Columbia government dug its trenches even deeper. Before spring came to the region, the wolf slaughterers had gunned down 283 wolves in the Muskwa and Kechika regions. Then, in December of 1984, the killing began again. But this time the kill area had been expanded. In the Kechika region, some 250 kilometers northwest of Fort Nelson, which is entirely composed of primal wilderness, the government has doubled the kill area to 18,400 square kilometers; and in the Muskwa region, about seventy kilometers south of the town of Fort Nelson, the kill zone has increased 50 percent to include 19,000 square kilometers.

Ray Halliday, assistant director of the British Columbia environment ministry's wildlife branch, made the following statement to the Vancouver *Sun* daily newspaper in early December: "Our objective is to reduce the density of wolves in both regions from one wolf per 26 to 31 square kilometers, to one wolf per 260 to 390 square kilometers after the treatment. The population will bounce back to about one wolf per 156 square kilometers and we hope it would remain stable at about that level."

The best that I can say for the above statement is that the assistant director of the British Columbia Ministry of the Environment is obeying orders. Indeed, the entire statement reflects biological obfuscation, to say nothing of the fact that the official, in using the word "treatment," evidently sees the wolves as a sickness that should be stamped out.

In a report entitled *Canadian Wildlife Administration*, prepared by Ontario's Ministry of Natural Resources in June 1980, W. G. Macgregor, a biologist in the department of ungulate management of the British Columbia Department of Wildlife, contributed a paper entitled *Allocation of Hunting Use of Wildlife Between Residents and Non-residents*. In the introduction to this report, he says: "In recent years, the increase in resident hunting, particularly for thin-horn sheep in the northern areas of the province, has resulted in demands for more restrictions on non-resident [i.e., out-of-province, or out-of-Canada hunters] hunting. An organization formed in 1976 called RAMS (Residents Action for Mountain Sheep) and the B.C. Wildlife Federation have been the main proponents of that position."

Macgregor then explained the argument that existed between resident hunters, who felt that nonresidents were making inroads on their hunting preserves, and the Association of Guides and Outfitters, who earn a good living by importing hunters from the United States but especially from Germany. The biologist noted that there were 314 licensed guide-outfitters in the province in 1978, including thirty-one who operate in the Peace River–Omineca region, where the wolves are being slaughtered. Collectively, the outfitters grossed $11.63 million, 53 percent of which was earned by those who operated in the wolf-kill area. Macgregor also noted that nonresident hunters spent a further $2.26 million in the province.

In early 1985, Minister Brummet was moved to a new post by the British Columbia government, a spokesman for which explained that this was not because of the controversy that arose over the wolf-killing program promoted by Brummet, but rather because it is policy to move ministers from one portfolio to another. The new minister, Austin Pelton, has at least hinted that he would favor a halt to the killing. Meanwhile, the biologist who is in charge of the kill program has asked that it be extended for another three years. There the matter rests. But the British Columbia government has added a new twist to its wildlife management program by offering to sell trapping licenses to nonresidents, who may now come from Germany, the United States, or any other part of the world to kill animals for their fur.

YUKON TERRITORY

The wolf-killers of the Yukon Territory are also active. They too are using questionable "evidence" to try to justify a three-year wolf kill over 30,000 square kilometers, a program that includes the use of poisons such as strychnine and the infamous 1080 (sodium monofluoro-

225

acetate), trapping, and shooting from aircraft. Once again, a government is claiming that wolves are depleting ungulate populations and also killing dogs and livestock. Once again, hunters and particularly guide outfitters have put pressure on officials of the territorial government's Department of Renewable Resources, who have bowed to these vested-interest groups at the expense of a sane conservative program.

Sharon and I know the Yukon well. We lived there in 1977 and 1978; before then, I had lived in the territory for a combined total of seventeen months, studying its wildlife and traveling over the entire region. Because of this experience, my wife and I know that the claims that wolves kill livestock are greatly exaggerated. There is little ranching in the Yukon—at temperatures of forty to fifty degrees below zero, in winters during which the sun shines only sporadically and only in the southernmost part of the territory, livestock cannot prosper. The so-called stock-killing mostly involves horses, which, after they have been used for hunting and other purposes, are turned out into the wilderness to shift for themselves—to live or die, that is, because it is cheaper to buy new mounts the next year than to import expensive feed to keep the old ones through a long winter. Such animals often die of starvation and cold. The wolves make use of their carcasses; the wolves also kill some that are dying, thereby bringing their suffering to a quick end. Then, of course, the horse owners claim that the wolves are killing the stock.

In the matter of dogs, anyone who has spent any time at all in the territory will have seen the many stray dogs that roam in packs in practically every community. These animals are at times killed by wolves; at other times they mate with wolves, creating hybrids that may well pose a serious threat to other animals and to people. While we were living at Watson Lake, the authorities in Dawson City issued a warning to its citizens that any dog found straying would be shot on sight, this warning coming after yet one more child had been savaged by strays. In addition, many Yukoners are in the habit of staking out their dogs in the front or back yard. In winter—and I remind the reader that temperatures of fifty below zero

226

are not unusual—these animals are huddled up in the darkness in a small town or village that is otherwise completely deserted. Wolves may well come in and kill such dogs.

The Yukon is the jumping-off place for outfitters who operate in that territory as well as for outfitters licensed in the western part of the Northwest Territories. Watson Lake, not far from the borders of British Columbia, is a major fly-in staging area where it is not unusual to see parties of German hunters strolling the town, clad in traditional German hunting costumes while they sightsee and wait for their flight to the hunting area, where, well housed, well fed, equipped with every modern aid that will facilitate their killing lust, the nonresidents spend from one to three weeks, shooting animals that have been first located by aircraft, after which the hunters are guided to the quarry by two-way communication between the air-spotters and the ground.

As I noted earlier, Sharon and I again visited the Yukon in 1984, having decided to see what was going on in the Peace River–Omineca regions and then, since we were about seven hundred kilometers from the Yukon border, to drive the Alaska Highway and check on the wolf situation in the territory. During this visit, I spoke with government biologists, whom I cannot identify here because they would lose their jobs if I did. They were completely opposed to the government's wolf-killing program. One, whom I have known for some years, summed up the Yukon wolf slaughter in these words:

"Poachers, local hunters, destruction of habitat by mining and exploration, imported hunters, severe winters, and damned bad conservation policies have made a mess of our big-game populations. The government won't accept the blame for that stuff, so we've just got to blame it all on wolves. And that's the way it is! I'll tell you, as soon as I can find another job on the outside, I'm getting the hell out of here! You can quote me, but I'll sue you if you use my name. . . ."

ALASKA

The history of wolf-hate in Alaska is a long and sorry one. It actually began in the nineteenth century, but the real rape of the land was noted in 1900, when extensive hunting by miners, who sold the moose meat they gathered, reached a peak. In that year, sledloads of dead moose were dumped near Fairbanks when hunters learned that the price of moose meat had dropped. Dall sheep *(Ovis dalli)* were sold in Fairbanks by the hundreds. Meanwhile, the carcasses of the dumped moose were poisoned in order to kill wolves.

Year by year, ungulates were slaughtered for their meat and for profit; wolves were shot, trapped, and poisoned for their fur. And so the record goes. Sometimes authorities sought to control wolves to protect "game animals"; at other times, authorities killed wolves indiscriminately. In 1975 the real battle started when the Alaska Board of Game approved a plan to hire private pilot-gunner teams to shoot wolves. Conservationists launched a lawsuit, spearheaded by the Fairbanks Environmental Center, Friends of the Earth, and some private individuals. An injunction to stop the killing was secured. The battle has been raging ever since, neither side achieving a clear victory, but neither side admitting defeat. Wolves are still being killed in Alaska, however, which gives the edge to the wolf-haters thus far.

In a newsletter dated November 6, 1984, the Alaska Wildlife Alliance noted that wolf hunts had already started and that expansion of the killing grounds was proposed by the Alaska Board of Game. At that time, it was the intention to shoot wolves over an area of 13,900 square miles, and as the Alliance said: "By the time you receive this newsletter, wolves will likely have already been killed from airplanes and helicopters."

Once again, those who opposed wolf killing were accused of acting on emotion and without real knowledge, this charge being made by members of the Alaska Department of Fish and Game; but after I read the Alliance's seven-page newsletter, there was little doubt in my mind that this conservation group does, indeed, know what it is talking about. Emotions were high, of course, but these were to be noted in both camps. In any event, it is clear that in Alaska, as in the other wolf-kill areas, the real reason for the slaughter of these predators is to be found in human greed. Hunters want to kill more animals, trappers want to sell more wolf skins, and politicians respond to that which they believe is the strongest party.

In 1985, however, pressure from conservationists caused the Alaska Board of Game to order its Department of Fish and Game to try alternative methods of reducing wolf populations before resorting to aerial shooting, and further adopted regulations limiting the circumstances under which such killings may be authorized. It also repealed two wolf-kill programs that had been previously approved, but left a third in place.

Undoubtedly this was a victory for conservation, but only a partial one, for the control of wolves in Alaska is going to continue.

The four regions here discussed have been selected because the wolves that live in them have been slaughtered more systematically and unmercifully than those living elsewhere in North America. But let it not be supposed that wolves are not being killed in other parts of the United States and Canada. Even in those areas where wolves are so scarce as to be considered near extinction, the animals are being shot and trapped, most often illegally and, especially in Canada, for their fur. Although Canada's provincial governments no longer pay bounty money to wolf hunters, local municipalities are yet allowed to reward wolf-killers in this way, the blood-money coming out of the pockets of resident taxpayers.

The arguments used to justify this continued persecution are always the same. The fur lobby claims that economic hardships will result if trapping is curtailed or abolished; the guides and outfitters sing the same song. The hunting lobby, backed by some government-employed biologists, insists that wolves are seriously depleting the stocks of "game" animals. Indeed, in recent years, some biologists have been promoting the view that wolves do not maintain the healthy balance among their prey species that has been long established by unbiased scientists. The proponents of this kind of specious reporting claim that now it has been found that wolves seriously reduce the numbers of deer, moose, and caribou in most parts of their ranges. To "prove" this, figures are cited showing that, in given areas, wolf kills have indeed reduced prey populations. But what such reports *invariably* fail to mention is that such reduction comes about after hunters have swept through the study areas and reduced the numbers of prey animals to the point where natural predation becomes a threat to the local species. Nor do these reports mention that severe winters, coupled with logging, mining, and other so-called development, negatively affect animal populations. Rather, because the political winds favor it, the entire blame is placed on the wolf.

The fact is that man is the most wanton, irresponsible destroyer to be found on our planet, as the following figures clearly demonstrate.

The U.S. Fish and Wildlife Service, in Washington, D.C., made available to me a document entitled *A Summary of Selected Fish and Wildlife Characteristics of the 50 States*. The eighty-three-page report includes a summary of fishing, hunting, and "wildlife-associated recreation." It shows that in one year, 1980, *human hunters in the United States killed a total of 65,552,792 mammals belonging to ten species!*

The number and species of animals killed were as follows: deer, 2,975,732; elk, 108,197; bears, 22,052; antelope, 77,783; moose, 7,661; mountain goats, 951; sheep, 1,413; rabbits and hares, 25,876,000; squirrels of various species, 36,483,000.

A second document the USFWS made available to me, *Special Scientific Report—Wildlife No. 215*, contains a summary of the annual bird mortality related to human activity. This shows that 196,887,810 birds of a wide variety of species are killed each year in America. Of this total, *120 million* are shot by hunters, and a further two million die from lead poisoning after the birds ingest spent shotgun pellets; another 57 million birds are killed in collisions with cars, trucks, buses, and aircraft, while picture windows, transmitter towers and powerlines cause the deaths of 4¾ million birds.

Added to the above slaughter, the Animal Welfare Institute, Washington, D.C., notes that *66 million* fur-bearing animals belonging to twenty-six species were killed by trappers in the United States during a seven-year period (1970–1977). Here are some of the kill figures: muskrats, 38,480,192; raccoons, 16,934,598; opossum, 3,498,691; red fox, 1,642,562; mink, 1,581,785; coyote, 929,211. In Alaska, 7,420 wolves were killed for their fur, which yielded the trappers a total of $1,054,827, for an average price per pelt of $142.16. No wonder people want to kill wolves in that state!

In May 1977, President Jimmy Carter commissioned a global study of environmental problems that, in his words, "do not stop at national boundaries. In the past decade, we in our nation have come to recognize the urgency of international efforts to protect our common environment."

The report was duly completed. On page 402 it says:

At no time in recorded history has the specter of species extinction loomed so ominously. Largely a consequence of deforestation and the "taming" of the wild, the projected loss over two decades of approximately *one-fifth of all species* on the planet (at *minimum*, roughly 500,000 species of plants and animals) is a prospective loss to the world that is literally beyond evaluation. The genetic and ecological values of wild and newly-identified species continue to be discovered. This represents an irreplaceable evolutionary legacy. . . . [Emphasis added.]

RECOMMENDED
READING

Many books have been written about wolves. Some, although good at the time of their publication, have now become outdated and can be misleading; others are hard-to-read biological treatises that may well baffle the layman; yet others are notable more for their prose than for their accuracy. A few are excellent sources for those wishing to further their knowledge of wolves: I include the latter in the following list and recommend them highly.

Allen, Durward L. *Wolves of Minong*. Boston: Houghton, Mifflin, 1979.
Fox, Michael W. *Behaviour of Wolves, Dogs and Related Canids*. London: Jonathan Cape, 1971.
———. *The Soul of the Wolf*. Boston: Little, Brown, 1980.
Leydet, François. *The Coyote*. Norman, Okla.: University of Oklahoma Press, 1977.

Mech, L. David. *The Wolf*. New York: Natural History Press, 1970.

Peterson, Rolf Olin. *Wolf Ecology and Prey Relationships on Isle Royale*. National Parks Scientific Monograph Series 11. Washington, D.C.: U.S. Government Printing Office, 1977.

Rutter, Russel J., and Douglas H. Pimlott. *The World of the Wolf*. New York: J. B. Lippincott, 1968.

CONSERVATION ORGANIZATIONS

For those readers who may wish to become involved in the cause of conservation in general and of the wolf in particular, the following organizations are recommended. All are worthy of support and will, upon request, provide details about themselves and about current issues relating to conservation.

Group 1 includes organizations directly involved with wolves, and can supply up-to-date information on the species and on the efforts that are being made to counteract its persecution. Group 2 comprises organizations that are generally involved in matters pertaining to animal welfare, environmental protection, and natural history. Although addresses listed refer to headquarters of these associations, they may have chapters in local areas.

GROUP 1

Canadian Wolf Defenders, Box 3480, Station A, Edmonton, Alberta, Canada T5L 453.

HOWL (Help Our Wolves), 4600 Emerson Avenue South, Minneapolis, Minnesota 55409, U.S.A.

Northern Michigan Wolf Sanctuary, 117 Case Street, Negaunee, Michigan 49866, U.S.A.

The Alaska Wildlife Alliance, P.O. Box 6953, Anchorage, Alaska 99502, U.S.A.

Wolf Haven, 3111 Offut Lake Road, Tenino, Washington 98589, U.S.A.

WOLF Newsletter, P.O. Box 112, Clifton Heights, Pennsylvania 19018, U.S.A.

GROUP 2

Defenders of Wildlife, 1244 19th Street, N.W., Washington, D.C. 20036, U.S.A.

Fauna Preservation Society, Zoological Society of London, Regents Park, London, England.

World Wildlife Fund, Avenue du Mont Blanc, CH 11, Gland, Switzerland.

The Fund for Animals, 200 West 57th Street, New York, N.Y. 10019, U.S.A.

INDEX

235

238

239

240

242

244

ABOUT THE AUTHOR

Born in Spain and educated at Cambridge University, R. D. LAWRENCE is a field biologist and naturalist whose work has taken him to four continents. The recipient of numerous awards for his writing and his contributions to the understanding of nature, he has lived in Canada for over thirty years, studying its fauna and working for conservationist causes.